To Dianne
Barbra Sullivan
Proverbs 3:5,6

A Rose from the Thorns

Barbra Sullivan

Printed in Canada

ISBN: 978-1-4866-2147-7
eBook ISBN: 978-1-4866-2148-4

Word Alive Press
119 De Baets Street Winnipeg, MB R2J 3R9
www.wordalivepress.ca

Cataloguing in Publication information can be obtained from Library and Archives Canada.

Dedication

The first part of this book is written in honour of my mother, six brothers, and three sisters. It's about how we survived inexpressible tribulation. What I've experienced seems trivial in comparison to what most of my siblings had to endure, and I'm so very sorry for the torment and anguish we all endured at the hands of the evil man called our father, who as long as I can remember was a violent alcoholic.

The second part of this book is dedicated to my three amazing sons, my daughters-in-law, my ten grandchildren, my two great-grandchildren (so far), and all the others who are still to come.

I was asked to write my story not only for the healing of my soul, but perhaps so that my experiences could one day help others. The cry of my heart is, "Please, don't follow in my footsteps. The practices I indulged in—drugs, alcohol, gambling, and promiscuity—took me to places I never planned to go and caused me to do things I never wanted to do. I hurt the ones I loved the most and destroyed my dreams, even the ones that didn't have a chance to be born. My lifestyle and choices wreaked havoc on my family and stole my sons' right to a good upbringing. I regret what I've done and will carry it in my heart until my dying day. I never want to forget where I've come from, so that I will never return to it."

I wish to thank all my faithful family and friends who helped, encouraged, and believed in me to share my story. I pray:

> *The Lord bless you and keep you; the Lord make his face shine on you and be gracious to you;*
> *the Lord turn his face toward you and give you peace.* (Numbers 6:24–26)

And above all, I thank my heavenly Father for saving me from myself!

I waited patiently for the Lord; he turned to me and heard my cry. He lifted me out of the slimy pit, out of the mud and mire; he set my feet on a rock and gave me a firm place to stand. He put a new song in my mouth, a hymn of praise to our God. (Psalm 40:1–3)

You plucked a filthy, disgusting thing
Out of the miry clay
Then breathed the breath of life
Into this body of sin and decay

You set my feet upon the Rock
And turned me the right way
And as we walk together, Lord,
This is what I have to say:

Thank You for the cross, Lord
Thank You for all those who prayed
If it wasn't for You and all of them
I wouldn't be where I am today

Introduction

I found myself standing in the quiet midst of one of the most elegant flower gardens I'd ever seen.

"Where am I?" I whispered to myself as I looked around in bewilderment and awe. The spaciousness and solitude caressed my soul with peace and joy.

A very tall and ancient stonewall guarded this mystical garden. Unbelievable colours radiated from the varieties of flowers, and their fragrance was beyond anything I'd ever experienced.

Glancing down, I realized that I was standing on a path made of the same stone as the wall. Curiosity getting the better of me, I eagerly set out. The path meandered into the midst of the garden, then suddenly disappeared around a bushy shrub.

My breath caught as I rounded the corner and beheld a magnificent display of exotic trees and shrubbery, surrounded by the most remarkable species of flowers on planet Earth. What a paradise! I simply had to inspect each variety of flower while I made my way along the path.

Coming to another blind bend, and anticipating more splendours, I came around the corner and stopped short. To my utter dismay, what I saw caused my heart to pound in fear. What at one time must have been a magnificent bush had become enmeshed in spiked vines. The area around it looked entirely dead, and appeared to have been so for quite some time. The thorns were the colour of driftwood one might find on the shore of a lake. Darkness permeated the scene and I wanted to run from it, but instead my feet dragged me closer—and the closer I got, the harder my heart pounded and the greater my fear grew.

Finally I stopped a short distance from this foreboding sight. Overcome with dread and feeling a desperate need to escape, tears streamed down my cheeks. I could feel the hand of hopelessness entwining its webbed fingers in my brain, coaxing me to fall into this tangled death trap.

Moments before succumbing to its seducing call, I caught a brilliant flash of light from the corner of my eye. With great effort, I tore my eyes away from the thorny bush and looked in the direction of the rapidly moving light, which slid past me and entered a hole halfway down the bush. The beam of light was pure and translucent, and from it I heard a whisper in my ear telling me to look inside.

With great apprehension, I leaned forward and peered into the hole, expecting to see something even more hideous than the bush itself. But much to my surprise, in the midst of all these lethal thorns, grew a beautiful blue rose in full bloom, the light bathing its delicate petals. The rose literally emanated life.

How could it possibly have survived amongst all these dreadful thorns? I asked myself.

A movement caught my attention, and there, pushing back the threatening vines, was a man's large bronze hand. Each time the vine attempted to grow towards the solitary rose, the hand forced it back, allowing the rose all the room it needed to continue to blossom.

Then I woke up.

This dream depicts my life. The stone wall represents God's protection for his children, the stone path represents the narrow road we take, the flowers represent all the different nationalities of people who belong to God, and the thorns represent the hardships and failed relationships that threaten to destroy us.

The stream of light represents the Holy Spirit, which has empowered me to triumph over the challenges life has thrown my way, and the hand is the Lord's, protecting me even before I ever knew Him.

The blue rose represents me, struggling and succeeding against all odds. And as for the colour blue? It represents a mystery hidden until the time comes for it to be revealed.

> *And you, son of man, do not be afraid of them or their words. Do not be afraid, though briers and thorns are all around you and you live among scorpions. Do not be afraid of what they say or be terrified by them, though they are a rebellious people.* (Ezekiel 2:6)

What follows is my journey, to the best of my memory.

One
Camp Shilo

My father was born in Prince Albert, Saskatchewan where he finished school at fourteen. To make money, he did odd jobs; to mention one, he cut wood.

He also spent much of his time in jail, as he was a hard child to manage. At the age of sixteen, he lied about his age to join the army. He was blind in one eye but managed to pass the physical exam and was recruited in 1940. He went overseas to England and Scotland and it's said that he spent time in France as well for training. He became a paratrooper.

Another member of my family told me that Dad fought in the Korean War while Mom lived at Rivers, Manitoba. He had made sergeant by that time but got demoted to corporal after being disrespectful to a sergeant major.

When he came home after the Korean War, he put in for a transfer to Camp Shilo in Manitoba to serve as the chef. There, he became an accomplished cook, baker, and butcher for the generals.

One day, a general complained about the food. Being hot-headed, my dad mouthed off to him, which got him demoted again, this time down to private.

It has been said that he was never the same after his time at war, but he was trouble in his early years anyway. He was also given three months in military jail when it was found out that he had beaten his wife.

He left the army after twenty-one years of service.

My mother was born on the family homestead north of Hazenmore, Saskatchewan. She was raised in the house my grandparents built.

When she left home, she went to work in a tuberculosis sanatorium at Prince Albert. She worked there for ten months, preparing and serving food and cleaning afterwards, until she developed tonsillitis. From there she cleaned houses and worked in restaurants until she met and married my father.

They met in Prince Albert, and I've been told that my mother's parents were against their meetings. My mother would sneak out to meet my father by the Saskatchewan River.[1]

Mom married Dad at the tender age of seventeen without her parents' blessings. My father's mother was against the marriage as well; she didn't accept my mother, and she let it be known by her actions and nasty words. So the families didn't visit or social with each other.

Not a good beginning for their marriage, I'd say.

Ten children came from this union. I was number six, following five older brothers. There's a great deal I don't remember about my upbringing, which is mainly because of all the trauma in our home, which I've blocked out. To the best of my knowledge, and from what information I've gathered, I will share a few stories of my life at home and after moving away.

Childhood Eczema

I was born in 1954 at Camp Shilo and lived there for about five years. Since it's an army base, that would make me an army brat. The word *brat*, of course, refers to an unpleasant child or a spoiled kid, so that wasn't a good start. Name-calling right from the beginning.

I had a serious skin disease that became full-blown about a month after I was born: eczema covered my whole body. My paternal grandmother and several of my brothers had it, but not to the extent I did. So it's hereditary.

The term eczema is broadly applied to a range of persistent skin conditions, including dryness and recurring skin rashes that are characterized by redness, swelling, itching, flaking, blistering, cracking, oozing, bleeding… I had them all.

Mom told me there were times in my first year when the only things she could see on me that weren't oozing and bleeding were my eyes. Many nights she had to tie my hands and feet to my crib bars to keep me from scratching and tossing myself about the crib. I kept her up most nights while she rubbed me, trying to soothe my tormented body.

My crying probably drove everyone nuts. How my mother managed to care for me, deal with an alcoholic husband, five active sons, and pregnancy is beyond me.

My condition was so severe that I was taken to the Camp Shilo Hospital so doctors could find out what was wrong with me. I'm told they tried everything they could think of to heal the eczema, but nothing worked until, out of desperation, they used an old army salve called Laser's Paste. It was a thick, white, gooey substance that didn't rub into the skin but sat on top of it. Whatever I touched, the paste would stick to it, such as clothes and furniture.

The paste's job was to dry out the skin, which caused it to look ghostly white and scaly. Most times it worked, but I suffered dearly, physically and emotionally, as I was so embarrassed and ashamed of how I looked.

I wasn't allowed to have hair until about three years of age because being bald made it easier for Mom to clean my head, and my fingernails were clipped short to keep me from scratching.

---

[1] Mom's closest friend told me this when I visited her in Prince Albert. She pointed to the very spot by the river where they'd secretly meet.

In my preteen years, large sores formed on my scalp and I picked at them because they would become matted with dried blood. Brushing my hair was dreadfully painful, as the scabs would catch on the bristles and rip my flesh open.

The winters were the hardest times. Most mornings I wouldn't be able to move or bend my fingers, and when I could they would split open at the knuckles, sometimes to the bone, and bleed. Very painful. At times the itch would drive me insane; there was no satisfying it. I'd scratch until I bled and then just keep on scratching. The skin between my toes would split and bleed, too, which made walking hard.

At times I had to wrap my hands and arms with gauze bandages to keep from getting blood and salve on everything. Many times my clothes stuck to the open wounds and when I pull the cloth away from my skin, the hardened blood would come with it, tearing open the sores again.

The embarrassment and shame was unbearable. I felt so ugly that I wished I didn't have to go to school. I desperately wanted to stay home and hide. It was on my face, and it even separated the bottoms of my earlobes from my head; the backs of my ears would split open, causing blood to ooze from the cuts. The whole area around my ears would be covered in dried scabs.

My knees and elbows would need to be covered as well, causing every movement to sting. Many times the wounds would dry and stick together, so that when I straightened my arms and legs the skin would rip away.

What young man would want a girl who looked like me? I felt isolated from almost everyone.

Finally, at about the age of eleven, the eczema began to disappear. But even after it had disappeared, I still felt alienated. Still feeling ugly, I didn't allow too many people to get close. I share this because most don't have a clue how much suffering people with eczema endure. I've often heard it said, "Oh, it's only eczema." But it's more than just a skin disorder. It's painful and debilitating, and it caused me deep emotional wounds that affected the way I saw myself.

I vaguely remember the duplex where we lived. It was an army house, and Mom's job was to keep the place spotless since the army inspectors could come at any time to inspect it. She also had to take care of Dad's uniform and boots, which should have been his job. With eight children, she carried a lot of responsibility on her small shoulders.

One afternoon after my five older brothers had gone back to school, Mom put my two younger sisters, Ann and Darlene, down for their usual afternoon nap. She then took me along with her to visit a friend who lived across the street and a couple houses down from our place. We sat outside on her front veranda and drank the most delicious iced tea. I played quietly with a toy while they talked and enjoyed their rare visit together. It was a warm and sunny day and everything was so nice and peaceful.

But like all good things, it came to an abrupt end. We suddenly heard the sound of sirens screaming by and Mom jumped to her feet, looking towards our house. I turned my head in the same direction and watched as a fire engine came to an abrupt stop in front of our house. Smoke was seeping out from under the front door.

Like a shot, my mom grabbed my hand, pulled me to my feet, and ran in the direction of our house. My short little legs could hardly keep up with her.

People were already gathering to watch the firemen hook up their hoses while others put on masks so they could go inside.

My mom broke through the crowd. "My babies are sleeping upstairs!" she screamed.

She dropped my hand and made a mad dash for the front door, but a fireman quickly grabbed her arm and pulled her back. He told her she couldn't go inside and she struggled against him, panic-stricken and desperate to get to her children.

Somehow, she managed to shake off his hold and rushed into the house before he knew she was gone. I watched in horror as she disappeared into the smoke now billowing out through the open front door. Two firemen, with masks on their faces, followed right behind her.

"Mommy!" I screamed after her. "*Mommy!*"

My body was stiff with terror as I watched the fire devouring the drapes in the living room window. Where was she?

Again I screamed with everything I had inside me. "Mommy!"

The seconds dragged into minutes, and still there was no sign of her. The firemen were doing their best to put the fire out and water was flying everywhere. I could hear voices, but was unable to make out what they were saying.

It seemed like an eternity before Mom finely stumbled out the front door, coughing and choking while clutching a little body tightly in her arms, followed closely behind by a fireman who protectively held my other sister in his big arms.

Afterward the firemen checked them for smoke inhalation and found them to be okay.

Once the fire was extinguished and the house aired out, it was deemed suitable enough to live in. The living room floor would have to be replaced, though. I was shocked to see the damage the fire had caused. Everything that hadn't completely burned was blackened from the smoke. Where there had once been a floor, all I could see was a hole to the burnt-out basement. The acrid smell of smoke was overpowering and nearly took my breath away.

After the investigation, it was determined that the cause of the fire had been a piece of clothing hanging on a clothesline too close to the coal-burning furnace. Possibly the last person to shovel in the coal hadn't closed the furnace door all the way.

I thank God for those firemen who put their lives on the line to save my mom and sisters. I was proud of her, even though years later I learned she had done the wrong thing by running into the house. However, through her actions she showed me what true sacrificial love was.

Greater love has no one than this: to lay down one's life for one's friends. (John 15:13)

A Traumatic Childhood

I was five years old when we moved to Brandon, Manitoba. We lived there about two years, but it could have been even shorter if Mom hadn't been so quick on her toes.

We lived in a civilian house which sat on a lot at the end of the block, and we had lots of room outside to play. It was a two-story with a veranda running along the front of the house and halfway around the side. We also had a large shed in the backyard with a fence that connected it to the house. My siblings and I would climb the fence, then get onto the shed's roof or up onto the roof of the house. But when we were caught, we got into serious trouble.

There was also a great big wooden barrel under the eaves trough that was used to collect rainwater. Mom used this water to wash our hair, which made our hair feel like silk. On hot summer days, we'd climb into the barrel to cool off.

I think we had three bedrooms upstairs and one down, along with a large living room and even larger kitchen. With a brood of eight kids, we needed a large kitchen. Quite often we ate porridge for dinner, since we didn't have a lot of food—or anything else, for that matter.

Mom had just finished cleaning up of the kitchen one day after a meagre meal of hotdogs, bologna, or porridge—can't remember which—when she left for a few minutes to have a cigarette. While she was gone, I set the highchair on fire; it was old, having been used by several of us kids, and the plastic was torn and stuffing hanging out. I don't know how I did it, or why, but Mom must have smelt the smoke because she came rushing back in, grabbed a large pot from the cupboard, filled it with water, and dumped it over the blazing highchair.

I just stood back in shock, watching her and the smouldering chair. There went her sparkling clean kitchen! There was water and burnt stuffing everywhere.

What happened to me after that? Fortunately, this was one of those times when I don't remember the consequences.

Now, as long as I can remember, we always had a cat, dog, or both. This time, it was a cat and her name was Fluffy, probably named after her long grey and white hair. She owned the hearts of all who resided within the walls of her domain.

Fluffy was allowed to run free, so she came and went as she pleased. She'd had several litters of kittens and we kids enjoyed watching them grow, although we had a hard time when it came to giving them away.

One night after dark, we noticed Fluffy wasn't home, which was unusual for her, especially because she was due to have another litter at any time. We searched the house and then the streets where she usually prowled. No sign of her. I was upset and didn't sleep well that night.

Come early morning, Fluffy dragged her tired and beaten body into the yard. Mom carefully picked her up and brought her inside. She had been in a fight, probably with another cat or dog, and was in poor condition. Her hair was matted with blood. Mom tried to make her as comfortable as possible.

Later that day, after giving birth to her kittens, she died. We cried for her and our loss. I wondered what was going to happen with her babies.

Wanting to be alone, I went into the backyard and moped around in my misery. I didn't understand death. What was wrong with my cat? I'd been told she was never coming back, but that was too big for me to comprehend.

I looked up when I heard the back door open. Mom was coming out, carrying a milk carton in one hand and a tea towel with something in it in the other. I followed her with my eyes as she made her way towards the shed.

I followed to see what she was doing, all the while hearing tiny meows. Realizing that she was carrying the kittens, I asked what she was going to do with them.

"Without Fluffy to feed and raise them, the kittens are going to suffer and die," she said.

Next she told me to leave, but I didn't. Instead I watched her take the kittens, one at a time, and put them in the cartoon that she'd filled with water. She later explained that it had been the quickest way to put them out of their misery, since they were hungry.

I knew it was a hard thing for her to do, so I didn't hate her for it, but I cried.

One of the rare times Dad was home, he surprised us all by taking us on a holiday to Sandy Lake. We'd never been there, nor did we know where it was. Magically he produced a station wagon that would hold our whole family, food, and borrowed camping gear.

With great excitement, we piled in. Mom and the youngest sat up front with Dad, three went in the back seat, and the rest of us lay on the gear in the back. We set off with the radio blaring the latest tunes. On a scale of one to ten, my excitement was at an eleven. All was truly well in our world that day.

We arrived at our destination by late afternoon. Dad found a great location to set up camp under some trees and a short distance from the beach. To get to the store, we had to walk along a deeply rutted dirt road between tall bushy trees. We could hardly wait to get out and explore this enormous place that would be our new home for the next few days.

First we all had to pitch in and unload the car. I did what I could, which didn't amount to too much, since I was only six years old. Fortunately Dad was in a good mood, which meant everyone else could be too. It was official: we are now allowed to have fun!

As soon as we could, we hit the water and splashed around and began to make new friends. The beach was crowded with people of all ages. It looked as though the fine white sand stretched around the whole lake. It was truly a paradise, with the sun shining in a clear blue sky and diamonds sparkling off the dark blue water. Boats and canoes crisscrossed the lake while people lay stretched out on towels and blankets, soaking up the much-welcomed sun.

We played hard and enjoyed ourselves immensely. Come bedtime, we were all packed into the tent like sardines, but that didn't seem to matter. We were doing something as a family, a very rare and exciting experience.

The next morning, we ran and screamed all over the beach. This was heaven on earth. The water was smooth and inviting and there were people everywhere. I bravely made my way into the water alone, sand squishing up between my toes, and got used to the cool water. I waded out a little deeper, and then a little deeper, and before I knew it I was up to my chest. I didn't know how to swim and was getting a little panicky, so I tried to step backwards.

Instead, the waves from the boats began to pull me forward. I tried stepping backwards again, and the same thing happened. I felt myself being pulled forwards until the water came up to my neck. There was no one around and the current was like a tentacle, grabbing and tugging at my legs.

My breath came in shallow gasps as I tried to call for help. I didn't think anyone heard me. Finally, on my tiptoes and feeling desperate, I stretched my arms out behind me and used my hands as paddles, thinking I could propel myself backwards. This only caused my feet to lift off the floor of the lake.

Now the water was up to my chin and I could hardly breathe.

Out of nowhere, a man and a woman in a canoe came alongside of me and gently picked me up and set me in their canoe. Once we were close to shore, they put me back down in the water and paddled off without a word.

I was scared, yet truly grateful for the couple that had saved my life. I know I would have drowned if not for them. God surely had his hand on me that day.

I quickly got out of the water and for the rest of the day didn't have any desire to go back in. I stayed close to my family.

Thankfully, the lake was cheated of a young soul that day.

On our second night at the lake, Dad decided to get gas for the car, but instead of returning he went off on his own adventure. We thought nothing of it at first, but then he didn't return that night... or for the next several nights after.

He had abandoned us and we were left to fend for ourselves.

We didn't have much in the way of food, nor did Mom have any money to purchase some. To add insult to injury, the sun disappeared and it poured buckets of rain. It didn't take long before the tent and all our clothes and bedding became soaking wet. We sat shivering in the cold.

To say we were miserable and afraid doesn't come close to describing what we felt. All our joy and excitement had escaped us and time dragged by unsympathetically.

We didn't know if Dad was even coming back. Mom didn't know if he was dead or alive. For all she knew, he could have gotten into an accident. She had no way of contacting him and felt fretful and angry all at the same time.

Then, after about four or five days of this torture, he finally graced us with his presence. I truly believe I hated him that day. What would possess a man to do that to his family? How cruel and totally selfish he was at times.

Solemnly, we broke camp. In no time, the tent was taken down and all the gear quickly packed away into the back of the station wagon. We all clambered in and slammed the doors with finality.

The ride home was nothing compared to the ride there. We were just grateful to be going home. We never went camping with him again.

Because Dad spent most of his paycheques in the local bars, food was a scarce commodity in our house and we were always hungry. Actually, we were close to starvation.

One day, like so many other days before, Dad didn't come home to join us for supper. I was still six years old and I remember sitting at the supper table with my seven siblings. Mom must have been pregnant with my youngest brother at that time.

With Mom running around serving us, and everyone talking at once, along with the sounds of clattering dishes, it was a noisy affair.

When I noticed that some of the others had eaten one more hot dog than me, I asked Mom about it in a whiny voice. Because her nerves were so frayed, probably because Dad had been beating her the night before, without thinking she picked up a fork, screamed something, and threw it at me.[2]

I didn't see it coming, but I felt it land with a powerful thud. Bullseye!

I remember plucking the fork from my face and dropping it to the floor with a loud clang. Then I looked at all the blood that covered my right hand.

Everyone in the room went deathly silent and I looked up to catch the horrified look on my mother's face and her terrified screams of apology. She gathered me up into her arms and from somewhere a clean cloth was produced and pressed against my eye to stop the bleeding.

Someone must have gone to the neighbours to phone a taxi, but I don't remember much after that until we were already in the taxi. I probably was in shock.

On the way to the hospital, Mom struggled to stay calm, but I could see with my one eye how frantic and fearful she was. She was holding me tightly to her side while I kept my injured eye covered with the bloodied cloth.

---

[2] I always understood that she threw it directly at me, but my brother Lawrence says that he saw what really happened: Mom tossed the fork down onto the table and it bounced off the table and struck me in my right eye.

To keep the cab driver from hearing anything, in a trembling voice she leaned down and whispered into my ear what I was to tell the doctors, or anyone else, if they asked me what had happened: I had tripped and fallen onto a fork that was lying on the floor. She pleaded with me not to tell them that she had thrown the fork. In earnest, she explained that if Children's Welfare found out what she had done, they would take all us kids away from her and that Dad would beat her to death.

I understood quite clearly what she was saying to me and agreed to do as she asked.

When we got to the hospital, I was put on a gurney in the emergency ward. What a strange place I had been taken to! There was a lot of activity around me. People were lying on gurneys and nurses were hustling back and forth. A radio played softly in the background. Of all the things I can remember, the song on the radio was an advertisement for Peter Jackson cigarettes. It was a very simple jingle: "More, more is what you get / with Peter Jackson, Peter Jackson, Peter Jackson / the king size cigarette." Why a little girl would remember that is a mystery to me.

Hearing a kind male voice on my right side say my name, I turned my head sideways to bring him into view. That was when I first noticed how limited my vision was. I focused in on this young doctor who was bending over me and smiling.

"Wow, have you ever got yourself a shiner," he said. "What happened?"

Mom was sitting close by and I remembered what she had said.

"I tripped on something and fell onto a fork that was lying on the floor," I said.

He believed me and gently began to clean the dry blood away from my eye. He closely examined the wound, then covered it with a white gauze patch and held it in place with tape. He then took Mom aside to talk with her and it was agreed that I was to stay in the hospital for a few days to make sure there was no serious damage done.

Fortunately, only one prong of the fork had poked into the white of the eye. The other three prongs had dug into the eyelid.

When I went home, no one in the family said anything about the accident and Dad never found out about it. Mom must have told my siblings not to tell the story, but I found it to be a hard burden for a six-year-old to carry.

While waiting for Mom to come home from the hospital one day after getting all her teeth extracted, Dad had the job of watching us kids, although he didn't know what me and Ann were up to. We were hiding in the basement, eating raw potatoes from storage. We knew we weren't supposed to be down there, but we were hungry.

After I had my fill, I got worried that Dad would catch us. I told Ann we had better get back upstairs, but she wasn't ready to leave yet, so she took a bite out of another potato. I told her if she didn't come with me, I would tell Dad she was down there. Still she said no.

I went upstairs, hoping she would follow me, but she didn't. So I told Dad she was downstairs. For the life of me, I don't know why I did that.

When he got up from the couch, I ran upstairs to my bedroom and listened. I knew I would be in trouble, too, because Ann would tell him I'd been with her. I heard him yelling angrily for Ann to get upstairs—

And then I heard the most godawful scream come out of her. When her screams didn't stop, I wondered what had happened. She just kept screaming over and over again. What had he done to her?

In fear, I opened the closet door and climbed onto the highest shelf, shut the door, and tried to make myself so small that I'd disappear. My heart was pounding.

Ann just kept screaming and screaming, until I heard Mom's frantic voice. She'd just gotten home. I wanted to go to her for protection, but I couldn't. Whatever had happened, I knew it was my fault.

I strained to hear what they were saying over Ann's screams, and soon I realized that they needed to take Ann to the hospital. Reluctantly I crawled down from my hiding place and made my way downstairs.

I was horrified at what I saw. Ann's mouth and the front of her clothes were covered in blood and Mom was trying to stop the bleeding by holding a cloth over her mouth. When she took it away, I could see that Ann's top four front teeth were hanging from her jaggedly cut gums.

Mom took Ann to the hospital and came home several hours later. Where there had once been four beautiful white teeth, there was now a gaping black hole. Her lips were very swollen and bruised. I felt so terrible.

I found out later that Dad hadn't laid a hand on her. When Ann had heard Dad calling down, in her rush to get up the stairs her foot had slipped on a step, causing her to fall face-first. She hit the step in front of her with her mouth, causing her front teeth to be pushed inside her mouth, gouging out her gums at the same time.

It took many years before her next set of teeth grew in. Many times I wondered if they'd ever grow back. Every time I looked at her, or even looked at a picture of her, I was reminded of what I had done. This was my fault.

When her teeth finally made their appearance, they were beautifully white and straight and she had a great smile.

Keep in mind we were a wild bunch of kids. Mom had her hands full keeping up with all of us. My brother Michael and I were no exception. He was a year and a half older than me and I followed him everywhere. We had wanderlust.

One of our favourite places to go was the trainyard, where we would climb over and under the train cars. One time I slipped and almost fell into an empty coal car. No one would have known, not even Michael, because he was off exploring somewhere else.

Near to the train tracks there was a pile of *giant* tractor tires. When we first found them, we climbed them just for the sake of climbing them. We were excited to reach the top and discover a mattress lying on the ground inside the tires. We climbed down to check the mattress and found that it had great bounce, so we climbed back up the tires then jumped down onto the mattress. We had an awesome time!

These tires were so big that I could easily fit inside of them with plenty of room to spare. It became our secret fort and we went back every opportunity we got.

Another time, Michael and I went down to the horse racetrack and discovered a large, reasonably deep swamp just behind the grounds. Finding a dilapidated old raft and long pole, we did the Huckleberry Finn thing. If our raft hadn't held up, we probably would have drowned because neither of us knew how to swim. It really was a very spooky and dangerous place.

Another time at the racetrack we found small paper bags and filled them with manure, then climbed up to the highest seats, took aim, and tried to drop them on anyone who came by. Then we'd duck out of sight. Oh, we were bad! And if we would have hit anyone... game over.

Several times, Michael and I went downtown to ride the elevators in the various buildings. Can you imagine a seven- and six-year-old wandering around the busy city streets? No one stopped to inquire if we were lost. We would ride the elevators until we got kicked off.

Then there were the times when we'd head down to the Assiniboine River on our own. The water was dangerously swift, yet people were fishing and hanging out nearby so we decided to join them. We didn't even consider the danger, since we already had that in spades at home because of our violent father. Now *that* was danger.

Naturally, with all that adventuring, we worked up an appetite. We knew of a fenced-off garden located in a back alley not far from our house, so cautiously we crawled under the wire fence one day, careful not to catch our clothes on it. Mom would kill us if we ripped our second-hand clothes.

After eating a few carrots, we figured we'd better leave before getting caught.

Too late! Halfway out from under the fence, we heard our mother's voice loud and clear: "Michael! Barbra!"

Busted! She was mad, and we were in for it—again.

We spent a lot of time getting lickings and being grounded. Understandably so. We were so bad. What she really should have done was lock us in cages or tie us up like dogs. It's truly a miracle that something really terrible didn't happen to us.

Because we had a shortage of money, one Christmas it seemed as though we weren't going to get any presents. As it was, our pantry was nearly bare, but Mom still decorated and went on as usual, taking care of us as best she knew how.

Two days before Christmas, I watched a pair of people dressed in black suits and hats come to our house and talk with Mom. I couldn't make out what they were saying, because she shooed me out of the room like they were sharing some kind of secret.

The next day, Mom opened the door to two more people who were dressed just the same. With a look of thankfulness, she eagerly invited them in. They carried in large boxes and Mom directed them to our nearly empty pantry. It took several trips before they were finished and Mom happily thanked them and closed the door behind them.

Of course we were all curious, but Mom wouldn't allow us to snoop. She locked the pantry door.

I stayed up on Christmas Eve, hiding behind a chair in the living room so Mom and Dad wouldn't find me. I wanted to see if Santa Claus was real and if he was going to come to our house.

Sometime early in my watch, I fell asleep. But when I woke up, wow! Did we ever have presents! There were dolls and teddy bears for us girls and cars and other toys for my brothers. I was so excited that I felt like I would bust. On top of all that, there was lots of food to eat. Our pantry shelves were full.

To my young mind, I thought this was the greatest Christmas ever!

Years later, I discovered who the mystery people were who had come to our house with such overwhelming compassion. They were from the Salvation Army. When I think back, I realize that God, in His mercy, took care of us in our time of need even though we didn't openly acknowledge Him.

I have since looked upon the Salvation Army with respect. They do a great service in God's name and may the Lord continue to bless them.

Three
Thompson

Not long after the accident with my eye, Dad left the army after twenty-one years and we moved to Thompson, Manitoba. It was 1961 and Dad got a job working for the International Nickel Company of Canada (INCO), a nickel mine.

One afternoon, while Dad was lying on the couch, I walked by the living room window and the sunlight struck my right eye in such a way that Dad could tell there was something wrong with it. He called me over and had me lean in close so he could look directly into both eyes. He told me to cover my left eye with my left hand, then asked me if I could see anything. I was stunned to find out that I had gone completely blind.

Panicking, I snatched my hand away from my good eye, so I could see again. I looked at Dad nervously and saw genuine concern. He immediately hollered out for Mom. She came into the living room, drying her hands on a tea towel. He motioned for her to come over and have a look at my eye.

After she'd seen it for herself, I could tell that she was shaken. At that moment, I just wanted to disappear.

Oh no, I thought. *He's going to find out what Mom did.*

Dad calmly leaned back against the couch and told Mom to get me to a doctor as soon as possible. What a relief! And at the same time, it was very strange to discover I was half-blind.

The doctor took one look at my eye and declared I had a cataract. In those days, a cataract operation required a week's stay in hospital. Because these kinds of operations weren't done in our small town, I was sent to the Children's Hospital in Winnipeg, about five hundred miles south of Thompson. My parents didn't have the money to pay for such a trip, so Dad contacted the Shriners Association for help and they kindly paid the train fare for me and Mom to go.

It was my first train ride and I was nervous and excited all at the same time. We were given first-class tickets for the sleeper car and dinner car, which had white tablecloths with fancy dishes, silverware, and water glasses. I was in awe! There was also a male lead service attendant dressed in a white coat and cap. He treated us as if we were royalty, and the food tasted incredible.

I felt like I was in a fairy tale as I looked out the massive train windows, hung with curtains on both sides of the car. I watched the landscape slip by. Because the north has so much muskeg and permafrost in the ground, the trains move at the slow pace of twenty-five to thirty-five miles per hour, so it would take us approximately twenty-four hours to get from Thompson to Winnipeg. Oh, but what an experience!

Not only that, but it was the first time I had Mom all to myself! We were relaxed and I believe she even enjoyed herself.

While on our way back to our seats after supper, I was surprised to see a porter turn our bench seats down to form a bed. He then pulled out sheets, blankets, and pillows from the compartment above our heads. He proceeded to make up our bed, which we were to share, and then pulled the curtains together to make a makeshift door for us. It was the most incredible thing I'd ever seen. The whole car had been transformed from a regular train with bench seats to a closed-in private sleeping compartment. The aisle was made up of floor-length black curtains swaying gently with the train's constant movements.

The next day, a conductor came by and asked if I wanted to go up into the engine. Mom gave her permission and so the conductor walked me through the many cars that made up our train. I couldn't believe my fortune!

It turned out there were two engineers running the train, and when I came in one asked if I wanted to drive it. He gestured to a huge iron brake wheel in front of two large windows. Was he kidding? With great excitement, I gazed through the windows looking at the tracks stretching for miles ahead of us.

"Yes," I whispered.

I walked up to the wheel, stretching out my arms on either side of me, and tightly grasped the wheel. It was nearly as tall as I was; I was probably all of four feet at the time. He told me to be careful steering the train around corners. So when a turn came up, he showed me how to turn the wheel ever so carefully so that we don't run off the tracks, and of course I believed him and turned it ever so carefully.

They must have got a good chuckle out of that. I know I did!

All too soon, we stepped down from the train in Winnipeg. I'd never had such wobbly legs in my life as I tried taking my first few steps on solid ground again. My whole body still swayed from the motion of the train. It took us a little while before we got our land legs back.

The train station was huge, with a lot of people going in every direction. I was afraid I'd lose Mom, so I stuck very close to her. It didn't take her long to find a taxi to take us to the hospital.

At the hospital we were directed to a person who had a lot of questions. As I watched Mom, I was amazed that she had all the answers. She was the smartest person I knew.

With the paperwork finished, I was taken upstairs to the ward where I was to stay. Mom remained with me while they settled me in, but all too soon she had to leave to find a hotel room for the night.

I met and made friends with a girl a year older than me, but I can't remember her name. She had to lie on something similar to a gurney. When she lay on her stomach, her head hung through a large hole and a wide strap went across her forehead, supporting her head. This was so she could see what was on the table below her as well as giving her back a rest.

In order to talk to her, I had to bend down and look up or sit on the floor in front of her. She had a mirror on the table below, so she could see what going on around her. She told me that she came from Churchill, Manitoba, and had been struck by a car while riding her bike, resulting in a broken back. She had already been in the hospital for almost a year and it would be some time yet before she could go home.

When she lay on her stomach, she didn't need to wear the formfitting cast they had made for her back, but every so often a couple of nurses would come by to switch her over onto her back. They'd fit the cast into place, then place a matching board on top of the cast, sandwiching her in. The board was then screwed into the place. On the count of three, they would flip her over quickly, so she wouldn't fall out. Lying on her back would cause her so much pain that she would cry. It broke my heart. Sometimes I felt mad at the nurses for hurting her, because I didn't understand at the time that this treatment was what was needed to recover.

She and I spent a lot of time learning new games to play and talking about all the important things which girls that age talk about.

Two Operations

On the morning of my first operation, I was given a needle to prepare me for surgery. A nurse placed me in a small room with cartoon pictures on the walls. The bed I was placed on was high off the floor; I guess they didn't want me jumping down and running around.

My mom wasn't with me and I was scared. What were they going to do?

When they were ready for me, a nurse came in, put me on a stretcher, and wheeled me into the operating room. I was okay up until the moment when a nurse tried to put a big mask over my mouth and nose. I was suffocating and couldn't stand the smell of whatever it was that was coming through that awful mask, so I began to struggle. It took three nurses to hold me down until the ether took hold and put me to sleep.

When I woke up, there was a thick bandage covering my right eye—and to my relief, Mom was sitting next to me. She stayed with me a short time, but then she had to leave to catch the train home because I was to remain in the hospital for a week and there was no one to watch the other kids back in Thompson.

I cried when she left, but my new friend calmed me down.

Time passed quickly and soon the day arrived when Mom returned and the doctor removed the bandage. Much to our dismay, I was still blind. The operation had failed. It turned out that the cataract had separated when they'd tried to scoop it out, and so they'd removed as much of it as they could. I would now have to wait another year before they could operate again.

When the time came to leave, it was hard to say goodbye to my friend. I missed her terribly.

A year later, I went back for the second surgery. Mom couldn't take me this time, so she had my brother Garrett, who was only twelve years old, accompany me by train to Winnipeg. Before boarding the train, Mom instructed him to put me on the top sleeper and he was to sleep on the bottom to make sure that no man got to me.

Once in Winnipeg, Garrett took me to the Children's Hospital and signed me in, then later came to pick me up and take me home. What a heavy responsibility for one so young! He told me that he got lost a few times while he was in the city. That would have been very scary.[3]

At the hospital, I was taken to the same floor as before. I asked if my friend was still there, but it turned out she had just left the hospital a day or two before. She had finally gotten to go home, but I was sad to have missed her. Every now and then, I still think about her and wonder how she's doing.

Again they operated, and again I fought the ether mask. Again, the cataract broke up, and again it was a failure. I went home still blind. There was no use trying again.

My First Jobs

Michael and I used to set up our own drink stands. Back then, we used plastic glasses and sold lemonade and Freshie. Maybe we didn't know it, but we were working. We had created our first jobs.

The two of us also took on other jobs. You see, we didn't just get into trouble together; we actually did some beneficial things! There was no such thing as an allowance in our house, so if we wanted to buy something we couldn't get at home, we had to work and earn our own money.

In the evenings, especially on Friday and Saturday nights, Michael and I would stand outside the doors of the toughest bar in town, called the Thompson Inn.[4] I sold copies of the Nickel Belt newspaper for ten cents and Michael shined shoes for ten cents. When he got tired, we'd switch jobs.

Because we were serious and good at what we did, we had plenty of customers. If we didn't get them going into the hotel, we got them on their way out—and by then they were drunk and very generous with their tips.

Another job of ours was bottle collecting. With a large metal wagon we'd go to apartment blocks, knocking on doors and asking if anyone wanted to get rid of their bottles. The people were very generous. We'd pile that wagon three or four cases high with beer bottles, then carefully push our heavy load, on groaning wheels, downtown to cash them in. We made good money, but it took a lot of hard work.

At the age of twelve, Mom gave me permission to get my own paper route. It consisted of eight apartment buildings, each of them three stories high and containing twenty-three units. Not everyone got a copy of the *Thompson Citizen*, but there sure were a lot who did. I had to tote those heavy papers up and down three flights of stairs every night of the week except Sunday.

Most people paid their paper bill, but at the end of the month many who still owed money just didn't answer their doors—either that or they'd moved. I would go back many times for several days trying to collect, but after a while I owed the newspaper company quite a bit of money. Mom was mad, but not at me. She knew I worked hard at this job. She managed to scrape together enough money to help cover my debt, but then I quit in disappointment. There went my dreams of making it big.

---

[3] Thank you, Garrett, for helping Mom by taking such good care of me, and for helping Mom to support the family by delivering newspapers and collecting bottles. You are so appreciated and loved.

[4] Of course, Mom didn't know about this.

My job for the next few years was babysitting. My first experience was for a lady who had a beautiful, blond, blue-eyed two-year-old girl and set of twin boys about three months old. Did I ever have my hands full with them! It didn't take long to fall in love, though.

All these years later, it has occurred to me that Michael taught me how to work. He taught me how to put my best into what I was doing, and for that I was well rewarded. Thank you, Michael!

Meet My Father

Our childhoods were sabotaged from the beginning as we tried to survive in a home with an abusive alcoholic father. He terrorized his wife and kids. When he was in the mood to reign over his kingdom, there was no one to stop him. He had an iron fist and an evil mouth that could destroy you right where you stood. His tongue was sharper than a serpent's poisonous bite, a bite which I felt many times. Just thinking about it still causes me to shiver.

In our home, we were dissected and re-dissected until we knew we were hated just because we were who we were. He hated us with a hate so evil that there was no mistaking it. He wanted to kill us, and there was no one strong enough to stop him—and he felt that he had the right to do things to us *because* we couldn't stop him. We were helpless.

He even seemed to be bigger than the police. No one dared to stand up to him.

He liked to hurt people. When he'd drink, he'd sit on the couch and everyone in the room would cower in fear. He'd sit there looking pleased. He would order my brothers away and let them starve, threatening anyone who would try to help.

He also said that he would live forever, which frightened me because I believed it. "I'm the meanest bastard that ever lived, and I'll never die," he said.

I felt condemned to a life of hell.

Yet when Dad was sober, he didn't have much to say. Nor was he physical. As a matter a fact, he could be a really nice guy. But when he was drinking, he was a true bully. He'd be like a cat with a mouse, giving you a little freedom and then, when you least expected it, he'd pounce. He blew hot and cold, so frightfully unpredictable.

It was said that when Dad got into a fight in the local bars, people would clear out until the fight was over. He'd take on anyone and usually come out on top. He was a trained boxer, a street fighter, and even a trained killer from his years in the army. People literally stepped out of his way.

He reminded me of a mafia boss, and he looked the part. He could have been the Godfather.

He was also a womanizer, hustling women in the same bar where I went to drink. He'd go so far as to introduce them to me and have them sit on his knee. Then he'd look me straight in the eyes, challenging me. Who would do that kind of thing in front of his daughter? I couldn't tell Mom. I had to keep my mouth shut. He had me well trained!

As for my mom, he would beat her severely and leave terrible bruises on her body. She'd cover them up so no one would know what was happening. He also abused us kids, mentally and physically. My five older brothers received the brunt of his wrath.

And so we lived in a home of secrets: secrets from outsiders, secrets from Dad, secrets from Mom, and secrets from each other.

As I've mentioned, Dad was an army man of more than twenty years. He owned two rifles and a colt-45, issued by the army. He liked guns and the power they gave him. He was also a hunter, so after he left the army he purchased several different handguns, rifles, shotguns, and 22s. He kept them in our basement, and having these weapons close at hand made him even more dangerous.

My oldest brother, Lawrence, told me there were times after Dad had been drinking that he'd take out a gun to clean it. He'd point it at objects in the house, and sometimes those objects were his own kids. One night he opened the basement door and emptied his clip, causing bullets to ricochet off the walls.

Another night, he came home and decided he was going to kill the whole family. He was going to use his 303 to commit this unpardonable act. I believe that God intervened. Mom had hidden all his bullets and shotgun shells, because he'd apparently attempted this once before. Lawrence found out where she'd hidden them this time, and he took them, without her knowledge, and hid them under the front step where no one could find them.

It was a good thing, too, because it turned out that Dad had found her hiding place as he tore up the house looking for them. Mom was unbelievably shocked when they weren't there. Imagine her relief!

In his rampage to find the shells, he came across hidden boxes of clothing and household items. It was the emergency boxes Mom had been secretly packing for the day we'd try to escape to another town or province to start over without him. This, of course, made him even more livid, causing him to explode. He beat her badly that day.

Four
Mom

Mom was a very special person in my life. There are times when I miss her so much that I find myself going to the phone to call her and then remember she no longer walks the earth but rather walks on streets of gold.

She had such a gentle and loving spirit. Whenever she had the time, she would play cards and marbles or put together puzzles with us. Many times I would find her singing hymns down in the basement while she washed the many piles of dirty clothes. She told me it helped her to hold herself together when times got too hard.

She had a beautiful voice and I loved to hear her sing. This is probably the reason my brothers, sisters, and I have such a love for singing and music.

Here's a song I wrote, sang, and recorded on tape for her, called "Precious Memories":

The years have passed so quickly
Only now do I see
How much I really miss you, Mom
And the times you shared with me
Come, let's walk back in time
To a kitchen I hold dear
Sharing pots of coffee
I remember it so clear

Those precious memories
Rolling through my head
Treasures of times past
No, they're not dead
Those precious memories
Of just you and me
So sweet, so special
So very much alive in me

I recall the times of challenge
Those famous Scrabble games
Concentrating for long moments
Wracking our tired brains
Ain't isn't in the dictionary
And how I vied for time
La, couldn't hold a note
And qua worked out just fine

Do you remember
That special dress you made for me
We modelled it in a contest
At that grand Ladies' Tea
Even though we didn't win a thing
A winner you were to me
Mom, I loved that dress
Just as much as you loved me

Mom and I became close friends after I moved out on my own. I would visit her quite often. We would sit at the kitchen table drinking coffee, and we'd often play cards or our favourite game, Scrabble. We were both exceedingly earnest in our play and had a big dictionary sitting on the table to prove it. We'd try all sorts of words, like qua, to win the big points. Sometimes that little word would win us up to thirty points.

Then there was the grand Ladies' Tea. I call it grand because it was for people who had money, which we didn't. For entertainment, the ladies would sew an outfit for their child between eight and ten years old. Then their child would model it in hopes of winning a cash prize.

When Mom heard about the contest, she decided to enter. I didn't know anything about it until the day I walked into the kitchen and found her putting together a very unusual-looking dress. The top had tiny pink roses on a white background. The knee-length skirt kind of flared out, and it had the same material as the top only she'd sewn green-panelled pleats into it, using the same shade of green as the stems on the flowers. When the skirt moved, the hidden panels became visible and then disappeared again, which made it look mysterious and attractive. I thought the colours and design were really pretty! When I asked who the dress was for, she explained that it was her own design and I would be modelling it. I felt truly honoured!

Mom completed the dress just days before the contest. When I tried it on to see how well it fit, it couldn't have been more perfect. She was proud and satisfied with her handiwork and so was I.

On the day of the contest, Mom curled and styled my hair. I was to change into the new dress shortly before the modelling was to begin. I was really excited and nervous at the same time!

Upon entering the tearoom, the level of activity, noise, and anticipation engulfed us. Some mothers were fussing over their kids; others rushed to and fro trying to get ready everything they needed, while still others talked a mile a minute with their friends.

Standing close to Mom, I anxiously waited to see what she would do. We soon moved into the room and found an empty table where we made ourselves comfortable. While she was talking with a woman about the event, I nervously glanced around. Not far from where we sat was the elevated stage where we would model our outfits. Seeing it caused my heart to beat a little faster.

There were also large bouquets of flowers scattered about the room. Everything looked very pretty, even the many tables that could seat four to six people. They were draped with snow-white tablecloths and decorated with fine china teacups sitting on saucers with tiny teaspoons lying next to them. In the middle of the tables were delicious platters of quartered sandwiches and dainties. Now things were looking up! I could hardly wait to sample one of those dainties!

Soon everyone was seated, and several women and their kids had joined our table. I think Mom may have known them. Anyway, the place was quite full.

A hush fell over the crowd as the master of ceremonies came to the podium and began her introductions. She talked for some time, but I didn't have a clue what she was saying. When it came time to eat, though, that I understood! The lunch tasted every bit as good as it looked.

With all the formalities taken care of, it was finally time to get ready for the main event. Mom and I were directed to a small change room. With pride, Mom took her creation out of its bag, shook it out gently, and then carefully pulled the dress over my head so my hair wouldn't be disturbed. When she'd zipped me up, the crisp newness of the material felt wonderful against my skin. It made me feel like a little princess. After all, new clothes weren't common in our house.

Then she magically produced a pair of special shoes to match the dress. Now I really felt like a princess!

Nervously, I waited in line with all the other contestants, each of them wearing great outfits. I really wanted to do Mom proud, and I wanted her to win.

When my turn finally arrived, on shaky limbs I climbed the stairs to the stage and moved shyly across it, knowing every eye in the room was on me. I did everything I had been told to do, to the best of my ability, and after it was done I could hardly wait to get off the stage so I could go and sit with Mom. When the time came, she gave me a big hug and a smile. I knew I had done okay!

It was interesting to watch the rest of the show, but it was also agonizing having to wait until we found out who the winner was. In the end, we didn't win, but to me, my mom was a winner. I really loved the dress she made for me!

Mom was a hard and steadfast worker, and it was common to see her up and working first thing in the morning. She'd get up before everyone else and be the last one to bed at night.

She was the type to take up a challenge, such as starting her own businesses. She did whatever she could to make extra money to put food on the table. She'd learn what she could about a business and proceed. Whether or not it succeeded, she would pursue it with so much tenacity that you couldn't help but admire her.

She took up a job called "invisible reweaving." A customer would bring in a pair of expensive dress pants or suit jacket that had a burn or tear in it and she would cut a matching piece of the material from some hidden place inside the garment, about half an inch larger than the hole, then lay the frayed patch over the hole. With a special tool, she used the loose strands of thread from all four sides, to weave the threads through the garment. She would concentrate for hours under a bright light, using a magnify glass to accomplish the task. When she was finished, no one could tell where the hole had been. She had many customers because no one else did this kind of work, nor have I ever heard of anyone else doing it since.

She was also hired to bake cinnamon rolls for a local restaurant. I've never tasted a cinnamon roll that matched hers. It was a privilege to be her daughter. That woman could bake.

Not long after we moved to Thompson, she took in boarders in order to feed us. She worked so hard as she cared for nine kids, seven boarders, a drunken husband, and whoever else might be around, having passed out after one of Dad's drinking parties.

To generate more income, she applied to work for a clothing company, selling their product. I don't recall the name of the company, but she was sent a catalogue filled with pages containing pictures of men, women, and children wearing the latest fashions. Along with the pictures were swatches of fabric to showcase the materials. She must have sold quite a bit, because the binder was around for a long time and new pages were always being added to it.

Out of the blue, Mom came up with the idea one day to change the look of our living room. She decided she wanted to build two wooden shelves that reached from the floor to the ceiling, with an artificial fireplace in the middle. Dad mocked her for these types of endeavours, but she'd just prove him wrong.

On this occasion, she bought the required materials and plywood and went to work. She measured, cut, nailed, and stained the whole thing with the help of a couple of my brothers. We were really proud of her. Even Dad went so far as to try to take credit for doing it when he showed it off to his friends, thinking Mom wasn't in hearing distance. However, Mom would catch him and correct him on the spot. Yet he wouldn't tell her she'd done a great job. That would mean he was wrong and she was right. That just wouldn't do. After all, he was "the man."

When Mom was no longer taking in boarders, she had two bedrooms built in the basement so the boys could have more space. After most of us had married and left home, she came up with the brilliant idea of turning one of those rooms into a store. She cleared out the room, then purchased enough shelves to line the walls. She carefully considered what kind of product she wanted to sell and then sent in her order to a company she was dealing with. When her product began to arrive, we found that she had chosen the most interesting trinkets, ornaments, and jewellery, none of which could be found in the stores downtown.

She placed ads in the newspaper and posted them on bulletin boards. She got a lot of customers, but of course Dad again ridiculed her. But as with other things, she was tenacious and determined to prove him wrong. To me, she was a winner and I very much admired her. I also became one of her best customers.

Mom was quite a feisty woman, and she absolutely hated booze; drinking had caused her more than her share of pain, abuse, and disappointment. When she did try to drink, she would get really sick on it.

She and Dad would get into major fights, and she'd often stand her ground and take the beating, especially if it meant saving us kids, which happened far too often.

As mentioned in the previous chapter, when she came to the end of her rope with Dad, she secretly packed our clothes and anything else we would need on the day we finally ran. One of my aunts told me that every time she tried to leave Dad, and then come back to him, she got pregnant. So she must have left him ten times.

On those occasions when we left with her, we would move to one of her sister's homes. I remember living for periods of time in Churchbridge, Wadena, Prince Albert, and Lloydminster.

My first memory of us leaving Dad happened when I was seven years old and we went to live with my aunt in Wadena. I don't know how long we were there, but I do remember the feeling of living in peace. We didn't cower when we did wrong or made mistakes. I very much liked living there and meeting our cousins for the first time.

Coming into the house one day, I heard the sound of my father's voice and stopped dead in my tracks from the anxiety that shot through my body. He had found us.

He and Mom were talking at the kitchen table, so I cautiously made my way to the staircase just outside the kitchen and listened to what they were saying.

No, don't listen to him, I silently pleaded. *He's lying, can't you see? Please, please say no.*

I held my breath, hoping for the best, but in the end we lost and he won. I ran upstairs and cried. We went home with him and in no time life returned to normal—more drinking, more fighting, more fear, more everything. Nothing changed.

When I was nine, during an extremely cold winter, Mom made plans to leave again but didn't let us know until the day we left. She wouldn't take any chance of one of us slipping up and telling Dad. It was sort of like a surprise vacation; our clothes and necessities were packed in boxes and suitcases and everything was ready to go.

Six out of nine kids sat at the kitchen table with Mom, anxiously waiting for our taxi to come. My other three brothers had been sent away prior to our leaving.

We were a desperate-looking lot and jumped nervously at every sound. The air seemed to crackle with electricity. My mind kept telling me that Dad was going to walk through that door any minute, coming home from work early, and we were all going to be in big trouble.

The minutes crawled by like a snail and my heart felt like it would explode from all the pressure we were under. Every sound sent shockwaves through my body. I was beginning to think the clock's hands were stuck.

Then I heard it—a car pulling into the driveway. My first panicked thought was that Dad was home, but to my relief it turned out to be the taxi. We quickly grabbed as much as we could, packed it into the taxi, and drove away without any mishap or regret.

At the train station outside of town, I watched Mom buy our tickets as the boys gave our luggage to the station attendant. We still had a while to wait for our train to arrive, so I walked outside onto the platform, willing the train to get here as soon as possible. None of us would be safe until we were on board, with the doors securely shut, and the train speeding down the tracks as fast as it could. Only then could we unwind.

Back inside the shabby little station, every sound echoed as it bounced off the grungy panelled walls and squeaky unpolished wooden floor. Old beat-up benches leaned against the walls, forcing you to look at the people on the other side of the room while you waited.

Every time one of the doors squeaked open, on either side of the building, I'd catch my breath and jerk my head around to see who was coming in or going out. I could hardly move a muscle for the tension.

It was all I could do to sit on the wooden bench and try to breathe. The train was taking forever to get here. Didn't they know how important it was for us to get away? He'd kill us if he found us. The fear and impatience were overloading my young mind.

After what seemed a lifetime, I heard the familiar sound of the train pulling in. I jumped to my feet and ran to the door to watch. Ever so slowly, the train backed its way into the station. I trembled with excitement.

Suddenly, lots of new people seemed to show up from out of nowhere, crowding in to get on or off. At least my dad wasn't amongst them.

When it was my turn to board, my legs felt like wooden pegs, making it difficult for me to walk up the steep steps into the car. The porter had to hold my arm and guide me. It was becoming more and more possible for me to believe that we were actually going to make our escape.

Inside, we had many seats to choose from, but Mom wanted us all together. I chose to sit on the side of the train that overlooked the platform. Through the window, I kept watch to see if Dad was going to appear. My ears were attuned to the slamming of the train door.

Impatiently, I watched as the porter made his way down the long aisle to check each and every passenger's ticket.

Come on, come on, my brain screamed. *Let's get out of here.*

Then, with a sharp jerk and a loud bang, the train began to nudge forward. We'd done it! He hadn't caught us! I could see the relief written on the faces of my family. They were just as strung out as I was.

We were headed for Prince Albert, where my grandmother and grandfather lived. I didn't know them very well, but I remembered that they were really nice.

When we arrived in Prince Albert, Mom found us an old two-story house that supported a veranda with big white pillars out front. The house itself was tall and narrow with a steep roof; we called it the Crackerbox House. It was rather ugly, but it was safe and it was ours.

On entering the house, one came face to face with a chipped wooden staircase. To the right was a small living room with scuffed hardwood floors. The only furniture it contained was an old, beat-up table and wooden crate that we came to use as a chair. A big picture window overlooked the front yard.

There was a door under the staircase which led to a partial dirt basement. All that we found down there was a hanging lightbulb, the furnace, the hot water tank, a roll of ancient linoleum, some canned jam, and a million cobwebs. It was really a spooky place and I kept away from it.

One time someone purposefully locked me down there with the light shut off for hours. Or at least that's how long it seemed; it may only have been about fifteen minutes. I was absolutely petrified and screamed over and over again for my jailer to let me out. My skin literally crawled at the thought of all those ugly spiders down there, the ones that had made all those horrible cobwebs. It was a living nightmare.

Finally, someone came to my rescue and freed me. It took a long time for me to get over the experience, and to this day I can't stand spiders.

A door in the living room led into a tiny kitchen. There was no fridge, stove, table, or any chairs to be found, but it did have a couple of cupboards, a sink, and a short counter. It boasted a two-paned window, which became our fridge. By lifting the inside window, there was enough room to hold a carton of milk and meat. For cooking, we had a hot plate.

There were two rooms upstairs, a fairly large bathroom and a small bedroom. The bedroom's only furniture was a metal-framed single bed with a worn-out mattress. Every movement caused it to squeak loudly.

It was decided that Lawrence would take the bed, as he had to work and needed his sleep. He was only fourteen years old, but he looked older and had found work with a drilling company out of Saskatoon. His job was soil-testing for a pulp and paper mill. He worked hard to help support us, and for this I am very grateful.

Because we had no furniture of our own, the rest of us slept on the hardwood floor in the living room, but we didn't mind.

First off, Mom enrolled us in school and then went on a job search. She found work cleaning five houses during the week. Her meagre wages paid for our scant meals of milk, bread, and bologna wrapped in waxed brown paper. Aside from inexpensive staples, we didn't have much for food, but we were content. There were days when all we had to eat before going to school were a few tablespoons of jam that had been left in jars in the basement.

On special occasions we'd visit our grandparents. We had to walk a couple of miles to get there, but it was well worth it for a full-course meal. My grandma made the best cabbage rolls ever!

Our school was about six blocks straight down the street from where we lived, and in the winter we didn't have the warmest of clothes. The few clothes we did have were shared between us three girls. It was first come, first served. We had the barest of necessities.

I found it hard to start over with school in the middle of a term. I was in Grade Four and didn't understand the way they taught math here. They did it differently and I couldn't grasp the concepts. I don't know how many times the teacher called me to her desk to show me. I just didn't get it, which made me feel dumb and out of place.

Then, on top of everything, I caught a cold and didn't have tissues to wipe my nose. So it would just keep running and I'd sniff it back in. Because I was always so shy and afraid, I couldn't ask the teacher for tissues or to go to the washroom. I had been told no one was allowed to go to the washroom during class. It was humiliating and caused me to shrink even more inside myself.

Because we were so poor, I felt nervous and lonely. I had a hard time communicating with others, but after a month or two I finely made friends with a girl my age. After a while, she invited me over to her house for a visit. Her mom talked kindly to me and made me feel special. It was nice to feel, for just a short time, that I was normal.

One day Mom brought home an inexpensive paper bingo game, and for prizes she used pennies and matchsticks. We laughed and shouted with great excitement when we won or got close to winning. Mom sat on the wooden crate and called out numbers while we used the stairway for tables and chairs. We also used the stairway to do our homework on, and to eat dinner on.

We had to entertain ourselves with one another, because there was no TV or telephone. But that was the beauty of it; we actually had to communicate with each other and Mom had time for us. It may have been hard, but we were happy. It's the only time I remember us having our own place and not staying with others when we moved away from Dad.

One evening, around springtime, just as the sun was starting to go down, some of us kids were outside playing on the front lawn when, unexpectedly, a strange car pulled up in front of the house.

You guessed it.

Dad slid out from behind the steering wheel and instantly all play came to an abrupt end. Not a sound was heard as we cautiously backed away from the sidewalk, filled with fear and dread.

I guess the best way to describe the situation would be to say that we were basically like a family in the witness protection program—and we'd been caught. Doom hung over our heads.

He greeted us in his cool, gruff voice, then confidently strutted straight into the house without knocking. We didn't follow him in.

Anger and resentment rose up in me. We knew what was coming next. We'd been here about six glorious months, and before long he would sweet-talk or threaten Mom into returning back with him.

Lawrence didn't come home with us this time, because Dad hated him and didn't want him around. Fortunately for him, he could stay with our grandparents. At least he was safe there. I would have gladly joined him.

The next day, we were on the train heading back to Thompson in a really old passenger car with several other people. Half the car had wooden benches lining its outside walls, so that our backs were to the windows and we had to face one another. The corner had a big pot-bellied wood-burning stove to heat the car when it got cold. Gas lanterns hung from the walls. I'd seen trains like this in the old western movies.

As kids, we had to explore and found out that the far end of the car was considered first class. It was partitioned off by a wooden wall, and the bench seats in there were stuffed and covered with thick black leather. It would have been much more comfortable, but it was closed off.

Sometime during the night, our car somehow disconnected from the rest of the train and we were left stranded in the middle of nowhere. It was so dark outside that all we could see were our reflections in the windows. It was getting very cold, so many of us huddled up to the stove. Listening to the adults, one mentioned that another train could be on the same track as us and not know we were stranded there; it could run into us. That was a scary thought!

We were stranded there for several hours until we were discovered missing and the train came back to get us.

That ride was the most interesting experience I'd ever had on a train, and it was the only thing I had to be thankful to Dad for. Once we were settled back at home, it didn't take him long to break all his promises and go back to the old routine. He just loved his booze more than he loved us.

This pattern continued for years to follow—new homes, new friends, new schools, new fears, and a lot of disappointment.

The one thing I learned from all this was how to run away from problems. If I didn't like how things were going, the solution was to say, "Screw this, I'm out of here." Eventually I came to a place in my life where I couldn't stay in one place longer than a year before I'd get that overpowering urge to move on. Sometimes it was just to move across the road, but I had to start over somewhere new.

I battled long and hard to break the habit of running, but with God's help I eventually managed to stay put in the same home for ten years.

Five

Lawrence

It was known among us kids that Dad tried to kill our mother on several occasions. Lawrence remembers being in the same room with them while they fought one day. In a rage, Dad picked up a sharp knife and threw it at her while she was walking away from him and it stuck in the back of her neck. How she survived, only God knows.

Another time, Dad beat her severely enough to put her in the hospital for five days. While she was recovering, out of pure hatred he sent Lawrence to a particular store for a package of cigarettes and instructed him to return in ten minutes or else. Lawrence ran as fast as his legs could carry him, knowing full well he wouldn't make it in time. Dad knew it, too. When Lawrence returned, Dad forced Lawrence into a kitchen chair and bound his hands and feet with ropes. He then went to the cupboard, took out a large pot, filled it with water, and set it on the stove to boil. When he was satisfied that it had boiled long enough, he picked up the pot and poured the water over Lawrence's feet.

Who does that to their little boy? I can only imagine the screams that must have come out of his pain-wracked body. The thought just nauseates me, the terror that must have gone through this boy as he sat, tied up and helpless, while the person who was supposed to be his protector prepared an injustice too monstrous for the mind to fathom.

When Lawrence later told me about this horrific act, and showed me his feet, I cried at the injustice of it, at the cruelty. That's how evil my father was. He was a monster that only his family ever witnessed.

I have no doubt at all that I was somewhere in the house on that day and witnessed what happened. But like I said, there is much I don't remember.

Not long after, a friend of the family came by to visit and saw Lawrence's wounds and immediately took him to the hospital. He was flown by air ambulance to Winnipeg where he was to undergo weeks of skin-grafting to learn how to walk again. He received a total of thirty-six skin grafts over the years.

For Dad to have gotten away with that, he must have told one whopper of a story to his friend and the staff at the hospital. Still, I'll bet Dad wasn't too happy having to pay the cost of the trip.

On release from the hospital, Lawrence tried running away to Vancouver, but he only made it as far as Brandon before the police caught up with him. He was taken back to Thompson on a Greyhound bus, with a police escort, and delivered back into the hands of a madman who the very next day beat him severely with his fists and cracked some ribs. This resulted in Lawrence being hospitalized for another seven days.

No one outside our family would have ever believed what Dad was capable of doing and what he'd gotten away with for far too many tragic years. Even now, my heart pounds. How my brother must have suffered at that monster's hands.

As of today, there are scars covering the tops of Lawrence's feet, and when touched it feels as though razor-sharp knives are being stuck through them, while the bottoms of his feet are numb yet tender to the touch. It just makes me want to scream.

On other occasions, Dad broke Lawrence's ribs, first when he was only three years old. He vaguely remembers crawling on the floor, hearing a scream, feeling a sharp pain, and then blacking out.

Years later, the memory was verified when one of Mom's sisters, who was visiting at the time, said that she saw it happen. Dad had been drunk and in his usual violent mood. While having choice words with Mom, Lawrence must have gotten in Dad's way because Dad kicked him across the room, slamming him into a wall. Dad always wore hard shoes; they made for a good weapon.

Another time, two of my mother's sisters came to visit. During their short stay, Dad got so drunk that he fell asleep while standing up in a corner. One aunt took it upon herself to go over to him and wake him up, so he could go and lay down. Mom saw what her sister was about to do and screamed for her not to touch him. My aunt stopped dead in her tracks. Who knows what would have happened if she had woken him up? When he passed out and someone touched him, he would come to swinging.

Lawrence once shared with me that Dad took him and another brother out for target practice one day, only they didn't know that they were the targets. Lawrence was maybe ten years old at the time. The boys were told to put apples on their head, so Dad could shoot them off. They were told not to move or cry or he'd shoot them in the leg. Dad also shot coins from between their fingers. He was a deadly shot for a man who could only see out of one eye.

Lawrence shook with fear, but he dared not defy our demented father.

My brothers came home that day, and all the other days that he did this to them. God must have protected them, and of course Mom was never told what happened. Dad had warned them to keep quiet.

There were times when Dad would come home from the bar stinking drunk and revert back to his old army days. He was no longer a slim and fit man and weighed well over two hundred pounds. Not caring about what time of night it was, he'd stand in the middle of the living room and holler out for each of my brothers to get out of their beds and come downstairs. He'd make them stand at attention in a perfect line for long periods of time—and if they didn't comply, there would be hell to pay. Dad would sometimes stand on their feet or have them kneel on a floor register made of metal. If they so much as moved, he'd backhand them or worse. Mom would stand by, helpless. Although she would step in if it got too far out of control, she would end up getting beaten. It did get him away from the boys for a while.

My two sisters and I didn't know everything that Dad did to them, but we could hear it loud and clear because our bedroom was right above the living room. All we could do was lie in our beds, shaking violently with fear at every bark of order or slamming of something against a table or wall and wondered who was the chosen victim.

I would get so angry at what he was doing to them, but all I could do was cry silently into my pillow and scream internally, *Stop! Leave them alone!* We had to keep quiet or else he would come to our room and start in on us.

I hurt so much for Mom and my tortured brothers. I wanted to be brave and strong, to go down there, sneak up behind him, and strike him on the head with something really hard, either to knock him out or even kill him... but I couldn't do any of that because I was just a terrified little girl who wanted it all to end.

These despicable games would go on and on until he tired of them.

The next day, I would get up and put on a pretend mask as though nothing was amiss, just smiling and saying hi and walking away, hating his guts. The fact that he acted as though nothing unusual had happened caused me to despise him even more.

Who Cares?

My secure home is gone
I'm out on the crowded streets
Pounding the pavement daily
Looking for food and a place to sleep

My only treasured possessions
Are the clothes upon my back
And a battered ol' suitcase
Held tightly in my grasp

Rejected, tired and scared
Meals scrounged from a garbage can
I am now a public nuisance
To be hassled by The Man[5]

---

[5] A reference to the police.

Shelters hold some protection
But only for the night
They're filled to such capacity
And often there could be a fight

Homeless, helpless and still trying
Lost in the big city streets
Hundreds and thousands just like me
Holding fast to our dignity

For many there is no way out
We may die in the stinking gutters
When poverty has its way
The rich can't hear us utter

We're not recognized by society
Though characterized as bums
Most won't try to help us
To them we're classified as scum

There were times when I could hardly wait until I was old enough to leave the house. I figured by the time I hit my teens, it'd be my turn to be booted out onto the streets, just like my other siblings before me. That scared me to death. They slept in old cars at the garbage dump, at a friend's place, and who knows where else.

When Dad was at work, they'd sneak home to the back door in desperate need of food. Mom would secretly bag them sandwiches, although she had been warned by Dad not to. I saw her do this many times, and would often help, but I was sworn to secrecy.

It broke my heart to see them treated in such an inhumane fashion. I hated him even more for this. I'd do the best I could to talk to him with great respect, even though I didn't respect him at all, or I'd stay out of his way altogether. I had no idea how to survive out on my own.

For my brothers' safety, when Mom had enough money saved, she would send them to live with one of her sisters. They would be gone for long periods of time, working on their farms and going to school. Because of this, I never got to know them well, but at least they were relatively safe. That's all that mattered.

Before Mom died, she had the chance to talk with Lawrence and told him that she'd feared that he, out of all the kids, would be most like his father. Instead she was proud that he'd turned out nothing like him. Now, that's precious!

Although I've only written about Lawrence's stories here, there are many others from my siblings. They have no desire to venture back into the past, though, and who can blame them? It would only wake the monster, and they'd just as soon let it sleep.

Throughout Lawrence's suffering, I know I was there. I must have heard or witnessed most of it. What I don't remember, I'm sure, must be a blessing from God. What I do remember is bad enough, and I'd love nothing more than to erase it all.

Later in life, I read the story of another family that was similar to ours. I cried uncontrollably, identifying with those kids and what they'd endured. I was able to feel everything written on the pages of that book, and it made me want to scream. At least it helped me to know that we weren't the only ones who had a father like ours, not that I'd wish him on anyone.

Six
More Family Violence

We received no real parental nurturing from either of our parents. Mom did what she could, but she wasn't able to spread herself around to give us the kind of attention we needed. She tried to keep the peace between her and Dad and at the same time protect us and maintain her own sanity.

Our lives were overloaded with terror, torment, anger, and hatred towards our father—and because we learned so well from him, the same dynamic spread into our relationships with each other. We had plenty of verbal and physical fights, from the oldest to the youngest. I remember having a butcher knife fight with one of my older brothers. Fortunately neither of us got hurt, but the intent was there. The same brother used to bend me over and drive his fist into my back. Just venting his frustration, I guess.

Violence became a way of life. If you didn't strike first, you may not get another chance.

When I was about eight years old, Dad got drunk one day and engaged in his usual bullying of Mom, but this time my older brother Paul protected her. From what I understand, Dad was harassing Mom in one of the upstairs bedrooms when Paul took hold of a bunkbed rail and tried to hit Dad over the head with it, only he struck Mom instead, cutting a large gash in her forehead just above the eye. She bled profusely, and when they came downstairs, yelling and carrying on, Paul was pleading that he hadn't meant to hurt her.

Dad was in a rage, probably because Paul had meant to hit him, not because Mom was hurt. I don't know what all happened, but somehow Dad came into the kitchen in a rampage and several of us kids grabbed sharp knives and surrounded Dad. We threatened to stab him if he didn't leave Paul and Mom alone.

He didn't know what to do, nor did we. All we knew was that he had hurt Mom one time too many and he wasn't going to do it again.

What a horrible feeling it is to hold a knife on someone you really hate and are terrified of. As I stood there with the knife pointed at his midsection, I knew I would stab him if I had to. I was that determined.

I don't recall exactly what happened after that, since my mind must have shut off from the fear, but Mom went to the hospital where the doctor stitched her up without any kind of anaesthetic, since she was allergic to everything they had. She suffered terribly. I just can't imagine what that must have been like for her.

My poor brother was so tormented because of what he'd done. We never blamed him, since we knew he had only been trying to protect her, but he must have had a hard time living with himself after that.

How we managed to get away with surrounding Dad that night, I'll never know, but you can bet that he would get his revenge.

I often witnessed Dad grab hold of Mom's long wavy hair and yank her head backwards. She would cry out in pain, pleading with him to let her go while he looked down into her face with a snarl on his lips. I would be fuming, screaming silently inside, as the nerves in my body trembled and tears rolled down my face: *Stop hurting her. She didn't do anything. It's your fault that everything is so bad. You ruin everything. You take all the money and drink it away then come home drunk and miserable and hurt her. Get out and leave us alone. We didn't do anything wrong, yet you hate and hurt us and kill whatever happiness we have.*

I hated him with a passion and truly wished he would die and get out of our lives once and for all. He was the monster of all monsters. It would have been safer for us out on the streets than to live in the same house with him.

When he was gone, Mom was different. She was relaxed and even laughed sometimes, but when he was home she walked on eggshells.

Why can't you be like the other fathers? I wanted to yell from years of pent-up resentment. *My friends aren't scared to go home. Their moms and dads talk to each other, and laugh and talk to them. I can feel the peace in their homes. I see my friend's bedrooms and they don't have beds stacked up on each other like our barracks. Most of them have their own rooms full of their own stuff. They have their own clothes. We have to share and wear whatever fits us. They have privacy. I don't have any of these things. I have a father who drinks, runs around on my mother, steals, cheats, and beats on her and my brothers. If you hate us so much, why don't you just leave? We're the sum total of your sexual abuse on our mother. How many of us were conceived by rape?*

I shared a small bedroom with my two younger sisters and a baby brother. Many nights we lay in bed listening to Dad through the thin closet wall that separated our bedrooms. I'd hear the sound of a slap, then my mother's moan of pain, followed by a bang as she was slammed into the wall. I also heard him raping her and her pleading cry for him to stop. I wanted to go in there and scream at him myself, but I couldn't do anything. I would lie there in tears and scream in my own mind.

Many other people have talked about being scared of their parents separating or divorcing. For me, I was scared mine would stay together.

I've lived a lot of years in apartment buildings and sometimes I'd hear neighbours fight. Whenever I heard a woman screaming and crying, I'd suddenly find myself back in my old bedroom, shaking in fear. The fear from those triggering sounds would grip my soul.

One time, while I was standing at the top of the stairway of our home, I saw Mom race from the kitchen into the living room, trying to get away from Dad. Right behind her, he chased her buck naked, reaching out his big meaty hand to grab her by the hair while calling her filthy names. I ran back to my bed and covered my head with my pillow. I didn't want to hear it. I was terrified for Mom.

Another time he dragged her by her hair, pulling her up the stairs. I could hear her body hit the steps and walls, and her cries for help, but there was no one to help. There was no calling the police, either, because we feared the consequences that would follow once they were gone. We'd already been down that road. Several times he'd disconnected the phone by pulling the wire out of the wall.

Years after I left home, I met up with an old friend of our family who was a neighbour. She told me that Mom sometimes came over to visit on scorching hot days wearing long-sleeved shirts and sunglasses. Mom would say she'd hurt herself doing something. My friend was utterly shocked when I told her what Dad had done to us throughout the years. She said she wished she had known, so that she could have put a stop to it.

"No one could have stopped him," I told her. "He was unstoppable."

She looked at me with tenderness and earnestly assured me that if she and our other neighbours had known what was going on they could have done something about it. Somehow I knew she was telling the truth, but growing up under his tyranny we had felt it was an impossibility. Even though this little ray of hope came too late, it somehow made me feel better.

As long as I can remember, up to the ripe old age of twelve, I sucked the two fingers closest to my thumb on my right hand for comfort and security. My nerves were frayed from the constant fighting and bickering in the house. Sucking my fingers soothed my troubled emotions and brought some kind of calm to the stormy seas called home. Even when the waters seemed calm on the surface, underneath there were gigantic riptides.

Nights were when I most needed comfort. I'd lay in my bunkbed, rocking back and forth and sucking hard on those fingers in the hopes that sleep would overtake my fear-ridden mind. Sometimes, without realizing it, I even shoved those fingers in my mouth during the day. It was an embarrassment, especially when Dad yelled at me to get them out.

Not only was I ashamed for sucking my fingers, I also became a bed-wetter. I don't know how many nights I dreamt of climbing down my bunkbed ladder, walking to the bathroom, and sitting on the toilet to relieve myself only to wake up and discover I had wet the bed. Not again! I had to lay in my own urine the rest of the night because I couldn't call out for help. I couldn't take the chance of waking or angering my father and facing the shame and embarrassment that would come with his words of scorn, or even a spanking.

I believe the bedwetting stems from my early childhood. If Dad heard anyone was out of their rooms for any reason, he would yell at us to get back to bed and he'd better not catch us out of bed again. In fear I'd run back to bed and try my hardest to hold on until he fell asleep, but unfortunately I wasn't always successful. The nights when I could wait him out, I'd carefully climb down from my bunk and as slowly and silently as possible turn the knob on our closed bedroom door and hope the door didn't make any sound when it opened. In the dark I'd tiptoe along the pitch-black hallway, hoping my bladder didn't give way before I could slip by my parent's open bedroom door. Carefully stepping into the bathroom, I'd softly close the door, then turn on the light and do my business. Flushing was out of the question.

To get back to my bedroom, I had to do everything in reverse. What a nerve-wracking ordeal it was.

The mornings after I wet the bed, I would have to somehow cover up my shame so the others wouldn't find out. This continued until I was about nine years old, maybe even older.

I determined one night that the finger-sucking habit had to stop, so I lay on my hand all night every night until I quit. As for bed-wetting, Dad slowed down enough on his drinking that I eventually felt brave enough to face his wrath. That's when the bed-wetting stopped.

I didn't understand until I was much older that these were symptoms of trauma, fear, and abuse. I had to come to the place of acknowledging that it wasn't my fault. I was a victim of circumstance.

Dad was like a roaring lion, prowling around the house seeking someone to devour. When he was like that, it didn't matter whether you were big or small; he was coming for you.

On nights when he drank, he'd patrol the upstairs hallway to check if there were any noises coming from the bedrooms, and make sure everyone was home. When his footsteps neared our door, my heart would pound wildly. No matter what happened, I pretended I was asleep and didn't move a muscle.

One night, he opened our bedroom door and reached down into the crib of my crying four-month-old baby brother, Andrew. He grabbed him by one foot and lifted him upside-down, shaking him violently, then threw him back down into the crib and told him to shut his f—ing mouth. Then he slammed the door shut on his way out.

I watched this through narrowed eyes, but not a muscle flinched. I waited anxiously until Dad had gone downstairs before climbing down the ladder to see how badly Andrew had been hurt. Carefully, I picked him up and cradled him in my arms, rocking him gently while whispering a soothing, shushing sound into his ears, hoping to quieten him before Dad came back to do more harm.

My two sisters watched me with fear on their faces. I wanted to tell them it was okay, but no one could promise such a thing in our house. It wasn't okay and never would be. We were his property to do with as he pleased.

Later in life, Andrew was told of another incident that had happened to him when he was only a baby. Dad must have been looking in the fridge for something when Andrew crawled up to look inside, too. Dad purposely slammed the door on his head. Another time, at the age of five, Andrew went outside to meet Dad as he was coming home from work, so he could carry Dad's lunch kit into the house for him. For no apparent reason, Dad backhanded him. Just because he could, I guess. From that day on, Andrew stayed as far away from him as possible.

On another occasion, Dad backhanded one of my sisters across her ear and destroyed her eardrum. She hasn't heard out of it since.

The man had a mean streak that ran deep into his soul. It didn't take me long to learn not to tell him about certain things, like when I had a loose tooth. Immediately he shoved his big, tobacco-stained fingers deep in my mouth, digging with his dirty nails down into my tender gums, causing the most horrible crunching, grinding sounds. Then he brutally yanked that tooth out, whether it was ready to come out or not. Triumphantly, he held up the tooth with blood on his fingertips.

"Don't be such a baby, or I'll really give you something to cry about," he said.

I wondered if the man had any feelings at all.

Christmas

It seemed that whenever anything nice was about to take place, something horrible would happen instead. That was the way of it.

Christmas was the worst time of year in our house. It always started out okay, with Mom pulling out the Christmas ornaments in readiness to decorate the living room. A pine tree would be brought in, cut down from somewhere along the highway.

Several days before Christmas one year, I went with Mom and a couple of the other kids to find that special Christmas tree. One of the boys drove Dad's station wagon down the highway until we stopped at a place where we thought we'd find a good tree.

We had to trudge our way down through a deep, snow-filled ditch to reach the edge of the forest where pine and poplar trees grew for miles and miles in every direction. Most of the pines were sparse because of the harsh northern winters, so they didn't have much on them and looked pretty shabby. Yet there were also some newer and fuller trees growing under the protection of the older ones.

After much deliberation, Mom settled on a fair-sized tree that looked the best and asked my brother to cut it down. We then had the pleasure of hauling it back to the car. It was an enjoyable hunt and we returned home victorious.

At home, Mom had the tree brought straight into the living room and stuck in the traditional corner. When it thawed and the branches settled into their natural form, she could see where it was bare and where more branches were needed to fill out the tree to make it look even. Mom would take a handsaw and cut branches off the backside of the tree, then reattach them to the bare spots in front. The tree was beautiful because it was real, its fragrance filling the living room. She always put the lights on first, and then we decorated the rest. When we were finished she would put on the final, wondrous touch: angel hair tinsel.

Next, we'd decorate the rest of the living room. Mom used red and green twisted crepe-paper streamers that crisscrossed the ceiling from corner to corner, forming a gigantic X. In the middle, a paper bell would hang down. Tinsel was hung all along the length of the streamers, shimmering and sparkling when the furnace ran. Along with other decorations, the living room would take on the magical appearance of a fairy land, inspiring feelings of awe.

Days before Christmas, a few presents would appear under the tree, the ones we bought for Mom and Dad. We didn't get too many new things, but our fun was in looking through the department store catalogues and dreaming big.

With the Christmas shopping done, we'd turn our attention to the different varieties of foods we only had at Christmastime. Dad made the most fantastic hors d'oeuvre platters I've ever seen, along with meat, cheese, and pickle trays that looked far too beautiful to eat, and they tasted even better than they looked. There were the usual nuts, tangerines, and varieties of candies, not to mention the pop and homemade eggnog.

We'd sit in front of the large black-and-white TV watching our favourite shows and gorging ourselves on all these wonderful foods. On such days, it felt like we were a real family.

Christmas Eve would soon arrive. Only one more sleep! A mixture of anticipation and excitement would give me an adrenaline rush… a rush that would cause me to forget what came next. You see, Christmas Eve is when Dad's celebrating would hit its peak. Almost like a ritual, we'd anxiously watch the clock tick away the minutes to see if Dad was going to go to the bar or come home after work.

Please, please come home, I would silently plead. *Don't ruin this Christmas like you did last year.*

Shortly before five o'clock one year, while supper was waiting to be put on the table, I sensed the tension emanating from Mom. She began to pace. When 5:15 struck and he still hadn't shown up, I could see the disappointment and fear etched on her face. The inevitable was going to happen. He was out celebrating with his buddies.

In anxious anticipation, we ate our supper in silence, hoping he'd still come home and join us.

We managed to watch a Christmas special on TV without him coming in and destroying it for us. Then it was bedtime and still we heard not a word from him. It was the calm before the storm.

While lying in a fetal position in bed, I jumped at every unwelcome sound of a car driving by, or a door closing. Even the creaks of the house sent shockwaves of fear through my rigid body. It wasn't so much that I thought he'd hurt me or my siblings; it was because I worried one of these times we would find Mom dead.

The later it got, the more I knew it was going to be a brutal night. Mom was like a caged lioness pacing back and forth from the kitchen to the living room below. I could hear her moving around restlessly. She knew what was coming.

Well, here it came. Long past midnight, we heard the loud crunching of tires on ice and snow in the driveway. The thud of the car door told me Dad was on his way in.

With each approaching footstep, my fear escalated. Because my room was at the front of the house and my bed the top bunk, almost level with the window, I cautiously looked down to see if it was Dad. There was no mistaking that silhouette. Ready for a scrap, he yanked the front door open and right on cue roared, "Elizabeth, where the hell are you, you miserable b——?"

By slamming the front door, he let us all know that the master of the house was in residence. Everyone was awake now, anticipating the next move. It had begun. Mom would answer, but it wouldn't matter what she said.

"Where's my supper?" he demanded.

Mom would be going to the kitchen to reheat what she'd made for supper earlier, but of course that wasn't good enough. He'd ridicule and belittle her, always putting her down.

Whatever joy we'd had that day became swallowed up in misery. The peace was shattered by the sound of loud music coming from the stereo. Added to that we heard a mixture of arguing, filthy name-calling, accusations, and lies. They echoed through the whole house. Mom tried to reason with him, but he wouldn't listen. In his books, she was stupid and useless, and only put there for his amusement and pleasure.

What began as a verbal fight became physical, and soon we heard the inevitable sound of a crash and breaking glass. That would be the Christmas tree thrown to the floor. It was just another one of his ways to hurt her because he knew she'd decorated the tree, and of course it was also a way to get at us kids. She would try to stand her ground, but it only encouraged him to react in a more hostile manner, if that were possible.

When he finally passed out on the couch, after she'd managed to get some food into him, she cleaned up the mess and put the tree back together as best she could. Its beauty was lost, but at least it resembled a Christmas tree once again. Just before dragging her exhausted body off to bed, she retrieved all the gifts she'd hidden and placed them lovingly under the tree. She knew once he passed out, he was out for the night.

Come morning, I hesitated going downstairs to see if there was still a tree, let alone anything under it. One never knew what to expect.

The stench of stale whisky and cigarette smoke hung in the air instead of the wonderful scent of pine. And there, sprawled on the couch, was Dad, still out cold, snoring up a storm, not a care in the world.

Nope. Presents could wait for another time.

I quietly backed away from the living room door and made my way to the kitchen in search of breakfast. Those who were awake spoke in whispers. Whatever you did, you didn't wake the lion or you'd get growled at.

"What the f— do you think you're doing? Get back to bed right now."

"Get out of my f—ing sight, you horrible beasts."

"You're nothing but a bunch of Yucks."

Yep, I'm sure those were his favourite words for us. I can still hear them in my head. Was it possible that he couldn't remember our names? He used many other vile names, spoken in the most demeaning way. I'd cower on the inside, very careful not to show fear—or to show fear, whatever kept you from being hit.

Anyway, when Dad finally woke up and began to be a little more civilized, he behaved as though nothing out of the ordinary had happened.

We were finally allowed to open our presents, and for a short while we, too, could forget and get excited.

When it was Dad's turn to open his gifts, like most Christmases, he said he'd open them later and get up and leave the room, leaving the gifts behind. That was his way of taunting us and not letting us know what he thought of our gifts. He never would tell us.

As tired as Mom was, she wouldn't be defeated. She did her best to put on a good show and try to make it a special day for us. She spent hours preparing an enormous turkey dinner that day and we showed our appreciation by gorging ourselves on it. She was such an awesome cook!

Seven
Dad's Extracurriculars

Dad's drink of choice was Crown Royal whisky on the rocks or with water, and he could slam it back, no problem. Maybe it was no problem to him, but it sure was for the rest of us. When he brought it home, it was usually the largest bottle he could find.

He also loved beer just as much. One day, out of the blue, he was hit with this brain wave that he should make his own homebrew. It would be more cost-effective.[6] So he went shopping and bought the biggest stoneware crockpot he could find, including all the ingredients he'd need. With great gusto, he then proceeded to mix up a healthy batch of beer. It needed a dark and cool place to ferment, so it was kept in my brothers' closet. I have no idea what they did with their clothes. This was more important.

I also think this might have been his way of setting the boys up to get in trouble. If he caught them stealing from it, he would have another excuse to assault them. Either way, he was very cunning. He somehow marked the level of the beer every day and would check to see if it had been touched… and also to add new ingredients when required.

This project became his obsession.

I've heard many stories about the time this beer spent fermenting and just plain stinking up the place. Some of the boys did help themselves to a few glasses, then replaced what they'd taken with an equal measure of water. I was surprised to learn that Mom also snuck in every now and then to take out a potful, dump it in the toilet, then replace it with the same amount of water.

It's a good thing they were all doing this, because it was a lethal batch after Dad drank a few bottles. The brew made him every bit as dangerous as when he drank the whisky.

---

[6] Very considerate of him.

Finally, Dad's experiment was ready to be bottled! The kitchen was turned into an assembly line, with every available kid designated a job. Dad directed the whole procedure from beginning to end. One or two washed and sterilized old beer bottles, another poured the precious liquid into bottles using a funnel, and then another capped the bottles. The filled beer bottles were then packed into empty beer cases and stored in the basement. It was quite the system Dad had going for himself, including cheap labour. We slaved while he drank the benefits and made everybody's lives miserable.

We didn't have what some people would call an ordinary lifestyle. Our household was kind of like an old western saloon. Gambling was a given in our house. We couldn't play a game of ordinary cards without a little wager on the side, whether it was for money or toothpicks. I mean, what would be the thrill in playing for nothing?

I couldn't even play a game of crib with Dad unless there was a $5 wager, and then he would skunk me and take $10. If he was feeling really nice, he would double skunk me and take $20. I didn't always have that kind of money on me, but I always paid my debts, even at a young age—and he didn't mind taking it.

I thought we were a competitive family, probably because in every other way we were losers—or at least, I felt we were, considering our family's reputation. We never had enough money for food and clothes, but there was more than enough to drink and play poker. Me and my sisters always had to share our clothing, including our underclothes, which would get so worn out that the elastics would come apart. But we had to wear them until there was nothing to hold them together. Our pants had holes in the knees and they where patched over and over again. Either that or we'd just have to wear them as they were, with holes. Having holes wasn't the style in those days. I even had to wear my brothers' jeans and shirts because sometimes I didn't have anything else to wear. You can bet that caused a fight or two.

So our large closet held very few clothes for three fast-growing girls, and what we had was second-hand and didn't always fit right or look good. I felt ashamed about the way we dressed compared to other families, so out of place and drab, but Mom did what she could. Her wardrobe wasn't much better. My five older brothers had the same problem.

As for my dad? Well, he made the money and could spend it as he pleased.

By the time I turned thirteen, Dad started bringing home a few people he'd met at the bar to play poker. At first they'd sit around the kitchen table chain-smoking, drinking, swearing, and telling coarse jokes. And of course the odd scuffle would break out, but at least the game would end that night and there wouldn't be another game for a while.

It didn't take long until it became a regular Friday night event. The game would start on Friday right after supper and end Sunday night or early Monday morning so Dad could go to work, even though he was still drunk.

I can say one positive thing about him, though: he never missed work. As drunk as he was, he'd go in to work and sleep it off there. At the nickel mine, he was in control of the tool crib in the smelter. He'd lock the door and make it look like he was out and about somewhere else.

If we kids managed to sleep at all through the shouting, fighting, and loud music of these poker weekends, it became commonplace to wake up to find men and women slobbering drunk and still playing cards. There'd also be men passed out in the living room. We'd just have to ignore them and stay away in case we woke them up.

Being a young girl, I didn't trust the men who came home with Dad. I'd pretend it didn't bother me and carefully make my way around the table in the kitchen and push aside the empty bottles, dirty dishes, and overflowing ashtrays on the counter, scrounging around for a clean dish to have breakfast.

Sometimes it was safer not to enter the kitchen at all. Just showing your face there could get you barked at or belittled, depending on how the old man felt at any given moment. Mom spent many nights staying up because otherwise he'd just keep waking her up to get them food to eat. And sometimes she'd have to break up a fight or, more importantly, keep the men from wandering into her daughters' bedroom.

When people came over, they brought cases of beer, as well as all kinds of liquor and mixes. The kitchen counter became the bar, and we kids became bartenders. Sometimes we'd even get tips if the players felt generous or lucky. We were allowed to hang out in the kitchen as long as we kept quiet and were useful and didn't bother anyone.

The players grew in number, and soon there were eight to ten people sitting at the table with others waiting on the sidelines, ready to take the place of those who lost or had to leave.

The game of choice was stook, which is like black jack. We also had seven boarders at that time and they'd come and lay their money down, which was okay as long as they still had money at the end to pay their rent. Dad was no respecter of persons, so he had no problem taking their money.

When Dad got too drunk to think straight, he'd become more arrogant than usual and bet ridiculously, so Mom would sit in and try to win back what he'd lost. When Mom played, she also played against Dad, because that's what he did to her. At first, she had thought they should play as a team to win money for the upkeep of the house, which only makes sense, but Dad would clean her out. He never considered her need to win so she could buy food or necessities for the family.

Dad was an exceptional player and had an excellent poker face. I watched him play and learned from him, so that when I was eventually old enough to sit in with my own money—money which I earned from babysitting—I was every bit as good. I held my cards, shuffled, and dealt like him. I'd hold the hand dealt to me between my left thumb and finger and shuffle the top card underneath the bottom card with my right hand, making the cards snap. I thought that was really smooth. It gave me the feeling of being a competent player with the grown-ups.

I soon became the one Dad focused on. He told me he could usually read anyone, but he found me difficult, so he was out to get me. I could bluff with such a straight face that I became a challenge. He liked that. He'd laugh and comment on my abilities, but at the same time he hated it because he didn't like to lose to his own little girl.

At first I liked this, because it meant I had his approval. But after losing my winnings to him too many times, I got frustrate… and even got mad. What Mom and I couldn't get over was that couples would come over to play and support each other, but Dad never supported us. My brothers would lose their paycheques to him. He derived immense pleasure out of beating us. It was as simple as that. It was all about him and he was good.

Anyway, it wasn't long before I became grossly addicted to gambling. My heart would speed up and excitement would take over. The exhilaration of the game made me come alive. It was a high of highs. I wasn't thrilled just by winning money; it was being part of a body of players and waiting anxiously for the right card to fall. When that happened, joy filled me to overflowing. I'd reach out both hands to circle the large mound of bills and loose change that made up my winnings and drag them toward me.

I counted the money nonchalantly on the outside while trembling with excitement on the inside. I stacked the quarters, dimes, and nickels into their own neat piles. The bigger the piles, the better I liked it.

I became known as the one to watch out for. I felt important. I'd even play some of the men's hands, because they believed I knew how to play. When I couldn't play, I would watch and the longing inside of me would eat away at me.

When it got to be too much, I'd borrow money to get in on the game. Dad would lend me $20 and then proceed to win it back. He'd then lend me more until I learned my lesson for the night.

I couldn't see it at the time, but I was addicted to gambling. I literally craved the game, so much so that when I got my own place years later I held my own poker games with all the drugs and booze that accompanied them. I couldn't even play a game of bingo without getting hooked. I had a very addictive nature and I paid dearly for it.

During the gambling days, we saw a lot of strange faces pass through our house. Lots of money exchanged hands, booze flowed, sordid language was spoken, and of course many bloody fights that erupted.

One in particular comes to mind. We kids were upstairs in our room when we heard a rush of shouts and angry retorts, then the slamming of the front door as Dad and some stranger took their fight out onto the front lawn for all the neighbours to see.

Kneeling on my top bunk, we hung out the bedroom window and watched as they pounded their fists into one another, wrestling each other to the ground. The stranger bit into Dad's shoulder and in retaliation Dad bit into the stranger's ear lobe, taking the bottom part right off. There was much blood and squealing. It wasn't the kind of entertainment children should watch, but that was our life.

If there was only one good thing to say about the gambling, it would be that it cut down on the fights between Mom and Dad.

Fishing was another source of gambling. I'd go fishing with Dad and his friends. The rule was that whoever caught the first fish collected one dollar from everyone else. I got lucky on several occasions, but I was even luckier when Dad didn't make me pay for the gas on the way home!

Eight
Sexual Abuse

I deliberated long and hard about whether to share these experiences, because they're painful and their secrets eat at my soul. I truly asked God to show me what He wanted in this book, and I committed to tell the truth, no matter what. The very fact that Satan builds his stronghold in the secrets of our lives and reinforces them by silence is why I'm going to break that silence.

The only way to break strongholds is to face them head-on, and the way to break the walls that have held me in captivity is to choose to forgive the paedophiles who played such a big part in helping to derail my life. I'm not saying, "What you've done to me is okay." No! Never! By forgiving them, I'm choosing not to carry them around on my shoulders anymore. I'm releasing myself from them. They will no longer have a hold on me.

Mentally, I don't have to walk in fear and disgrace. What happened was not my fault. I'm putting the ownership of their sin back on them, where it belongs. I release them to God, and one day they will have to face Him.

In this chapter, I'll speak out for myself and the many men and women who have been victims of these predators. They've taken away our right to give to whom we choose that which we hold most sacred, our bodies. They've violated our bodies and minds and, for some of us, destroyed our wills. They've made us feel ashamed and soiled. They've changed our lives so drastically that we can never go back to being the way we were before. They've robbed us of our innocence.

These painful encounters pushed my life far out of whack. I share these stories so that parents can reconsider what they allow their children to do. Parents should be armed with some knowledge of the danger their children could be in.

So, with tears and a mighty struggle in my heart, here goes.

My first encounter with a paedophile, or so I thought, happened when I was eight. Bert was about the same age as my father. He had separated from his wife and two boys and had moved from Ontario to Thompson to work at the nickel mine. He moved into our house as one of the seven borders Mom took in and stayed with us a couple of years, becoming entangled in our family's affairs. He once bought me a puppy and made me a beautiful heart-shaped ring by sculpting it from a stainless steel bolt.

Little did I know that he was grooming me.

Bert was looked up to and esteemed highly as an all-around nice guy. He and Dad were good drinking buddies, and we considered him one of the family. When Dad got into one of his moods to beat Mom, Bert would come between them and talk Dad into calming down and having another drink to get his mind off it. He took it upon himself to be our saviour, so to speak. I used to wish he were our dad instead because he was always in a good mood and had time to talk and play with us.

One afternoon, I found out that he wasn't all that he appeared to be. While everyone was out of the house, I went looking for him in his room. I found him asleep, and because we sometimes played tricks on each other I innocently thought I would wake him up by throwing my teddy bear at him.

When the bear hit him, he raised his head and saw me standing in his doorway. He called me over to his bedside. Giggling, I went towards him and he lifted me onto the bed and began to do strange things to my body. I didn't understand what he was doing and I didn't know how to stop him.

When he was finished with me, he warned me never to tell anyone. All I could do was put my clothes back on, drop my head, and leave the room, so very different than when I had first entered.

I didn't tell anyone because I became very scared of him. I felt dirty and ashamed. For a long time, I didn't want to be around anyone, especially him. I didn't like him anymore. I hated him. In secret, I cried and blamed myself, but I didn't know what I'd done.

No one noticed any difference in me, because I started to put on a mask to pretend that everything was okay. This helped to cover my shame.

I was an easy victim because I saw what a big man, like my father, could do to my mother. I kept my mouth shut, and this was the start of carrying another heavy weight—the other was the truth about my eye accident.

Not long after that, Bert met a beautiful woman who had two daughters who weren't much older than myself and I often wondered if he used them, too. This was the man who saved our family from being beaten. What a snake, though. The bastard was a paedophile. How many other little girls' lives did he destroy?

The second time, I was eleven. It wasn't unusual for an eleven-year-old to go alone to a Saturday afternoon matinee at the local movie theatre. I was sitting down front, close to the wall, and enjoying the solitude when a big man sat down next to me, blocking my way to the aisle. It was too dark to see what he looked like. He placed a big tub of popcorn on his lap and looked at the massive screen in front of us.

I didn't think too much of it except that there were a lot of empty seats all around me, so why had he chosen the one next to me?

Not long after he sat down, he calmly leaned sideways into me, so no one could see, and reached over and took my hand. I tried hard to pull away, but he squeezed my hand hard enough to get a whimper out of me. In a low, growling voice, he whispered into my ear that I was to be quiet or else he would really hurt me. Because of the darkness in the theatre and the volume of the movie, no one would have noticed or heard us. People would only think he was a brother, uncle, or someone I knew and had been waiting for.

He proceeded to molest me and forced me to touch him. I was utterly helpless; no one knew I needed help.

"Let me go. Please stop," I pleaded with him.

As scared as I was, I again tried to pull away, and again he commanded me to sit perfectly quiet. With tears of shame in my eyes, I did what I was told. When he was finished, in the same threatening voice, he told me not to say anything to anyone or he would find me and hurt me.

Then he got up and left.

I was so overcome by fear, shame, and filth that all I wanted to do was get out of there and go home, but my legs were too weak to carry me. What if I ran into him out in the lobby?

When I could finally make myself move, I left the theatre in disgrace. I went home and hid in my bedroom, hoping no one would look for me. I wanted to die.

The days that followed were black. Again, I could tell no one.

Not long after that, I had another encounter with a guy who lived in our house. This one raped me, causing me so much pain that I cried, but again I was warned not to say anything. He even promised me money to shut me up, but he didn't pay. And even if he did, it would only have doubled the shame and guilt.

The fourth time happened when I was twelve. I was babysitting for a couple I didn't know, taking over for one of my girlfriends who wasn't feeling well. The husband picked me up in his car and drove me over to their place. I was there a few hours, and when they returned he paid me and drove me home.

Halfway home, in the dark, he calmly reached over and began to fondle my well-developed breasts, all the while talking casually as he drove. I was small for my age and he was a big man, using his power to subdue me. There was nothing I could do to stop him.

When he let me off in front of my house, again all the filth, guilt, and shame infiltrated my mind. And again I said nothing, not even to my girlfriend. I can only assume she must have experienced the same thing.

The very first time my innocence was stolen, by the man I had believed would be the perfect father, I lost my ability to trust. He not only broke my heart, but any illusion of there being a good father anywhere. To think, *I* was the one who felt embarrassed and full of shame whenever that pervert walked into the same room as me. He'd just smile at me and carry on being the family hero, as if nothing had ever happened.

To this day, it really angers me when I see kids sitting alone in a theatre. Their parents are thinking, *They'll be all right.* If only they knew the kinds of predators who stalk dark theatres, just waiting for their innocent sons and daughters.

My small understanding of what love meant completely changed. It became something ugly and hurtful, and my world was never the same; the innocent little girl never returned.

I lost having power over my own body. I lost the right to come to my wedding bed as a virgin, pure and undefiled. I also felt I didn't have the right to speak out for myself because of the threats. And knowing what Dad was like with Mom, what would be different about these other men?

I didn't have the strength to protect myself from those who wanted to use me. I didn't have the right to say no. I didn't have any rights at all.

Only those who have walked this road will truly understand what I'm saying. I blamed myself. And it didn't stop there.

When I was twenty-two, I was assaulted for the fifth time. I'd hired a babysitter for my three sons and gone over to my brother James's apartment for a party. He only lived a few buildings down from me. At the party, I had a great time meeting some of his friends and visiting others I knew.

I grabbed a pop and relaxed on an overstuffed cushion on the floor, listening to the great tunes of the 70s. The strobe and black lights entertained my brain while I focused on the radical black-light posters on the walls. He had the coolest pad and I always felt safe there. I didn't get involved with anyone; I just wanted to unwind for a bit before going home and waking up to another day of babies and diapers.

When it had gotten late, I reluctantly said my goodbyes and made my way outside into a beautiful warm summer night. For once I felt peaceful and relaxed.

After making sure my babysitter had gotten home safely and the kids were fast asleep, I decided to take a bath. It was wonderful to enjoy this me-time before one of the babies woke up.

No sooner was I in the bathtub than the bathroom door opened and there in the doorway stood one of the guys from the party. To my horror, I'd forgotten to lock my apartment door after the babysitter left, and apparently the bathroom door as well.

I quickly grabbed the shower curtain to cover myself. What the hell was he doing in my apartment? In disbelief, I asked him what he wanted and he just said that he'd wanted to make sure I got home all right. I was in shock and didn't know what to do. I couldn't stay in the tub, so I asked him to step out and shut the door behind him so my children wouldn't be woken up. I didn't know what this guy was capable of and I needed to protect my kids.

Wrapped in a towel and in utter embarrassment, I faced him and longed to scream for him to get the hell out of my apartment, but instead I became that frightened little girl who had no control over the situation. Even though I didn't want anything to do with him, for some unknown reason I felt like I owed him because he'd caught me in a compromising position. So when he made a move on me, I froze. I felt I had no choice but to let him take advantage of me.

Before this, I had never once given him any sign that I was interested in him. He was James's friend and that was all.

He obviously had a different idea about that.

Once on my bed, he began to do what he wanted. When he entered me, I felt utterly defiled and sickened. Somehow my mind managed to fight its way back out of the black hole of insanity, and with all my might I shoved him off me and commanded him to get out of my apartment. Surprisingly, he did what he was told.

After he left, I showered and scrubbed at my skin to try to clean his filth off me. I lay in bed, trembling and feeling utterly destroyed and disgusted with myself. Every time I thought of that pig inside me, I wanted to vomit. My skin crawled from his touch and I couldn't get rid of that unclean feeling and humiliation.

Just knowing I'd see him again, because he hung around my brother, caused me to shudder. If I could have moved out of town right then and there, I would have.

But what really got to me was this question: why had I felt like I owed him my body and he had a right to it? I didn't understand. And yet this pattern in my life would continue for many years. A long list of men went through my life, and I frequently felt as though I owed them sex.

The only love I really understood was what went on between the sheets. If I was compatible with a man there, the rest would fall in place. I would meet a guy in a bar and within a few days we would be shacked up. But it never lasted long, two years at the most. I would know nothing about him, nor he of me. That didn't seem to matter, though, since I didn't know the difference between love and lust. To me, it was all the same thing.

Stranger yet, I couldn't stand to be alone. All I ever longed for was to be loved, wanted, and needed. I was a broken human being with no self worth. I didn't know how sick my conception of love was, since it was the only one I'd seen. I didn't know what a truly normal love relationship looked like. I sure hadn't learned it at home, and nor did I learn it from the kind of partners I met. My thinking was warped. I had come out of an insane home environment, expecting to be of a sane mind out on my own in the world.

Some time after writing this, I experienced similar dreams two nights in a row, both of which jolted me awake with my heart pounding. Through these dreams, a well-hidden memory of my past resurfaced. Remember that I said there were things that happened to me that I couldn't remember, or didn't want to remember?

When I was three years old, I was sitting with my back pressed hard against the bedroom wall one day, willing it to swallow me up. With my arms tightly locked across my heaving chest, my spindly legs tucked beneath my trembling body, tears of great anguish streamed down my cheeks. I tried to muffle the sobs that tried to escape.

I starred in horror at the door of my bedroom, dreading that the man who had just left would return. Dad had just finished violating me, and I was too paralyzed to move. He had really hurt me, and all the while he had covered my mouth with his hand, warning me not to make a sound. He had stolen my innocence.

For years after, I was haunted by questions. Why hadn't I bled when I had sex for the first time? Why hadn't I been able to tell my parents, or anyone else for that matter, that other men had molested me? Why had I felt like my body belonged to others and I couldn't say no?

My mother had once asked me if Dad had ever touched me. This had shocked me at first, and I said no. But a nagging feeling lingered and never left me in peace after that. Had he touched me? Something was stirred.

I believe that I experienced many traumatic things in my life, and my mind shut it out.

Mom, with great concern and shame, had gone on to tell me a few things about my father and his crimes. Sadly, it all makes sense now. My father was not only a whoremonger, but also a rapist and a paedophile, engaging in incest as well. I also believe he was a pimp, according to some of the stories I had heard.

To my astonishment, I've discovered that I was violated six times by six different men. When I add to this what I heard while my father was beating and raping my mother, plus all the perverted movies I watched and books I read in my younger years, it's no wonder that my thinking became so warped. When I read or watched a scene about someone getting raped, I would get turned on by it instead of being filled with anger at the perpetrator.

It's no wonder I've always felt so unclean and unloved when my common-law partners and husbands told me they really loved me. I could never quite believe it, because there was always an invisible wall that kept me separated from trusting them and receiving love. I wanted to, but it never connected in my heart.

Discovering all this made me physically sick to my stomach. I've had a lot of sexual partners over the years and I always felt like a sex toy, like I had to perform. I was like a prostitute, only I didn't think I was worth the pay.

As disturbing as this is, I'm not without hope. I now know that Jesus wants to heal me and set me free from Satan's hold. Jesus wants me to have a truly loving and beautiful relationship. As dirty and ashamed as I feel sometimes, I know that Jesus is better than any doctor or psychiatrist—and He's better than any medication I could take to stop the pain. I know without a doubt that when I pray and give Him my guilt and shame, He tosses it farther than the east is from the west and remembers it no more. He took all this upon himself when He went to Calvary and died for my sins.

When I took this to Jesus in prayer, He showed me that by keeping my mouth shut and not reporting my attackers, I was protecting them. I had thought I was protecting myself. But when I repented of my own sins and forgave my assailants, Jesus washed away *all* the guilt and shame. I no longer hate them. I have been set free to live in peace.

How do I know this? Because I left this chapter in the book!

Nine
School

Men and women are busy
Locked in everyday cares
Many cannot imagine
The burdens some children bear

School becomes their haven
A safe place to unwind
Merely thinking of their homes
Torments their fear-filled minds

School was a mammoth struggle for me. I barely had passing grades.

It wasn't until recently that I finally understood why I did so poorly. I always thought I was just plain stupid, incapable of learning anything. I couldn't grasp or retain the concepts being taught. I struggled with every grade, even kindergarten.

It never once occurred to me that this was because of the battlefield at home. I got very little sleep and was always nervous and fearful. The weekends were the absolute worst. And on top of all that, I was still dealing with eczema.

Since I was doing so poorly by Grade Six, I was introduced to a special class. In simple terms, it was a class for dummies. There were fourteen boys and four girls in the class and we were given an extraordinary female teacher who was very patient with us.

Except for the one time we really misbehaved during recess. It was in the middle of winter and our breath hung like fog in the frozen air. We had to stamp our feet to keep them warm. We'd just finished playing a game of soccer and were more than ready to put the ball away and go inside where it was warm.

While standing around and waiting for the teachers to take us to our classes, each classroom was to form a straight line. For whatever reason, our class didn't cooperate this day. Instead we defiantly stood wherever we wanted, and hence we weren't allowed back inside. Two of the girls were cooperating, so our teacher let them in. I was disgusted with them, figuring they were the teacher's pets.

Well, our teacher kept us out in the cold another twenty minutes. We were nearly frozen by the time she finally relented and let us back in. We figured we'd won—that is, until we were ordered to line up in a row along the wall of the class. One by one she laid the ruler down hard on both our hands. Oh, was she mad!

She had a hard swing and it hurt, but I wouldn't allow my face to flinch. That would be a sign of weakness. No one was going to see me cry, least of all this bunch of guys. Already my heart had been seared of my natural emotions. I had lots of anger and hatred, and I'd fight if I felt cornered, I was so defiant toward guys that I wouldn't let any of them get close enough to me to see any of my weaknesses.

Anyway, by the time our teacher was finished the punishment, she broke out in tears and rushed out of the room. Of course we mocked her.

But she proved to be a very good teacher and knew how to get our attention. She took us out of the classroom and into the auditorium one day where the piano sat on stage. She taught us to sing songs from *The Sound of Music*. At first we goofed around a lot because we thought it was silly, but as she persisted we began to pay more attention.

One day, because she felt we were good enough, she announced to us that we would be performing on stage for the rest of the school. After that, we really got into it and enjoyed ourselves.

A few days before the performance, she dropped a bomb: "All the girls are to wear dresses." Some of the guys grinned.

Now she'd gone too far. Fear overwhelmed my thinking, and I bucked it with everything in me. No way was I going to wear one of those disgusting things. No one was going to make fun of me, least of all one of these jerks in our class. I'd kill him just as soon as look at him, in dress or out of dress.

Just my luck, Mom found me a nice dress. Yeah right… like there was such a thing as a nice dress. When I put it on, I cried. I didn't want to go to school and tried to get out of it.

"Mom, I'm too sick to go to school today. Have a heart."

She knew what I was up to and wouldn't budge an inch. I had to go.

This was the cruellest request my teacher—and my mom—could ever have asked of me.

Go ahead, I thought. *Put a gun to my head and pull the trigger. Do me the favour!*

I was teased and laughed at by some of my brothers, even though Mom did her best to shut them up. She encouraged me by saying how nice I looked. She didn't understand the humiliation this was causing me, and I couldn't explain to her. Because of the sexual abuse and eczema, I just wanted to melt into the background and not be seen. I hated looking like a girl, yet alone being one. I felt so hopelessly vulnerable. If no one saw me as a person, that was okay. But wear a dress? It filled me with shame.

I considered skipping school that day, but I had no place to hide. Going to school that day was like a death walk, and I dragged my feet the whole way.

Once inside, I felt terribly uncomfortable and out of place. I didn't want to take off my coat. I just wanted to run right back outside, but I clenched my teeth and prepared myself for any remarks the guys made. Just one remark and I'd smash him right in the mouth, no matter the consequences. They were used to me being out on the soccer field, battling with them. I wasn't some frilly damsel in distress.

My defences were up and I was really angry. I had enough anger in me that I could have taken on most of those guys, even though I stood less than five feet tall. Scrapping I understood, but girly things, that was way out of my league. I didn't feel safe dressing up as a girl.

No one said anything to me and I was grateful. They were probably just as anxious as I was, knowing we would have to face the rest of the school.

We all managed to remember the words to the songs while our teacher kept up her encouragement, which we so desperately needed. The concert went off without a hitch and we were a success. The other classes looked at us with more respect, too, and that made us feel good.

That was the first and last time I tried wearing a dress for many years. I couldn't get home fast enough to change. I wanted to burn the ugly thing.

Anyway, most of us were a rebellious lot, myself included. I'd stand up against the boys and wouldn't back down. Something inside me drove me to have to prove myself to them. I needed to be as tough as them, if not tougher.

I once called a guy out for an after-school fight. He didn't show up. That was probably lucky for me, but I didn't care.

Looking back now, I can see that most of the other students came out of homes similar to mine. We were all troubled and didn't know it—nor did we know what to do about it. We had a lot in common!

After a year, I was moved on to the junior high school, where I joined a regular class.

Junior High School

It was a hard transition for me. Withdrawn, I'd watch other girls with envy. They stood before the bathroom mirrors examining themselves, primping, doing the makeup and hair thing, while I could hardly stand to look at myself. I knew I was dirty and didn't fit in.

Other girls flirted with boys and did all they could to catch their attention, but not me. I had the conflict of wanting a boyfriend but feeling soiled. I didn't want to draw any unwelcome attention to myself. I didn't dress like a girl and didn't want to be a girl. I was ashamed of my body and covered it with boy's clothes as much as possible.

I also needed to cover up the last of the eczema that still showed on my arms and hands.

The other thing that made junior high difficult was the fact that my five older brothers had already been through there and left quite the reputation behind. Knowing this didn't help my disposition. Many of the teachers remembered our last name and the memories weren't good. When someone asked if I was connected to our family, I would openly deny it. Our name carried a stigma—not so much because of my brothers, but because of my dad.

After finding my homeroom class on the first day, I searched out the back row of desks to see which ones were open for me to sit at. I did this in every class I attended. I felt more comfortable in the back than in the middle. That pretty much went with everything about me. I didn't ever feel like I belonged, nor did I like to participate in activities that involved groups and role-playing. It still causes me to have paralyzing panic attacks, to freeze up inside.

Of course, nobody would know this because anger would come to my rescue and relieve most of the pressure.

I had two very close girlfriends, Elaine and Leona, and was very fortunate to have Elaine in the same class as me. This alleviated a lot of the fear I had about entering a new system, since I didn't adjust to change easily. We shared the same table.

I so admired Elaine, because she was smart and full of confidence, while I only pretended to be. You see, I didn't know how to study. My mind wouldn't stay focused. I would read and reread, but no sooner would I finish a paragraph then I'd forget what I'd just read. It was so frustrating.

Many times I couldn't get my homework done because I didn't understand it and there was no one to help me because of what was going on in our house. When it came time to pass in our homework, I'd panic because it wasn't completed. Out of pure desperation, I'm ashamed to say, I would go so far as to cheat, pleading with Elaine to give me the answers. She tried saying no to me, but I was persistent and she'd give in.[7]

I only attended French classes three or four times before I managed to get kicked out for the rest of the year. I was told by someone that I was somewhat of a bully during those years. When I look back, I can see what that person meant.

There was this one guy who irritated me, and when I walked by his desk I would deliberately push his books to the floor and just keep walking. Why did I do that? I don't honestly know, but I got caught and had to spent the rest of the French classes in the library. That was all right with me, because I didn't like French anyway.

To top that off, I was also dismissed from music class. That was okay, too.

Going to gym class was unbearable. I hated it. It was bad enough that it required group participation, but at the end of the period we were expected to take showers. The first half of the year wasn't so bad, since I could undress in a shower stall, then shower and dress in private, even though we weren't supposed to. The second half of the year, we had to use the boys' change room, with its open showers. Here we were expected to shower in front of everyone. This didn't sit well with me at all. I was well developed by that time while most of those girls had flat chests. No way on God's green earth was I going to walk around in front of them naked.

My gym teacher threatened to undress me and put me in the shower herself, but I fought her on that and won. Needless to say, I was sent to the principal's office on a few occasions. Sometimes I didn't show up for gym—and when I did, I didn't shower.

Because I barely passed Grade Seven, I was assigned once again to attend another special class called the occupational entrance course. Actually, it was intended to help us find an occupation that would best

---

[7] I'm truly sorry, Elaine, for using you like that. It was wrong, wrong, wrong.

suit our learning disabilities. I was surprised to see that most of the people from my Grade Six class were back with me, and amongst them was Leona. This class felt familiar and I felt fairly comfortable.

Leona and I spent about three months skipping school and hanging out downtown. How she got away with it is beyond me, since she babysat for the teacher and his wife on many of those evenings when we skipped.

I also got caught smoking on the schoolgrounds twice and was kicked out for three days on each occasion. Mom wasn't at all happy about it, but she made sure Dad didn't find out. There would have been hell to pay if he had known.

For someone who didn't want to draw attention to herself, I seemed to have quite the knack for it. It seems I followed in my brothers' footsteps, full of frustration and not knowing how to deal with it. On top of that, I hated school. Actually, I hated everything about my life, period.

I managed to get through Grade Nine, but with very poor marks.

Ten
Boarders

Because Thompson was a fast-growing community and didn't have enough homes and apartments to accommodate the many men who came to work in the mine, many families opened their homes to offer room and board. Our home was no exception.

We had a large unfinished basement. One side held a giant deep-freeze, washing machine and rinse tub, dryer, clotheslines, furnace, and hot water tank. On the other side, Mom put out seven beds in a row, turning it into sleeping quarters.

The boarders moved in and out so often that there always seemed to be strange faces in the house. Some regulars stayed for a year or more, and they had access to the kitchen and living room when they were home. They just blended in with the rest of the family.

Mom washed and ironed their clothes, cooked their meals, made their beds, and cleaned up after them just as she did for us. She had so much work that she had very little time for us kids. We had our share of chores, as well, with dishes being a never-ending story. A job that should have taken only half an hour, tops, usually ended up taking an hour or more because of all the arguing. We fought about who'd wash, dry, and put away. We hated this chore. We would much rather have been outside playing ball or something.

Our house wasn't big, but there were usually sixteen or seventeen of us living there. Someone was always home. The living room held two long couches, two chairs with end tables, and a coffee table. The black-and-white TV had one channel. Since the room was often crowded, the smaller kids had to sit or lie on the bare wooden floor to watch.

Late in the evenings, Mom would make our lunches for the next day, and sometimes I would help. Lunch kits for the grownups lay open in a row on the kitchen table, along with paper bags for us kids. She'd cover the kitchen counter with freshly baked slices of bread for buttering. Mom would fill the grownups' sandwiches with lunchmeat, and for us it was mostly peanut butter and jam. There were always fresh pastries or fruit to complete the lunches. At least we had food in the house with all the boarders being there.

Our kitchen was like a cafeteria. Each morning breakfast was set out along with a coffee urn filled with freshly perked coffee. Dad and the boarders were usually gone to work before we got up to have our breakfast. It was quite the system.

Mom baked twice a week, depending on what she needed. When she baked bread, she made it in a square metal washtub that would make thirty or more loaves. When I was old enough to help, she taught me how to punch down and fold in the large batch of dough. This proved to be quite the workout because I'd have to keep punching the dough until it squeaked with air bubbles and had just the right texture. Because the tub was so big, Mom would join in and help me.

After the first six loaves were baked and cooling, the aroma would cause my mouth to water. It was hard not to cut the crusts off, slap butter and jam on it, and cram it in my mouth to savour the wonderful taste.

Many times Mom kept enough dough aside to make pans of cinnamon rolls, which were to die for. Then there were all the freshly baked pies, cakes, and cookies. She had a gift! And she didn't just make a few. No, the counter and kitchen table would be filled with these fine delicacies. When they cooled, they were wrapped and packed away into the deep-freeze in the basement.

I recall that a boarder once made the mistake of going into the freezer and helping himself to a pie. The evidence was later found under his bed in the form of an empty pie plate and fork. Obviously he had enjoyed Mom's baking, but it did cost him. He was asked to leave immediately. Mom would not abide stealing.

Once a week, Mom went grocery shopping, and she'd take several of us kids to help push the shopping carts around. On this trips she bought enough groceries to fill the store's delivery van from front to back. The till tape would stretch from one end of our long kitchen to the other. I'm sure the store welcomed her business, but the deliverymen must have dreaded it.

Eleven

Steve

I was thirteen when eighteen-year-old Steve moved into our house as a boarder. He appeared to be shy, and I found him to be very good-looking guy. I had an instant crush. I remember him walking past our supper table with a guitar on his back. Whether or not he played the guitar, I don't recall.

Although he was one of the many men who passed through our home, he was the one I would marry two years later.

Steve also introduced me to motorcycles. After he had worked and saved enough money to buy one, he picked up a little 150 Yamaha.[8] When I got my first ride on it, I was hooked. There was nothing like it!

I used to go target practicing with Steve and my brother Garrett. Steve owned the biggest gun I'd ever shot, which was a 410. It had a kick that almost ripped my shoulder off the first time I fired it. It sounded like a big cannon going off. It was deafening.

The gun was completely made of metal and extremely heavy, and you could unscrew the stock to transform it into a handgun with a rifle-length barrel. It was an odd-looking gun and I hadn't seen one like it before—nor have I seen one since. I preferred it as a handgun, because the butt kicked back too hard into my shoulder when the stock was attached. Holding it out in front of me, I had to use both hands to steady it. When I pulled the trigger, the kickback would jerk both my arms up into the air—still holding the gun, of course. Now that was power!

My dad had a fair arsenal at home and he'd lend guns to us for practice, but none of them ever had a kick like that one. In those days, it was commonplace to see guns hanging on living room walls. This was the case in my own living room when I was first married.

---

[8] Yeah, I know, it wasn't a Harley Davidson. But everyone starts somewhere, right?

I was fifteen at the time when Steve and Garrett suggested we go goose-hunting. Garrett had a friend whose father had built a cabin on an island out on Paint Lake, which was about twenty-one miles from Thompson. The plan was to meet with Garrett's friend and stay overnight and go goose-hunting in the morning.

We travelled by boat for nearly an hour, passing a lot of islands before Garrett steered us into a little hidden bay where the cabin was situated under a grove of tall and sparse trees. By this time the sun was about set and we could barely make out the trees, cabin, and shoreline. Any later and we would have been lost out on the lake until morning.

While still a short distance from the shore, we saw the cabin door open and Garrett's friend staggered drunkenly out with a rifle in his hand. When he saw us, he shouted some profanities at Garrett, then lifted his rifle to his shoulder and popped off a couple of rounds directly at our boat. I heard pellets drop into the water right in front of our boat. If that wasn't unsettling enough, Garrett stood up and shouted profanities of his own; he then lifted his rifle to his shoulder and popped a couple of shots right back.

Then they laughed at each other.

If ever there was a time I wanted to go home, it was then. I didn't want to get out of the boat—and when I turned to Steve, I could see that he was extremely angry. It usually took a lot to get him upset, but this triggered instant anger. He had some choice words to say about the incident.[9]

There were two other guys in the cabin, and they were just as drunk as Garrett's friend. To my understanding there were only supposed to be four of us that weekend, not six. I felt completely out of place and stayed close to Steve. Still, I managed to hold my own.

At the break of dawn, the three of us—Steve, Garrett, and I—went out on the lake to a place that Garrett knew would be a good spot for geese. He found his own hiding place a short distance from where Steve and I hid.

After close to an hour of patient waiting, geese began to glide in over our heads and land directly in front of us. As noisy as they were, it was really something to see these remarkable birds up close like that. I wasn't carrying a gun myself, because I was too young for a license, but Garrett and Steve had wanted me to experience this.

It was fascinating to watch Garrett and Steve concentrate as they held their breaths and slowly placed their guns to their shoulders, waiting for the right moment to fire.

Boom!

Garrett fired first and down came his prize. He was delighted!

Steve had decided beforehand to try out his 410 to see how it would perform on geese. He slowly took his bead, preparing himself for the kick he knew was coming. Ever so gently, he squeezed the trigger.

Boom!

---

[9] After I wrote about the shooting incident between Garrett and his friend, I felt seriously ill. As I prayed about it, God showed me that I hadn't forgiven Garrett's friend for shooting at us, so I bowed my head and forgave him. Instantly I began to purge, as in dry heaves, and while that was happening the Lord showed me that He had stopped the pellets from hitting us. That's why I had heard the pellets drop in front of our boat. God had put a shield in place to protect us. Even though I hadn't acknowledged Him at the time, He'd still had his hand on me.

After we recovered from the sound, Steve let out a victorious shout! He'd hit two geese with one shot! It was well worth the trip.

Our Wedding Day

On June 28, 1970, the sun was shining and the air felt blissfully warm. It was a beautiful day for a wedding.

I was fifteen, turning sixteen the next month, and had the consent of both my parents to wed. At last I was going to fulfill the dream of almost every girl: I was going to walk down the aisle of a little church wearing the most beautiful long-sleeved, floor-length white satin and lace wedding dress, one which Mom and I had picked out only weeks before.

My best friend Elaine was my maid of honour, and my sister Ann was my bridesmaid. They wore baby blue chiffon dresses and looked beautiful. My dad was dressed in a tailored suit, looking militant. He was giving me away and it was going to be the best day of my life. My parents really did me proud.

When the bridal party arrived at the church, we stayed in the tiny lobby waiting for our cue to enter the sanctuary. I was so nervous that I dared to take out a cigarette and light it in front of Dad. I'd never smoked in front of him before, so I expected him to say something, but he didn't. Instead he tilted his head back and drank out of what appeared to be a can of soda.

I later found out it had been filled with whisky. He'd no doubt started drinking early that morning, which would explain why he reprimanded us girls after my sister said something really funny that caused us to laugh. He would remind us that this was a serious occasion and we had better behave ourselves. That was so embarrassing and took all the joy and excitement out of my special day.

When he spoke in that tone of voice, something would happen to me that I can't explain. On the inside I'd cower and ball up in a fetal position, anxiety paralyzing my nerves. Yet the outer part of me would want to run as far away from him as possible. All the while, I'd know that I couldn't show any of this. I had to fight to keep my mind from shutting off.

Anyway, somewhere between the time I lit my cigarette and put it out, I managed to burn a hole in the skirt of my beautiful wedding dress. You'd have to look very close to see the burn, but it was there nonetheless and I hoped no one would notice, least of all Dad.

Soon everyone was in their places, as had been rehearsed the night before. The doors swung open and I hesitantly took hold of my father's extended right forearm and determined that he wasn't going to spoil this special day. Despite the fierce anxiety that washed over me, I put a smile on my face and readied myself to move forward.

This was it! It was really happening!

Elaine and Ann walked out ahead of me on the arms of Steve's best men. I could see our friends and family smiling as we entered the sanctuary. My legs shook nervously and my heart pounded. Would I remember my lines? If I forgot them, would I be in trouble with Dad? Would he yell at me in front of everyone?

Slowly we began the military walk down the aisle. Left footstep, then pause. Right footstep, then pause. I had to really concentrate hard to keep in step. I sure didn't want to be the one to screw it up. For a short aisle, it took a long time to reach the front.

When I finally dared to look up, I saw Steve and everything that had happened in the lobby was forgotten. He was as handsome as ever and all my fear dissipated. It felt as though I was bursting with sunbeams. Could it get any better than this?

Dad placed me directly before his future son-in-law, and when the minister asked, "Who gives this woman away?" he gave his consent and took his seat next to Mom. When the minister proceeded, I remembered to say what I was supposed to and before I knew it we were pronounced husband and wife.

Afterwards, if anyone were to ask me what the minister had said, I would honestly have said I couldn't remember a single word. I was a blur of nerves and excitement.

Once the congratulations were said and pictures taken, we all left the church and went to a reception hall to celebrate. Later, Dad and Mom invited close friends over to their house for a few drinks and socializing.

Steve and I went to our new home to change clothes before going to my parents' house. What could possibly go wrong in that short of time?

Somewhere between being in our small basement suite and driving over to join my parents, Dad and Lawrence managed to get into a fight. The story goes something like this.

My brother Michael was strumming on a guitar in the living room when Dad came along and said something nasty, like "Why don't you give that guitar to someone who can play it?" Then he tried to take the guitar away.

Lawrence, seeing what Dad had done, stepped in. "Why don't you pick on someone your own size?"

Dad, only too happy to oblige, picked up the challenge and threw a few badly aimed swings at Lawrence, along with some nasty remarks, and of course it had to take place in front of all their guests.

Enraged, Lawrence grabbed the front of Dad's shirt with both hands and hauled him to the front door where he proceeded to lift him up and send him sailing through the screen door, over the cement steps, and out onto the lawn for all the neighbours to witness. This would definitely give them something more to talk about. We kept the neighbourhood well entertained.

As the fight continued, there was a lot of screaming and shouting from those who were trying to stop it. Lawrence said he didn't hear any of this until Mom screamed his name: "Lawrence, don't! He's not worth it!" Somehow her voice filtered through all that rage and hatred, just moments before Lawrence had been about to dig his fingers into Dad's throat and pull out his juggler vein.[10]

Indeed, the old man wasn't worth going to jail for. With that, Lawrence got off him and left him lying defeated on the ground.

Dad was taken to the hospital after it was discovered he had a broken foot. That was about the time Steve and I showed up. When he came home later, he was wearing a cast.

There aren't any words to describe how I felt. Ashamed, disgusted, humiliated… I just wanted to get out of there and go to my new home.

Welcome to the family, Steve!

---

[10] Like Dad, Lawrence had been trained in how to kill.

After the Wedding

For our honeymoon, Steve proudly took me to his hometown in Nova Scotia to meet his parents and show me where he had grown up. We toured New Glasgow, Truro, and many other small towns that had the most interesting names.

I found Nova Scotia to be a beautiful place. No wonder he wanted to show it off!

His parents took us on a tour of the Cabot Trail on Cape Breton Island, where we also visited the old ruins of the fortress of Louisbourg. That was an amazing sight to see and experience, bringing to life lessons I'd heard in school.

Another day we took a ferry over to Prince Edward Island and circled the island by car and stayed overnight. I was especially thrilled to have stood on the porch of the home that inspired *Anne of Green Gables*. Her story came to life for me that day.

I was shown some amazing sights during that trip and had a wonderful time. I thank Steve for those beautiful memories. He showed me places I never would have seen or dreamed of otherwise.

Five months later, the doctor pronounced me to be almost two and a half months pregnant. We were so proud and excited that we were going to be parents and immediately began shopping for baby necessities. I discovered that some of our friends and acquaintances had been watching the calendar to see whether I'd already been pregnant at the wedding, but I proved them wrong.

Before our child was born, Steve and I had the care of Lawrence's baby girl, Elizabeth. She was only a few months old. We fell head over heals in love with her and even talked about adopting her. Unfortunately, after a couple of months her mother came to get her. It really tore our hearts out to give her back, but at least we'd had her for a short time. She still holds a special place in my heart.

My pregnancy went well, but on my due date my labour still hadn't started. I was taken to the hospital so that the doctor could induce labour if necessary. He instructed me to walk the halls all that day until I was exhausted. It must have worked, because by the next day labour started on its own.

Eighteen agonizing hours later, I delivered a healthy baby boy. We named him Joseph—or Joey, for short. Steve couldn't have been prouder. Joey was the apple of his father's eye. This little one had everything to look forward to when he grew up. He had a mom and dad who loved him.

We were content and wanted to have a big family. Steve figured twelve kids should do it.

One morning when Joey was only about a month old, for whatever reason he wouldn't stop crying. I had done everything possible to see that he was comfortable—bathed, clean diaper, fed, and burped. I held him in my arms, gently rocking him and talking to him for more than an hour, but no matter what I did he just kept crying.

At this point I was operating on very little sleep, because he was up at all hours during the night for feeding.

This particular morning, nothing satisfied him. Every time he finally fell asleep, I'd carefully place him in his crib so as not to wake him—and as soon as I began to walk away, he'd start crying all over again.

Suffering from exhaustion and frayed nerves, I came to the point where I couldn't stand his crying any longer and all I wanted to do was smash his tiny little head into the wall, just to shut him up. I wanted to throw him as far away from me as I could.

The instinct to do this was so strange and strong that I screamed for Steve to come immediately. When he entered the bedroom, I thrust Joey into his hands and told him he had better take care of him or I'd kill him.

I ran out of the room, locked myself in the bathroom, and shook violently. I couldn't believe what had almost taken place. I had wanted to kill my baby. I didn't understand what had happened to me and I couldn't tell Steve what I'd almost done. He would have thought I was insane, which I would have believed at that point.

It's quite possible that I experienced postpartum depression, which I knew nothing about in those days. Years later, I discovered that many new mothers experience it. I can only speculate that this may have been it, but it only happened the one time.

After that, I was afraid to be alone with him in case it happened again, but I determined to keep a tight rein over my emotions.

As it turned out, Joey was never that unsettled again. He was a happy baby.

But I never forgot what I'd almost done. I hid it in my heart until now, keeping yet another secret out of shame and guilt.

Twelve
Nova Scotia

Life was exceptionally good until Steve decided, less than a year later, that it was time for him to return to Nova Scotia. He had gotten homesick. So we sold all our furniture, packed up our household goods, and stored it all with my parents. We drove from Manitoba to Nova Scotia with our little one. What an experience that was!

Since Steve didn't have a job or home there, his parents invited us to stay with them out in the country. While Steve was looking for a job, I was kept busy by keeping Joey out of trouble. My in-laws' beautiful country home wasn't set up for children. They had a house full of very expensive furniture and ornaments and Joey liked to touch everything that was at his level while he was learning to walk and explore his new surroundings. It got so that the only places I could keep Joey out of trouble was out in the yard or in his crib upstairs. We spent a lot of time in that bedroom. I became very unhappy and stressed out over this situation.

We were with his parents for several weeks, and still there was no job to be found. Staying there became difficult for us all. I had no knowledge of the place and had no way to travel around and investigate my surroundings when Steve wasn't around. It was more than a mile's walk into town and I couldn't carry the baby that far. I also felt that my mother-in-law didn't like me much, probably because I was so young and because of my rough upbringing. I was rough around the edges, not the woman they'd expected their son to bring home. I didn't fit the criteria of a good wife for him. It wasn't said to me in so many words, but I felt it.

I unfortunately had a foul mouth because of all the cursing and swearing I'd grown up with. It's what I knew and how almost everyone talked back home. Steve warned me not to swear around his parents before we had moved, and I said I wouldn't, but it was a hard habit to break. I tried. But with great regret, I failed.

After several weeks of this stress, Steve and I talked about my returning to Manitoba until he could set us up with our own place. The prospect of taking a plane trip home with the baby scared the bejeebers out of me. I didn't know anything about air travel, and I was about to get a crash course.

I felt like I was being ripped in two by leaving Steve at the airport, but I trusted his decision and believed he would take care of us. Joey and I survived the trip home and we didn't get lost on the way.

So there I was, back in my parents' house, the very last place I ever wanted to be. I had gone full circle.

The days dragged into weeks, and weeks into months, and I missed Steve terribly. Then, a little over two months later, I discovered I was pregnant. It must have happened in the last few days I was with him.

With tremendous excitement, I wrote Steve to let him know that number two of twelve was on its way. I figured the reason he'd only contacted me once since leaving Nova Scotia was because phoning was too expensive. I thought I'd get a quick response by letter with this wonderful news.

The response I finally received was very slow in coming and didn't mention our new baby. I was really disappointed, but I kept my spirits up by looking forward to the day he would send for us.

Staying at my parents' wasn't easy for any of us, but at least my little guy could walk around and we had places to go. I heard from Steve only a few times. He sent very little money, so I had to sell some of our personal belongs in order to pay for rent and food.

I was seven months pregnant when he finally sent for us. The airline almost didn't let me on the plane in case I went into early labour due to the altitude.

It was a brisk late winter morning when Joey and I left Thompson to embrace our new lives. We changed planes in Winnipeg and from there flew on to Toronto. In all this time, Joey, being the happy and friendly little guy he was, interacted with the passengers in front and behind us. When he wasn't showing off for them, he'd sit on my lap chattering about who knew what, or played happily with the few toys I'd brought along to keep him entertained.

By the time we departed Toronto for Moncton, New Brunswick, where Steve was to collect us, Joey became restless. He'd had enough sleeps, seen enough strange faces, and had gotten bored with his toys. What he really wanted was to get down on the floor and run around. When he couldn't do that, he began to cry and wouldn't be comforted. The poor little guy just had enough.

The stewardess could see my predicament and asked if it would be okay if she took him up to the cockpit. For a few minutes of peace and quiet, I was only too happy to hand him over to her, and no doubt so were the passengers.

We left Toronto somewhere around suppertime, but we only flew as far as Montreal, with a severe snowstorm grounding our plane for several hours. We were extremely tired and all the activity around us had become overwhelming. My own body was tired from sitting for so many hours and my feet and ankles were swollen.

To top it off, the thought of staying in Quebec over night, understanding no French, compounded my anxiety. I remembered a previous trip through Quebec and found it hadn't been such a friendly place if you didn't speak French, at least from where Steve and I had been. I'm not saying there's anything wrong with Quebec, but my experience wasn't a good one.

Then there was the fact that I had only $7 in my purse. Getting a hotel room for the night just wasn't going to happen.

For whatever reason, Joey and I ended up taking an old four-propeller airplane that became available after the snow eased off. We flew to Halifax instead of Moncton, and the turbulence of that flight is something I have no desire to ever experience again. My heart was in my throat for most of the flight. There were times when it felt like the plane was going to fall right out of the sky, and being pregnant only added to my discomfort. What a relief it was to land safely in Halifax, with the snow really coming down.

With great excitement, I phoned Steve to let him know where we were, but there was no answer. It was quite late, so he should have been home.

I then called his parents' house, but there was no answer there either. I didn't know what to make of it. Now what was I going to do?

By this time Joey was crying and really restless. He just wanted to be at home in his crib.

Exhausted, I managed to retrieve our luggage and secure a bench where Joey and I could sit quietly and be out of the way of all the people hustling about. We were up on the second level overlooking the bottom floor where all arrivals and departures came and went. At least I had something to occupy my thoughts as I tried to rock my worn-out baby to sleep.

The minutes dragged by as I watched people come and go. Soon the airport was empty and the lights were being shut off one at a time. By 1:00 a.m., we were the only ones still sitting in the empty terminal.

A night worker came over to me and asked if anyone was coming to get us. Regrettably, I told him that there wasn't and I only had a little money left to feed my baby. I couldn't afford a hotel room. He went to talk to someone and came back to tell me he had arranged for us to use one of the pilot's rooms. He would have to take half my money, which left me with only $3.50 to care for my son.

Through tears, I thanked the man and let him know how grateful I was for the room. As soon as our heads touched the pillows, we were out for the night.

By early afternoon the next day, I managed to connect with my father-in-law. From the shocked sound in his voice, I could tell he was shocked to discover I was in Nova Scotia. He didn't know where his son was, but he promised to track him down.

By late afternoon, I was about done in, feeling sick from the lack of food and full of anxiety over our situation. I didn't have enough money to feed us both, so I only fed Joey. My ankles were painfully swollen and every part of my body hurt.

I just felt plain lost and scared. I hardly had the strength to deal with Joey's needs, because he was extremely vexed. All the noise had gotten to us. There were so many people coming and going that it felt like the whole world was closing in on me. The only thing that kept me going was the thought of Steve coming to get us at any moment.

Sometime around 6:00 p.m., Steve finally showed up. At the sight of him, I wanted to rush into his arms and feel his love wash over me, clearing away all those long, lonely months we'd been apart, and all the fear that had stuck to me for the last two days.

Much to my surprise and dismay, his only acknowledgement towards me was to say hi. In fact, he scarcely looked at me. He eagerly picked up his son, hugged and kissed him, then grabbed what he could of our luggage and made his way toward the door, leading us out of the airport. I awkwardly trailed behind with the rest of my luggage.

I was greatly confused and hurt, but I didn't say anything because I was at least glad to be out of there. He led us to a brand-new green sportscar. I asked him whose car this was, and he replied that it was his. Another unexpected surprise…

What was going on?

The ride took several hours because it was snowing and blowing hard, making it difficult to see in the dark. I let Steve concentrate on his driving, so the talk could come later. But the wait was emotionally draining. On top of that, Joey's crying and the radio didn't allow for conversation. He didn't seem at all pleased that we were there. I didn't get it. After all, he had sent for us.

By the time we pulled into our driveway, I guessed that our new home was a trailer, according to what I could see in the headlights. Steve still wasn't talking. Without a word, he got out of the car, reached into the back seat, then took Joey out and placed him in one arm. He then carried some of our suitcases towards the trailer. I crawled out of the little car, almost every bone and muscle in my body protesting. I was in a lot of pain.

The heavy snow was almost knee-deep, which made walking awkward. Nonetheless I gathered the rest of our things and carefully walked in Steve's footsteps towards the front door.

I felt hurt and unwanted by his odd behaviour. He was acting strange and distant and I couldn't understand why. What had happened to him? What had happened to us?

My first impression of our home was that it was really small. But at least it was ours! Walking through the front door brought us into the kitchen and living room, which was really one room. It took only four or five steps to get from the door to the kitchen counter. The kitchen boasted a single sink with a small window above it. Next to this was a small stove and fridge. Opposite the counter was a mini table with two chairs. The table was flush with the wall, under a picture window. It was crowded.

The living room contained a small closet that hid the furnace, a chair, and a short couch with another picture window looking out the other side of the trailer. It may have taken only a few steps to cross the length of the living room. That's how small this place was.

On the left side of the front door was a dark hallway. The first room was the master bedroom, which held a double bed. Next to that was a tiny bathroom, and then there was Joey's room at the end of the hall, which had a bunkbed and a small dresser. This room was dark and cold.

Steve remained distant and polite. I consoled myself that he must just be tired after a long day of work, driving the many miles to Halifax and then home again. That would do anyone in.

Because I was very hungry and Joey needed to be fed as well, he politely showed me what food was available. When we'd had our fill, I tried to put my little guy to bed, which he didn't want to do. His bedroom was too strange for him and he didn't want to be left alone. I had been trying to keep him entertain and soothe him for two days, so by this time I was completely done in and desperately in need of help. What I really wanted to do was spend some much needed time getting to know my husband again.

Because Joey wouldn't stop crying, I lost my temper and began yelling at him to shut up and go to sleep. My nerves were almost shot. I couldn't handle any more, and Steve couldn't be bothered to come and help me.

By the time I got Joey sleeping and went back out to the living room, I found Steve sound asleep on the couch. I tried waking him, but he was out for the night. I covered him with a blanket I'd found, then went alone to our bedroom. The bed only had a sleeping bag, which I unhappily crawled into and shivered from the cold. But I finally found a comfortable position, hard to accomplish being seven months pregnant, and fell asleep.

Upon waking the next morning, I found myself alone with my son. With great disappointment, I figured Steve must have gotten up early and gone to work. I didn't even know what he did for a living.

Sadly, I found very little food in the kitchen, and it wasn't proper food for a baby or a pregnant woman. I figured when Steve got back we would go grocery shopping.

Looking out the picture window in the living room, all I could see were fields of snow stretching out to the horizon. There wasn't a house in sight, only a few cows wandering around in the distance. From the kitchen window, on the opposite side of the trailer, I could see the driveway we'd come in on. As it turned out, we were quite far from the main road. All I could see was a bluff of trees and more empty fields.

When I went out into the freezing cold to see what was in the backyard, to my surprise I saw something like a huge fishing boat… and of course more snow-covered fields. We were out in the middle of nowhere and I didn't have a clue where. It was truly a frozen, desolate place.

Betrayal

The day was spent familiarizing myself with the trailer. I swept the carpets because there wasn't a vacuum, then washed the kitchen floor on my hands and knees so Joey would have a clean floor to play on. Joey's mood was much improved after having had a good night's sleep and room to move around as he pleased.

By evening, I knew something was terribly wrong when Steve still hadn't come home.

He didn't return that night or the next night. We'd been deserted.

For the life of me, I couldn't figure out what was happening. We didn't have a telephone, which explained why I hadn't been able to reach him when I was at the airport.

Each night I cried myself to sleep. This was worse than being in Manitoba waiting for him to call. The days dragged endlessly and anxiety occupied my mind.

When Steve finally decided to grace us with his presence, without saying a word he removed his boots and coat and sat in the living room chair. I walked over to him and awkwardly lowered my large body to the floor at his feet and looked up into his face.

"Where were you and what's going on?" I asked.

Struggling with the guilt of his problem, he confessed, "I found someone else."

He had been spending his nights with her, having met her only a few weeks after I had gone home seven months prior.

Hearing those unbelievable words was like having a sword plunged into my heart. My mind reeled. The pain was unbearable. He might as well have slapped me across the face.

I was devastated. It had never once occurred to me that this would happen. Why had he even sent for me then? Couldn't he have told me about her while I was still in Manitoba?

He proceeded to tell me that he still loved me, but he also loved her and that he didn't know what to do.

It took every ounce of strength I had left in my body to stand to my feet and look down at him through tear-filled eyes. There was only one thing for me to do—and that was to leave. I couldn't share my husband with another woman.

With a distraught heart, I told him I would go home. Little did I know that with this statement I solved his problem.

He then had the audacity to ask if he could keep our son.

"No," I told him firmly. "He's mine and I will care for him."

He didn't dispute my decision and left shortly thereafter to find consolation with his girlfriend. Meanwhile, I had only anguish, jealousy, fear, worry, and loneliness to keep me company. He had completely neglected his responsibility as a husband and father.

I also didn't know how I was going to get back to Manitoba. I didn't have any money or way to leave… and he hadn't offered any help before he left.

Thirteen
Abandoned

I had very little contact with Steve after that because he was gone for days on end without a word. I was out of my mind, left with the knowledge that he was with another woman while I had been abandoned to care for our son.

I don't believe I had ever felt so alone in all my life. The days passed agonizingly slowly. I'd sit at the small living room window for long periods of time, looking out over the snow-covered ground that stretched for miles in every direction. Tears ran down my cheeks as I listened to the sad songs playing on the radio. We didn't even have a TV.

I'd been so in love with him. He had been my whole world, my joy. All I had desired was this man. Not once during our life together—through dating, engagement, and marriage—had I regretted my choice of mate. I had truly given him my heart and soul and looked forward to spending the rest of my life growing old with him. I was proud to be his wife and bare his children. Before this, I'd felt like a priceless vase that had been chosen to sit in an honoured position in the middle of an elegant table for all to see.

Now it felt like an angry arm had swept across that table, sending me crashing to the floor, smashing me into a million pieces.

So many tormenting thoughts flooded my mind. What was this other woman like? How could he make love to her while I was still here? How could she be with a married man?

I felt like this was my fault. Maybe if I'd done this or had not done that…

My thoughts kept going back to the day I'd met his family, all of sixteen years old and immature. At that time, I'd done two things I was ashamed of.

One, while touring Cape Breton with his parents, I hadn't acted as a mature married woman should act, bringing embarrassment on my husband. I don't remember what I did or said, but I felt it in my heart that I had done something very wrong whenever I thought about that trip.

Two, he had asked me not to swear in front of his parents. But I had, without knowing it at the time. One day while talking to Steve's younger sister and boyfriend, who were older than I was, for whatever reason I'd suddenly began to use F-bombs and then the others followed. Little had I known that his mother was in the other room. Not that it should have mattered. I shouldn't have been swearing to begin with. But I'd grown up with that kind of language and it had become a part of my vocabulary. I knew without a doubt that I'd brought dishonour on my husband and his family. I cringed inside just thinking about it.

Had that been reason enough for him to find someone else?

On top of all these tormenting thoughts was the fact that no one other than Steve and his girlfriend even knew I was there. And I couldn't tell anybody what was happening because there was no phone. Joey and I were completely isolated from the rest of the world, and I didn't know for how long this would go on.

It was hard to keep Joey entertained, because there wasn't much room in our little trailer and we had only the few toys I'd brought on the plane with us. It was still really cold to play outdoors and the snow was too deep for either of us to walk around in.

Besides, where would we go?

After a week of seclusion, Steve's Aunt Grace came by to see him about his car insurance for the sportscar, as she worked for an insurance company. She was quite taken aback to see me when I answered the door. I invited her in to join me for a cup of tea.

During that visit, I told her how long we'd been alone and that I knew about the other woman. Grace knew we had come, but she'd understood that Steve had sent us home. It was embarrassing to know that everyone else in the family knew what my husband was up to, but no one had cared enough to warn me ahead of time.

That's when I found out why he must have sent for us. When he'd smashed up our old car, which I hadn't been told about, his insurance had required my signature for the new car loan. I not only felt abandoned but extremely used. I couldn't believe this was the same man I'd married.

I must have looked every bit as devastated as I felt because Grace took pity on us and took us home with her. She fed us a good hot meal and we visited for most of the day. After dinner, she had to take us back to the trailer, which I dreaded.

She said that she couldn't get involved with her family's affairs because she still had to live with them long after I was gone. She explained that they could make life miserable for her. She didn't agree with what was happening to us, but there was nothing she could do about it.

Grace never came by again and we were left to fend for ourselves.

As time went on, twice the oil furnace shut off for several days at a time. I didn't know what was wrong with it and the trailer became a deep-freeze. Dressed in our warmest clothes, winter coats, and boots, Joey and I huddled for hours before the open door of the oven, our only source of heat. We spent the cold nights shivering in bed together under the sleeping bag and all the blankets I could find.

On top of that, our food was running out. The first time Steve came home to get something, he found us in this frozen state. He showed me how to light the pilot light when it went out.

The second time it went out, I figured I must have forgotten how to relight it because it wouldn't start. When Steve next came home, bringing some food, he discovered that the furnace was out of oil. He said he would have to phone somebody to come and fill the oil tank.

He returned long enough to start the furnace and make sure it was going. Then he disappeared again without any indication of when he would be back.

We only had a little food to sustain us—bread, margarine, boxed cereal, milk, and frozen fish, which I very much disliked. I drank tea from a tall, brightly coloured tin tumbler which burnt my fingers. He didn't have much in the line of dishes either.

I dread to think what would have happened if I'd had a premature birth. I'm almost certain that my baby and I wouldn't have survived and Joey would have been left on his own, for who knows how long, before we were found.

Many nights I cried myself to sleep. I was stressed to the max and had a lot of back pain due to my pregnancy.

Going Home

On another one of those long and lonely evenings, friends of Steve's stopped by the trailer to see him. I'd met this couple, a man and a woman, on my previous visit to Nova Scotia. They must have figured Steve was home because the lights were on.

They, too, were surprised to see me there. I could see that they were uncomfortable, but they stayed and visited for a short time. They told me that they knew the woman Steve was with and they didn't agree with what he was doing.

At least that made me feel a little better, if that were possible.

They told me some of her history, including her name, and shortly after that they left. I had hoped they would take pity on me and come back to visit again because I was starved for company.

But they didn't.

In the second week of my being there, Steve's father dropped by looking for him. Like the others, he was surprised to see us. He told me that he wasn't happy with what his son had done, but he hadn't thought Steve would have been keeping us here. He'd assumed that Steve had sent us back the day I'd told him we were in Halifax.

I could see this man's disappointment and felt for him. He was a kind man and a man of principle. I respected and trusted him, so I asked him if he would mail a letter to my mom, so I could tell her of my situation. I needed to ask her to somehow find enough money to bring us home, since Steve still hadn't made any effort to tell me what his plans were.

I didn't see my father-in-law again until a week later when he brought back my mother's letter, which contained a plane ticket.[11]

---

[11] Years later, I found out that my mom had needed to borrow the money from one of my brothers. To him, I am forever grateful.

Steve came home while his father was there, and within minutes they got into an angry dispute over who was going to dump me and Joey off at the airport. As I stood watching them trying to out-yell each other, and talking about me as though I weren't there, I felt like we were bugs that had invaded the trailer.

"Quick! Kill and destroy them! Get them out!

"You kill them."

"No, you kill them."

Like discarded pieces of trash, they needed to get rid of us. I believe that this was the lowest point in my life. Never had I ever felt so unwanted as I did then. They actually hurt me deeper than anything my own father ever said or did to me. Yes, my father had been a despicable drunk, but these people, with all their wealth, had portrayed themselves as being special and important, and I had believed it. But who would do this to a helpless eighteen-year-old pregnant girl and her baby, never mind a baby which was of their own blood?

I didn't have a say in the matter, but I truly wanted my father-in-law to take us instead of Steve. It may have been Steve's duty to do it himself, but I dreaded the long and unpleasant ride to the airport in Moncton. I couldn't stand the thought of riding for hours in the same car as him. I meant nothing to him but a signature.

I don't remember if I signed the document, but somehow I don't think I did. At least I hope I didn't.

It was arranged that I would leave the next day, and it didn't take long to pack the few belongings Joey and I owned.

Finally, after three agonizing weeks of unexpected captivity, we were being released. I felt an enormous relief leaving my solitary confinement behind, yet my heart had been shredded, knowing that my husband was forever lost to me.

The trip to the airport was the longest ride of my life. The songs on the radio assaulted every nerve in my body: "These Boots Were Made for Walking," "These Shades Can't Hide a Broken Heart," "Tie a Yellow Ribbon Around the Old Oak Tree." They bombarded my mind and reminded me of the many hours I'd spent sitting at that living room window waiting for my husband to come home.

After an hour or so of this torment, we finally arrived at the airport. While Steve took care of our luggage, I managed to find an airport stroller and put Joey into it.

Then I turned to Steve, hoping he would say something like "Don't go" or "I'll change" or "Let's start over." Instead this final episode of our marriage came to an abrupt and unhappy end. As he turned and walked away, without once looking back, I realized it was truly over. I felt like a discarded piece of trash.

In a conscience effort to pull myself together, I held my head high and walked stiff-legged towards the waiting plane.

After Joey finally settled down and fell asleep, I had time to reminisce over everything that had taken place. The reality of it hit me so hard in the gut that I'm sure the baby inside felt it, too.

We had a layover in Toronto. While I was in the lady's washroom, changing Joey's diaper, the tears began to fall. It felt unbearable. I was only eighteen and didn't know what was going to happen to us. How was I going to raise these two babies on my own?

Just then a woman walked out of one of the stalls and asked what was wrong. I told her what happened and she said, "There's always someone who has it worse than you." I guess that was her way of consoling me. I figured she knew what she was talking about, so I shut down my feelings and hardened my heart.

That was the pattern I chose to live by for the many years to follow. I shoved my wounds deep inside, along with everything else that came my way, and it nearly destroyed me.

I don't recommend saying to anyone what this woman said to me. Pain is pain and it needs to be acknowledged when it's happening. We need to be comforted and understood by others. We need to be told that it's all right to feel and grieve, otherwise it gets held inside and festers until it comes out in other destructive ways, like blaming myself for Steve leaving me for another woman.

Years later, my sister Ann told me that Steve had hit on her in our bedroom during our first year of marriage. She had gone in there to see to Joey's needs.

For whatever reason, she hadn't been able to bring herself to tell me about it at the time. I wish she had, but then I never would have had my second son. That knowledge would have drastically altered the course of my life, so I'm grateful she never said anything.

When she did tell me, though, I realized that Steve was the one at fault for our marriage breakup. This realization removed the false guilt I'd carried all those years.

Fourteen
Restoration

J oey and I were back living with my parents, but only for a short time. Welfare helped us to relocate to our new home, a cute one-bedroom apartment. Fortunately, Steve and I hadn't sold our kitchenware, bedding, towels, and other household goods when we'd moved down east, so I only needed help getting furniture.

The first day in our new home was a blessing and relief, yet it was also a foreign, empty, and very lonely place.

As the days passed and I settled into a daily routine, the reality of everything that had happened really began to sink in. It was hard to accept the fact that Steve was never going to live with me again or share the raising of our children. I had just become one of those single parents everyone talked about. He had someone else to hold, but who was going to hold me when I needed it?

While I waited for the arrival of my second child, I not only battled the loneliness, but every day my body went into false labour. Sometimes the pain was as close as two minutes apart. Then the labour pains would stop as suddenly as they'd started, so that by the time my baby was due to arrive I didn't want to go to the hospital.

I was visiting Mom that day, and all afternoon the pains persisted. When she finally asked what was happening, I told her that this was a common occurrence and not to worry.

By the time Dad came home from work, I was tired and cranky. The pain hadn't let up. All I wanted to do was go home and lay down. Mom had a different feeling about this, though, and she wanted me to go to the hospital. I tried to compromise with her and said I'd go after I'd gone home to shower and change clothes. She'd have none of that and ordered Dad to drive me to the hospital right away. Too tired to argue, I left Joey with her and got into the car with Dad.

When we arrived at the front doors of the hospital, Dad asked if I wanted him to come in with me. I knew he really didn't want to do this, so I told him I'd probably be back home in no time.

With only my purse in hand, I walked to the front desk. Much to my dismay, they took my information and booked me in. I was taken immediately to a room and prepped.

Within fifteen minutes, I had given birth to a healthy and vibrant baby boy who I named Blayne.

As I was being wheeled out of the delivery room, I noticed a phone hanging on the wall and asked the nurse if I could phone my parents and let them know I wasn't coming home that night after all, and that they would have to care for Joey. The nurse dispatched me through and handed me the phone. I told Mom the good news, but she didn't believe me. So I handed the phone back to the nurse to confirm Blayne's arrival.

The brightest moments of my two-day hospital stay were when the nurses brought Blayne to me for feeding. My heart swelled at the sight of him. I couldn't hold him long enough. I knew I wanted to make up to him and his brother all that they would miss out on by not having a daddy.

Oh, Steve, I thought. *Don't you care at all about what you're missing out on?*

I was still eighteen when I gave birth to Blayne. He was a beautiful baby just like his older brother—and like his brother, he was a perfect baby; he slept through most of the night, ate hungrily, and smiled a lot.

I figured that if their father could only see them now, he would be so proud of them. Two very fine sons.

I hadn't received any money from Steve for our children, nor did I want anything from him, but the government insisted that I file for child support. I had to go to court, and the judge granted child support from Steve. He was to pay financial support for me as well. I hadn't wanted anything for myself, but the judge insisted that Steve pay at least one dollar per month to me, which he never did. The dollar was insulting enough, but not to pay it was worse. I wasn't even worth a dollar to him!

He sent maybe four cheques for the children that first year, and after that I received nothing. He and his family never inquired about the children, nor did they send them birthday cards or Christmas gifts. They simply never acknowledged their existence. I wish they had contacted the boys, at least for the sake of them knowing who their father and grandparents were, but not a word. I consider it their loss not to know my sons.

Return to Nova Scotia

While I had been at Aunt Grace's home, back when I was living in the trailer, I had taken her address and promised to write when I got back to Thompson. We kept in touch for several years and I looked forward to receiving her affection-filled letters, telling me about how she and her family were doing. We never discussed Steve or his family. That was best left alone.

Each Christmas, she sent a lovely Christmas card.

I flew back to Nova Scotia almost two years later to visit her for a week. Upon landing in Moncton, I got the feeling that this part of the country must not like me very much, because I was told that my luggage hadn't arrived with me. It had been sent elsewhere, and now it had to be tracked down and rerouted. In the meantime, Aunt Grace picked me up and we spent a wonderful week together.

During that time, I somehow met up with the couple who had come to visit me when I'd been in Steve's trailer. They took me over to one of their parents' place for dinner and then the woman and I went out to a pub and had a couple of beers. We had a good evening and I was able to part with good feelings. I never heard from them again after that.

Two days before my stay was over, I received a call from the airport in Moncton informing me that my luggage had arrived. I was so relieved, because up until then I'd needed to wash my clothes every night in order to have something clean to wear in the morning.

So Grace and I headed back to Moncton. She took me on a wonderful sight-seeing holiday tour there and back. We had no shortage of things to talk about.

I did, however, see Steve one more time on that trip. I was standing at Grace's kitchen window when Steve drove up and got out of his car. He just walked up to get something that was in the yard. He didn't come into the house, so I never talked with him. In fact, I don't even know if he knew I was in town or not.

That was the last time I saw him.

I also met up with my father-in-law, and that, too, ended on a good note.

It helped that I saw both of them, as it settled the anguish I still carried in my heart from our last meeting. When I left Nova Scotia, it was on my own terms.

I continued to write to Aunt Grace until her husband died. Then we lost track of each other.

Fifteen
Henry

Shortly after moving into my new apartment, I had the pleasure of meeting three women who were several years older than me. They each had their own apartments in the same building.

One was the property manager and she lived down the hall from me. She was happily married with three children. When Joey was put down for his afternoon nap and she was taking a break from work, I'd go over to her place for coffee and we'd leave our doors open, so I could hear if Joey woke up. She was an inspiration to me. After talking with her, I'd feel uplifted and hopeful. She was a good friend and always had something positive to say.

The second woman I met lived right across the hall. She was divorced and had two children. She had a strong character and just as strong a mouth. She made me cringe when she called her children horrible names, just like my father had done to us. I really felt sorry for those kids. But she was an interesting person nonetheless and I liked visiting with her.

She introduced me to the third woman, who lived two floors above us. This woman was also single.

Meeting them helped dispel a lot of my loneliness. We were all in the same boat, separated from our husbands, so we had a few things in common.

Another thing we all had in common was that our ex-husbands didn't make much of an effort to pay child support, and yet I noticed the other women always seemed to have new clothes, the latest household gadgets, and nicely decorated apartments. How could they afford it on their small incomes? After all, we lived on welfare.

After I'd had my baby and we'd gotten to know each other better, they introduced me to their little secret. They told me how easy it was to walk out of stores with large items, like full area rugs, small TVs, stereos, and anything else that caught their fancy. And the proof of their success was right there in their apartments.

They took me and my two sons grocery shopping one day and I put to practice what they told me to do. While in the meat section, I used my three-week-old baby, hiding several packages of steaks and hamburgers under his blankets. I walked apprehensively out of the store without getting caught.

My girlfriends were thrilled that I'd gotten away with it, yet I felt disgusted and full of shame by the time I got home. I had not only stolen from the store but used my baby as an accomplice. Three weeks old and he had been part of a robbery! What was I thinking?

Now I held the grand title of "shoplifter." My mother had taught me better than that. I had done it to fit in, but I knew it was wrong and I never wanted to do it again. I made a point of never shopping with either one of those women again. When we got together, I pretended that I had no problem with what they were doing, but that was only because I desired their approval and didn't want to lose their trust and friendship. I was a people-pleaser.

The woman who lived upstairs had the gift of fortune-telling. She used a deck of cards to read people's fortunes. Being curious, I allowed her to read mine and she was fairly accurate. Since this intrigued me, she taught me how to read the cards as well. Twice I read death in the cards, and twice someone I knew died within the year after having seen it. This was scary stuff.

One of the deaths was a new man I was about to meet.

When I became a Christian many years later, I found out what the Bible had to say about fortune-telling:

> *Let no one be found among you who sacrifices their son or daughter in the fire, who practices divination or sorcery, interprets omens, engages in witchcraft, or casts spells, or who is a medium or spiritist or who consults the dead. Anyone who does these things is detestable to the Lord; because of these same detestable practices the Lord your God will drive out those nations before you.* (Deuteronomy 18:10–12)

Divination is fortune-telling. An enchanter is a magician. A charmer is a hypnotist. A wizard is a clairvoyant. Observers of times are astrologers. A witch is a sorcerer. Consulters with familiar spirits are mediums. A necromancer is one who consults with the dead.

Upon finding this out, I renounced my involvement with the occult. I did this by going to God and acknowledging the wrong I had done. I asked Him to forgive me in Jesus's name for my involvement in fortune-telling (palm and card reading), astrology (horoscopes and the zodiac), and learning about magic (through stories, watching movies, and television cartoons containing magic). After I did this, I felt something lift off my shoulders. I felt clean!

The New Man

About a month and a half after bringing my new baby home from the hospital, my friends at the apartment noticed that I didn't go out much. They hadn't gone out much themselves, so they decided it was time we all did something exciting, like going to a bar.

At first I was reluctant. I'd seen enough drinking while growing up to know better. Besides, I'd only been in a bar twice and I'd found the experiences uncomfortable.

I told the girls no, but they were remarkably persuasive and I soon found myself sitting in a very noisy, smoked-filled crowded bar, nervously nursing a rum and coke. I felt completely out of place and desperately wanted to get home to the safety of my apartment and children.

The deejay had the music cranked so loud that I could hardly hear what my friends were saying across the table from me. I found it to be very frustrating. The place was packed wall to wall with high-spirited people having a good time, celebrating the weekend.

Not long after settling in, a good-looking guy came over to our table and offered to buy us a round. The girls were all for it. Myself, I was still nursing the drink we'd ordered when we first came in. I didn't much like the taste of alcohol, so I turned him down.

He confidently introduced himself as Henry and asked if he could join us because he was by himself. My friends had no problem with that, and so he sat down and kept the conversation flowing.

Henry seemed to take an interest in me, and after a bit he asked me to dance. I looked at my girlfriends nervously and they encouraged me to go and have fun. Shyly, I followed him to the crowded dance floor.

At first I felt awkward. I'd never danced in a bar before. While trying to get my confidence up, he leaned into me and shouted overtop the music to ask what I was angry about. I told him I wasn't angry about anything. He went on to say that when he'd first noticed me from across the room, it had looked like I was spitting daggers out of my eyes. I told him I just felt out of place.

After that, it didn't take long for the music to get inside me and I started to enjoy myself. We stayed on the dance floor for a few more songs before returning to the table. I felt more at ease with Henry and we fell into a casual conversation.

After another round of drinks, my friends decided to go home. Since I was enjoying myself, they offered to send my babysitter home and watch my boys. Just as quickly, one of them turned to Henry and asked him if he'd see to it that I got home safely, which he gladly agreed to do.

It was all said and done before I had a chance to stop them from leaving me behind. I felt rather awkward. I would have gone home with them if they hadn't tricked me into staying.

We stayed until the bar closed, at which time Henry called a taxi and took me home. Instead of letting me out in the parking lot, though, he walked me to my door. I invited him in for a coffee, which he accepted. I let my neighbour across the hall know that I was back and thanked her for watching the boys.

I went into the boys' bedroom to check on them and found that Henry had followed me in to see them as well. He told me that he had two sons with his ex-wife and missed them terribly. Looking down at my sleeping boys, I could understand why. As their mother, my heart swelled with love for them.

Satisfied that the boys were okay, we quietly left the room.

While drinking the promised coffee, I discovered that he liked to play crib, so I fetched the crib board and cards and soon the game was on. We played until seven o'clock in the morning, which was when the boys regularly got up. Henry stayed long enough to meet them. Joey took to him right off.

I saw him to the door, bid him goodbye, and figured that this would be the last time I'd see him. But he proved me wrong. He came over every available minute he had.

Because we enjoyed each other's company so much, within a month of meeting he ended up moving in with us. The only thing I can figure out is that loneliness will cause you to do things you'd never thought yourself capable of. It can also make you trust when you shouldn't.

One night as we lay together on the couch listening to music, Henry went to the stereo and put on a song by The Righteous Brothers called "Baby, Don't Get Hooked on Me." The song was about how the guy would use his woman and then walk away on his terms. Henry came back and lay back beside me.

"Listen to the words of this song and take heed," he said coolly. "Don't get hook on me because I may not stick around."

That was a cold splash of water to the face, but I didn't show him just how much those words affected me. What do you say to someone who has already set up residence in your heart—and your home—and then drops a bombshell like that? I guess it was his way of warning me that he didn't want to settle down.

All I offered was my own cool "Okay." But inside, I felt devastated.

In the days to follow, I was haunted by that song. When was he leaving?

That wasn't an inspiring start on which to build any kind of relationship, but it did keep me at arm's length. But I swallowed my hurt and refused to show it. After all, as the woman in the airport bathroom had said, others had it worse than I did.

My heart was hardening.

Henry had put a condition on our relationship, as though to say, "I'll live with you, bed you, and love you, but don't expect me to stay." It made me quite uncomfortable, but I accepted it—even though I didn't understand it. I was young, in love, and obviously very stupid.

I found out things about Henry that at times frightened me. He had a favourite buckskin coat and matching long-sleeved buckskin shirt. They'd been custom-made by a local Indigenous woman who had hand-beaded the back of the coat with the most beautiful wolf head I'd ever seen. This jacket was Henry's pride and joy. Nobody could touch or wear it except me, or so he told me as he placed it over my cold shoulders one night at the bar. I felt honoured.

Henry worked at the Thompson Inn, the toughest bar in town, as a bouncer, waiter, and bartender. The first time he phoned and asked me to bring him a clean white shirt to work, I thought nothing of it, thinking he must have spilt something on his shirt and needed a change. But when I showed up with the shirt, I realized how badly mistaken I'd been. The front of his work shirt was covered in blood. He explained that sometimes the customers got rowdy and wanted to fight. I didn't like that part of his job. I'd seen enough of this at home growing up, but he didn't seem to mind it too much.

On his days off, or after his shift was over, we would go over to the lounge and meet with his friends and dance. I'd order a rum and coke, which usually lasted all night. I didn't enjoy drinking, but I did enjoy being with his friends and being known as his lady. I was treated with respect.

Henry seemed to dote on me and his actions were gentle and loving. I was insecure after the treatment I'd received from Steve and didn't have a lot of trust, but Henry knew how to romance me and make me feel special. With him, I felt safe and secure.

Until one night, while Henry was working, someone took his buckskin coat from where he had hung it up with the other staff's coats. I was sitting in the lounge with two of his friends, waiting for his shift to end, when he came storming in and rushed me out to a waiting taxi. He told me what had happened and said he needed to take me home so he could go looking for his coat.

When we entered our small apartment, I sent the sitter home. Henry went straight to the kitchen drawer and took out a butcher knife, as well as several steak knives, and hid them on different parts of his body. I couldn't believe what I was seeing. I asked him what he was going to do, but all he told me was that he was going to find the S.O.B. who'd stolen his coat.

With that, he brushed past me and slammed the door.

I stood frozen to the spot, shaking in fear. I had never seen him so angry and full of revenge. What was he capable of doing? I was scared for the guy he was looking for and hoped Henry didn't find him.

The night had turned into a nightmare, something right out of a TV show. I waited about an hour for Henry to come home.

When I couldn't stand it any longer, I got my friend across the hall to listen for my sleeping children. Then I got a ride from someone I knew to go looking for Henry. After about an hour of searching, I found him sitting by himself at a restaurant. He was fuming over a cup of coffee and he still didn't have his coat.

Lucky for the thief, he was never found.

And as for my knives, I never got them back either. Henry said he'd needed to ditch them so the police wouldn't find them on him. He said that the police had found out he was out looking for the thief.

I saw a whole different side of him that night, one I never would have thought possible.

Because our one-bedroom apartment was too crowded for the four of us, we decided it was time to find a bigger place. Henry found us a two-bedroom apartment on the second floor of a two-story apartment building on Fox Bay, a cluster of the oldest apartment buildings in Thompson. It was also known as the slum area of our city.

Not long after we moved in, I discovered that Henry had a Jekyll and Hyde personality. He was unpredictable and subject to mood swings.

One evening, he came home later than usual from work and appeared to have had a few drinks, but he wasn't anywhere near drunk. I told him that his supper was heating in the oven in case he was hungry. No response.

Then I asked if he'd a good day at work, and for whatever reason he snapped back at me, telling me that I was prying into his life. I felt hurt and confused.

Angered, I took his supper out of the oven, wrapped it up, and put it in the fridge. With that, I gave up and went to our bedroom. The boys were already sleeping, so instead of getting into a fight I figured I'd just go to bed and read for a while. What had I done to deserve this?

It didn't take long before Henry followed me into the bedroom. He stood beside me just as I was about to climb into bed. He spoke to me in a calm and intimidating voice, dripping with sarcasm. I don't remember what he said, but while speaking he reached down and took my right hand. He lifted my arm until it was evenly stretched out, level with my shoulder. Looking straight into my eyes, he then placed his other hand around my forearm.

"You know, I could easily snap your arm in two and there isn't a thing you could do about it," he said.

I was stunned. What had brought this on? Again, what had I done?

Stifling my fear, I calmly looked back at him. "If it makes you feel any better, go ahead and do it."

He held my gaze for a few moments, then dropped my arm and left the room. Thank God he didn't take me up on it.

That shook me to the core of my being, but I had learned from Mom not to show fear. In her case, it had only fuelled dad's power trips.

It wasn't long before he confessed to me that he had a violent temper which had once caused him to commit an unpardonable act on another person. He claimed not to remember having done it. He'd blacked out. When he explained what had happened, he warned me never to repeat it... since he hadn't been caught.

Why I stayed with him after that is anyone's guess.

New Year's Eve

On an extremely cold New Year's Eve, Henry and I headed out to attend our first social dance together, being held in our local arena. I wore a formal dress, but because I didn't have an appropriate winter coat to go with the dress I was forced to wear a dressy knee-length summer jacket. The only shoes I had to match my outfit were opened-toed high-heels. I wasn't at all concerned about the way I was dressed, though, because we were going to and from the arena by taxi.

When we arrived, the dance was crowded with decked-out couples in high spirits, wandering about with drinks in their hands. The place was filled with excitement and it didn't take long for us to catch the spirit. The band was excellent and the light show dazzling.

Henry secured a table for us and ordered drinks. We met up with some people we knew and danced for most of the night.

We were having a fantastic time, until the inevitable happened. Around eleven o'clock, Henry had had a few too many and managed to find himself a fight. I don't know who or what started it, but he was determined to finish it. He even turned on me for some reason.

Somehow I ended up alone, and because I didn't have any money on me and couldn't find anyone who wanted to leave before midnight, I had no other choice but to walk home alone. It wasn't safe for a woman to be by herself, and I wasn't dressed for the weather, but I needed to get back to my kids.

Once I got outside, every moving shadow set my teeth on edge and my heart pounding. Thompson was a dangerous place at the best of times, but nights were the worst. As I walked, I kept looking over my shoulder. Fear had a tight grip on my heart.

Why did he have to do this to us? I asked myself. *And where is he right now?*

These thoughts only added to the fear, because I didn't know if he was going to come home or spend the night at someone else's place.

It seemed to take forever just to make my way out of the arena parking lot and all the people wandering around there. The snow on the sidewalk was slippery and it was slow going. The main roads were piled high with snow on both sides, so if someone was to intercept me I would have no place to run. And even if I did, I was wearing heels. I had no hat, scarf, or mitts, only the flimsy coat and open-toed shoes I'd left home in earlier that evening.

Home was nearly a mile away and the wind kept trying to snatch my breath away. The sky was so black and clear that I could see almost every star in the galaxy.

About a quarter of the way home, I felt both my ears go *ping* and I knew they were frozen. I did everything I could to keep them covered by using the collar of my jacket and holding it in place with my numb fingers, but my whole body stung from the cold. The blood in my veins felt like it had turned into ice.

It seemed like the longest walk ever and I wasn't sure if I was going to make it. There weren't any people around, since everyone in town seemed to be either out attending functions or waiting in their warm cozy homes for the clock to strike twelve.

The northern wind blew mercilessly, nipping at every part of my body. It didn't take long for the cold to zap my strength and make me feel lightheaded. With determination, and thinking of my children, I pressed on. I kept telling myself, *If I die out here, someone else will raise my children. I have to get home. These kids are mine and no one else is going to have them.*

My exhaustion beckoned me to lie down on that soft blanket of fluffy snow.

Just take a little rest. Then I'll make it the rest of the way…

Those were dangerous thoughts and I determined with the little bit of strength I had not to succumb to these lies. I felt Death walking behind me, waiting for the right moment to pounce.

What seemed like hours later, I came upon an apartment building that was only three buildings down the street from my own. In what seemed like slow motion, I staggered towards the front door and, with the last of my ebbing strength, I grabbed hold of the frozen steel handle with both hands and wrenched the door open and stumbled inside. The cold steel burned my hands like fire.

It didn't appear to be much warmer inside the hallway. The heaters in these buildings didn't work efficiently, but at least I was out of the driving wind. I was also relieved to see that there was no one in the hallway. I was in no condition to explain my reason for being there.

Stiff from the cold, I lowered my weary body onto one of the steps that led to the upper floor and sagged against the wall. My dizziness and feelings of disorientation were trying to overpower me, but I fought against them. I had to stay in my right mind in order to make it home.

When the room stopped moving, I glanced up and looked out of the large window halfway up the wall beside the door I'd just come through. Through it, I could see the next apartment building across the street; my apartment was only two buildings behind it, but it might just as well have been a million miles away. I couldn't go back outside until my body thawed out.

As warmth seeped into my skin, I began to shiver. My skin tingled with life and pain. I was also concerned about the condition of my ears. I battled these symptoms for almost ten minutes before I even felt close to being able to go back outside and face the unwelcoming night again. I really had to get home.

After all, it's only a short walk down the street, I reasoned. *Come on, you can do it. You've got to do it. Your kids need you.*

With that, I heaved my body off the step and pushed opened the heavy wooden door, only to be greeted by a powerful blast of frigid air.

The short walk took an enormous toll on my already worn-out limbs. It didn't take long for the cold to undo what the apartment had revived, and as I pressed steadily forward, my head bowed into the wind,

I willed my stiff legs to move, all the while slipping and sliding on the uneven ice. My feet ached in these ridiculous shoes, and it's truly a miracle I didn't slip and kill myself.

Finally, the door was in front of me and I knew I had won. Triumphantly, I latched onto the door handle with both hands and swung the door wide open. With newfound energy, I stepped inside, thankful to have survived.

As the door closed with finality behind me, Death was left standing outside alone, frustrated and defeated.

I literally pulled myself up one step at a time until I reached the landing at the top of stairs. With shaky hands, I opened the door to my apartment and finally knew I was going to be all right. I had never felt so happy to be home in all my life.

Not mentioning anything to my babysitter about what I'd just come through, because I didn't want to frighten her, I casually asked how the kids had behaved. She said they had been good and were now sound asleep. Fortunately, I had enough money at home to pay her and send her home in a taxi.

As the warmth began to seep into my frozen skin, I hastily pulled off my skimpy clothes and eagerly climbed into something thick and warm. Grabbing a heavy blanket, I made for the living room couch. All I wanted to do was bundle up and begin the process of thawing out and returning to normal, while waiting to see if Henry would show up.

All I knew was that my children still had their mom and I was very grateful to be alive. Happy New Year!

Henry eventually made his way home, only I don't remember if it was that same night or another night. I do remember that it took a few days to get over the pain of my cold walk home. After my poor ears thawed out, they swelled up. Because I wore my hair short, every time I wanted to leave my apartment, even just to go downstairs and do laundry, I'd check first to see if anyone was around to see me. If there was, I'd stay in my apartment until they were gone. My ears ached for a long time. I was very fortunate that no other parts of my body froze.

A few days later, I received some terrible news. My sister-in-law's sister, who lived on a reservation not far from Thompson, had taken a bombardier with some friends to a New Year's Eve party that was quite some distance away. On the way back, the bombardier had broken down and she had frozen to death. The temperature that night had been -40 degrees Fahrenheit, but the wind chill made it feel close to -60 degrees. It was record-breaking.

Indeed, I was *very* fortunate to have made it home.

Sixteen
A Third Baby

Before Henry and I had started living together, I'd told him I needed to go to my doctor and get some kind of birth control, but he had claimed there was no need for that. He couldn't have children because of something his ex-wife had done to him during a fight when they were still together. Being a trusting person, I believed him and didn't take any precautions.

Imagine my surprise when I found out in January that I was three months pregnant. I couldn't believe it. I felt like a baby machine. It seemed like I could get pregnant at the drop of a hat.

Now I had the responsibility of telling Henry that we were going to have a baby.

Unsure of what his response would be, I delivered my special news with caution. It resulted in an instantaneous explosion of denial. In righteous indignation, and with cold, glaring eyes, Henry accused me of having an affair.

Any hope I might have had that he would be happy about our child vanished. I couldn't believe his reaction, and of course I denied having had an affair. I was so angry at his accusation of my character.

"Before you came along, I was already raising two kids whose father didn't want them," I said. "So if you don't want to take responsibility, you can get the hell out. What's one more child?"

That wasn't exactly how I really felt inside; it was a defence mechanism. I wanted my words to spit in his face, but inside I was begging him to believe me and not abandon us.

I'd like to say he stayed, but he was infuriated beyond rationality and began to slam around the apartment, gathering his belongs and throwing them into his suitcases while I stood by and watched, holding my arms protectively around my unborn child. He never looked at me. In fact, he didn't say another word to me.

I wanted to scream, begging him to believe me, assuring him that I hadn't done anything wrong. Instead I silently watched him prepare to go.

After he'd collected his things, he headed for the door and without looking back he slammed it shut behind him. My resilience crumbled into a million tiny pieces. I stared at the closed door, unbelievable emptiness filling the whole apartment. Once again I was left to pick myself up and reconstruct my broken life.

I could feel Pain's bony fingers squeezing the breath of life out of me. It took everything in me to keep from screaming at the top of my lungs over and over again that I was innocent and to emphasize it by smashing and throwing and overturning whatever was in the living room. Instead all I allowed myself were the burning tears of rejection that streamed down my cheeks, because the boys were in their room sleeping and the neighbours might hear me and come running.

Abandonment had moved in to stay, but at least this time I didn't have to fly halfway across Canada to find a home, contact welfare, and start all over again. The apartment was already mine. It was a small ray of sunshine on a very stormy day.

In the span of about a year, I'd managed to end two relationships, my marriage and a common-law relationship, and get left carrying the bag—or in my case, carrying a child. Once again I found my life torn apart and there wasn't a thing I could do about it except rebuild.

As bad as that may have been, when I thought back to that dreadful New Year's Eve night, I discovered that I hadn't only been fighting for my own life, but also for the life of my unborn child. What a revelation that was! No wonder Death had wanted so badly to take me out. He would have had two souls for the price of one.

Henry Comes Back

Henry did eventually return after a time and accept the baby as his own, but we had a lot of problems.

In my life, the hardest thing to put up with was being with an unfaithful mate. I had never experienced loyalty. It had started with my dad, then continued with Steve, and now the same was true with Henry.

Our relationship was rocky. Over and over, he would provoke fights that led to separation, packing his suitcase and leaving with the intention of never coming back. In fact, he did this three times. Then I found out during one of those moves that he had started seeing another woman, after which he'd come back to me, stay a while, then return to her again.

Because we weren't married and there was no commitment between us, I didn't seem to have any right to be upset if he left and went to her. He wasn't cheating on me, because he didn't belong to me. In fact, the reality is that he still belonged to his wife, to whom he was still married, even though they had been separated for several years. Or at least so he'd told me.

I also belonged to Steve, to whom I was still married even though he was with someone else now.

Oh, the webs we weave. In the end, everything seems to come back around to slap us in the face.

It's a hard pill to swallow when you know you can be replaced so easily. My self-worth was at an all-time low. My children and I hadn't asked for this.

Each time Henry left, another piece of my heart shrivelled up. But that was okay, apparently, because someone else out there had it worse than I did. As long as I hung onto that saying, I could just take my anger, hurt, and rejection and shove it deeper inside in order to survive another day.

On a frosty winter's night, Henry came home late from work, only this time he came through our apartment door walking backwards, stopping long enough to close the door. Without a word to me, he continued walking backwards, passing by the kitchen table where I was sitting.

He headed for our bedroom.

Puzzled, I heard him rummaging around in our closet. I got up to see what he was looking for. Maybe I could be of some help.

On the bed, he had packed some of his clothes into a small suitcase. I also noticed that he'd changed into a fresh set of clothing and was now anxiously trying to bundle his discarded work clothes into a ball.

When he saw me, he shoved the bundle into my hands and barked out instructions for me to either burn them or dump them in a dumpster down the street. I looked at the bundle and saw a lot of blood on both his white shirt and black dress pants. Taken off-guard, all I could do was stare at him in dismay.

He'd gotten into a fight and beaten up a guy so bad that he didn't know whether he'd left him dead or alive. By this time, I could well believe that he was capable of murder.

Henry then asked if we had any pepper, to which I nodded. He figured the police might be looking for him with their dogs and the pepper would throw the dogs off his scent. He had been walking backwards so as to confuse anyone who was hunting him. He wanted it to appear as though his tracks were leaving the apartment instead of coming in.

He said that he was going to disappear until he found out whether it was safe to come back. If the guy died, he would be gone for good and I wouldn't hear from him ever again.

With that, he reminded me to get rid of the clothes because it had the guy's blood on it. And he told me not to forget to pepper his footsteps. Shrugging into his coat, he then grabbed up his suitcase, rushed out of the door, and out of the building.

I grabbed my winter jacket, found a brown paper bag, and shoved the clothes into it. Then I got the pepper and headed out the door to shake it onto the hallway floor. I continued down the stairs, even making my way out into the cold night, peppering all the footprints as far as the road. I hoped no one was watching me.

When I completed the task, I walked a long ways down the street in a daze, then dumped the bag of bloody clothes into another apartment's dumpster.

I couldn't believe I'd just done this. Why hadn't he dumped his own clothes in the dumpster? After living with my father, the only explanation I have is that you just get used to doing what you're told without asking questions.

I went back to the apartment and waited. The silence was deafening and I jumped at every little sound. I'd stare anxiously at the phone, but it didn't ring.

Placing my hands over my swollen belly, I knew this wasn't good for my baby. Fortunately the boys were sleeping and no police came knocking.

I didn't know what to do. I couldn't call anyone. My mind played all sorts of tricks on me. I was terrified for Henry, for myself, for my babies, and for the stranger who was left dying somewhere in a pool of blood. It was a night from hell.

Henry returned later the next day, saying that the guy was going to be okay. I wasn't all that happy to see him, but I knew to keep my mouth shut and not mention any of this to anyone.

After that incident, on several occasions he'd call me from work and ask me to bring him a clean white shirt and tie because he'd gotten blood spattered on the ones he was wearing. Working as a bouncer gave him many opportunities to get into fights. I'd get someone to watch the kids and bring him the fresh clothes without asking any questions. I often wondered whose blood was on his shirt this time, and how badly had Henry beaten him. Henry didn't seem to ever carry any bruises or cuts himself. I truly felt sorry for whoever it was.

Then came the blowout of all blowouts. It began subtly early one morning while the boys were still in bed sleeping. Henry was dressed for work while I wore one of his long white dress shirts that covered my protruding belly and reached down to my knees. At the door, I kissed him goodbye and bid him a great day at work. Happily, I closed our door and headed towards my bedroom to get dressed, so I could go over to my neighbour's apartment just down the hall for our morning coffee. She and I did this most mornings after our men left for work. We would leave our doors open so I could hear when my kids woke up. It was our quiet time for the day.

Anyway, about halfway to my room I was stopped by a knock at the door. Had Henry forgotten his key?

When I opened the door, I peeked carefully around it in case it wasn't Henry. To my utter surprise, standing at my door was a male friend I hadn't seen for several years. At the same time, my girlfriend from down the hall came out into the hall. I quickly introduced her to my friend and asked her to talk with him, out in the hall, while I went to get dressed.

After I was appropriately dressed, I invited him in and we visited for an hour or so, rehashing the good old days. In our early teens, we had lived just down the street from one another. There were about six of us who hung out together as a gang. We had so many stories to share and relive. Time seemed to fly by.

After he had met my kids and we were about talked out, he had to get going. He was only visiting town for a few days and had other people to see. Sadly, we wished each other the best and he left. It had been so good to see him again.

That evening, I had supper ready to be put on the table by 5:00 p.m. I waited anxiously for Henry to come home from work so I could tell him about my visitor.

An hour went by, and there was no sign of him. That was strange, since he hadn't mentioned working overtime and he usually phoned if that was the case. The kids began to fuss, so I fed them.

By 7:00 p.m., I gave up waiting and bathed and put the boys to bed, all the time wondering what was keeping him. Shortly after the boys were sound asleep, my brother dropped by for a quick visit. He wanted to see Henry, but he didn't stay long.

Discouraged, I cleaned up the kitchen, then tried to settle down and watch some TV until Henry came home.

Around 10:30, he burst through the door in a great huff and marched straight through our tiny kitchen and into the bedroom, leaving behind an odour of beer. Now what's wrong? I could hear him banging around in there, so I went in to see what he was doing. His suitcase lay open on the bed and he was once again throwing his clothes into it in a tangled heap. In anger, he grabbed at everything that belonged to him.

Taken aback, I asked him what he was doing. He turned on me in anger and told me that he was catching the next bus out of this town. His dad had wired him enough money to go home.

"Why?" I asked, frantic. "What happened?"

By the look on his face and the stance of his body, I could tell he wanted to strike me. Yelling, he claimed the baby I was carrying wasn't his, but he knew who the father was because he'd seen him earlier that morning while on the way down the stairs. My friend had passed him in the stairwell, and then Henry had seen him go up to our apartment door.

Henry then proceeded to call me a few choice names.

Shaken, I tried to explain that the guy was my childhood friend whom I hadn't seen in years and that my girlfriend had kept him company while I went and got dressed. I told him to ask her about it, but Henry wasn't buying any of this. No, he insisted that my baby wasn't his and he was moving out. All the while, he kept slamming around the apartment, gathering his things. Of course the kids woke up and were upset as well. Everything was going crazy. My world was being tossed out of its orbit once again.

I felt weak and confused. Why was he doing this to us? I hadn't done anything wrong. He was accusing me unfairly of messing around.

Before Henry left, out of anger and fear, and with a boldness I didn't really possess, I told him he could go—only in not so nice words—and that I would raise his child on my own. I didn't need him.

And with that, he left. I stood at the living room window, looking down and watching him get into the taxi and drive out of my life.

A great darkness descended upon me at this latest injustice. What had I done to deserve this treatment?

Out of all the times Henry and I broke up, this was truly the worst. I missed him terribly and cried off and on for weeks. I kept hoping he'd change his mind, but still he didn't return. I wished with all my heart that he'd realize that I would never have done anything to betray him. I loved him.

"Oh, God," I cried out. "Please bring him home."

But there was no answer.

I withdrew into myself, coping as best I could while feeling empty and depleted. At least I had my friend down the hall, but she couldn't pull me out of the dark cloud that wrapped itself around me and grew thicker with each passing day.

Somewhere in the depth of this despair a plan formed in my mind to abort this baby. How was I going to look after a third child? I was having a hard enough time keeping myself together to care for the two I already had.[12]

I heard somewhere that if you took a really hot bath, with some kind of powder in it, it would cause a miscarriage, so I bought the largest box I could find and later that night, after my children were asleep, I

---

[12] Oh, God, this hurts so much to write.

went into the bathroom and filled the bathtub with the hottest water I could stand. Armed with the magic powder, I poured it all in and ever so slowly submerged my body into the water, first allowing my feet to get accustomed to the heat, then my ankles, and so on until I was fully seated. Then I leaned back and waited for the promised results.

I had no plans on what to do next if it worked. How would I get to the hospital? Who would watch the kids? I simply couldn't think that far ahead. My mind was swallowed up in a thick fog.

Finally, when I couldn't stand the heat any longer, I climbed out and dried myself off—ever so gently, because my skin was raw. I waited and waited for the labour pains to begin, but nothing happened.

Now what was I going do? The fog seemed to grow heavier and darker.

Several weeks later, one of my brothers moved back to town with his wife. I remembered them saying that they couldn't have children of their own, and because I loved them and felt sorry for their situation, and because I felt like I was some kind of baby machine, I offered my baby to them for adoption. We talked about it and I believe we came to an agreement that he could take this one. I truly wanted my baby to have a good home and I thought my brother would be the good choice.

With what I had tried to do to my child, I had proved that any place would be safer than with me.

I never believed in abortion, yet my mind became so dark and twisted that I turned to this hideous "solution." It seemed the only way to end my dilemma. I didn't know anything about the illness of depression or what it could do to a person, but there I was in a full-blown depression. I'd descended rapidly into a deep, dark cavern and stayed there a long time. There was nothing rational about my warped thoughts.

It wrenches my guts to think that I tried terminating my pregnancy, neglecting my responsibility to my child. This little person was my child, my blood, my gift from God, and I almost destroyed him along with his right to live and be loved like his brothers. As his mother, I had scarred our relationship and I've lived with that regret ever since. I can't think about it without grieving. I know I've been forgiven, but I can't forget.

Seventeen
Unexpected News

Henry had been gone about two and a half months before he wrote to tell me that he had seen a doctor and found out he could still make babies, after all. He earnestly apologized and then asked if he could come home and marry me after we both got our divorces.

I was overjoyed and wrote back with a great big, "Yes!"

He said it would take about a week or so to make enough money for his bus fare. Then he would be coming home.

With that, I began to climb out of the pit and once again embraced life. Joy rose up within me and I could hardly wait to see him. Greater still was the fact that I wouldn't have to give up my baby. I had many misgivings about the poor decision I'd made, but I didn't know how to stop it now that I'd made that promise to my brother. I knew he would understand my change of heart once Henry came home, though.

The black veil was lifting. Sanity was returning.

Almost a week later, while having coffee with my girlfriend across the hall, I heard a knock at someone's door and got up to see if it was mine. I was surprised to see two very tall police officers standing in the hallway outside my door. When I asked what they wanted, one of them wanted to know if I knew anyone by the name of Barbra.

"That would be me," I said.

He solemnly handed me a legal document and told me to phone the woman whose number was on the paper. This woman had been trying to find my phone number to contact me, and when she'd failed to find it she had called the police for help.

With that, they left without another word—although years later, I learned that they had been supposed to stay with me while I made the call.

I told my friend that I'd be back as soon as I found out what this was all about. I understood very little about what was written on the paper. The woman I was to call was named Terri, and she lived in Ontario. This was very puzzling.

I bent over and dialled the mystery woman's number. It rang only a couple of times, and then a woman answered. I told her my name and how I'd gotten her number and she immediately introduced herself as Henry's sister.

With compassion, Terri told me the reason for the call. As it turned out, she had the misfortune of having been chosen to inform me about Henry's death. She'd tried to get in touch with me sooner, and it turned out that Henry's funeral had been held that very day.

She kindly told me that she'd placed two long-stemmed red roses in the coffin, one for me and one for the baby. She was also sending me a letter to explain to the best of the family's knowledge what had happened.

I politely thanked her for the roses, as well as for notifying me. I didn't know what else to say. I'd just been sucker-punched.

After our call ended, I calmly placed the phone back in its cradle. Feeling numb, I sank to the floor in slow motion. Surely this must be a mistake. Was this some kind of sick joke? My body was reduced to a puddle on the floor and I had no strength or desire to get up—couldn't have even if I'd wanted to. My legs had turned to jello.

I wished the floor would open up and swallow me.

My friend watched me through my open door and quickly came over to find out what had happened. I looked up at her and robotically repeated the news. She just stared down at me and asked the same questions I was asking myself. Was it true? How could it be possible? He had been due home in a week!

I don't remember getting off the floor or what happened the rest of the day. All I know was that I got through it somehow.

All the next day, a cloud of defeat hung over me. I woke, fed my children, I talked to those who called or dropped by, cleaned, bathed the children, and put them to bed. I functioned. When the day was almost at an end, I was exhausted. My body had been in pain all day long with false labour, as it had been every day for the last three months. I just wanted to go to bed, shut out the world, and succumb to the utter blackness of unconsciousness.

But that was not to be. By seven o'clock, my pain turned into the real thing. I felt the pressure in my abdomen. My baby was letting me know that it was time.

I phoned my mother because she had agreed to watch the boys while I was in the hospital, but she wasn't home. The pain was worsening. I then phoned my usual babysitter, but she was out as well. I tried my friend across the hall. She was out. I knocked on the doors of the other two apartments. Still no answer.

I began to panic. Couldn't anything go right?

I made my way downstairs to try the other three apartments. There was no response on the first two, but the third had a babysitter answer the door. Out of all seven apartments, everyone had gone out except me.

The pain was doubling me over, causing me to gasp for breath. I had to get to the hospital as soon as possible.

In desperation I talked this babysitter into checking in on my boys until I could find someone to relieve her. She agreed.

Slowly and painfully, I made my way back upstairs and phoned a taxi, letting the dispatcher know I needed it right away. In minutes, it was waiting outside. I quickly looked in on my boys and they were still sound asleep.

I grabbed what I needed and went downstairs. It was already dark outside as I awkwardly climbed into the backseat of the cab, but not near as dark as I felt inside. Once again I was alone, on my way to the hospital. Henry wasn't beside me. Another baby was being brought into the world without a father to greet it.

Pulling myself together, I told the driver my destination and asked if he could make it as quick as possible. I felt the pressure bearing down in my abdomen and knew it was possible to give birth in the backseat of the car, but I didn't tell the driver that. I wanted his full concentration to be on his driving.

I barely stifled the moans from the pain that was gripping my body. The swaying motion of the car only added to my discomfort and I hoped my baby would be kind and wait until we got to the hospital and had all the papers filled out.

I was never so glad to walk through the hospital's door as I was that night. I had enough time to complete the necessary paperwork, be put to bed, and phone my mother to let her know where I was so she could pick up the boys and take them home with her.

Now all I had to do was wait. I found a comic book about the true stories of unbelievable situations that had happened to people. How fitting.

I was totally engrossed in the first story when my little one decided it was time. Slightly disappointed that I didn't get to finish the story, I reluctantly laid the book down and hoped I'd get to read the rest after the baby was born. That didn't happen.

Anyway, I wasn't on the delivery table more than a few minutes before my third son made his debut. The doctor held him up and asked me if I was pleased with him. All I could do was look lovingly at this precious little being who instantly brought great joy to my heart. This was the wonderful gift my body had refused to let go of when I'd tried to abort him that night in the bathtub.

With tears of gratitude running down my cheeks and a tremendous ache in my heart, I told her how pleased his father would have been had he known he had a son, but now he would never know.

"Why not?" she asked, surprised.

That's when I lost it. Looking at the tiny form she held carefully in her hands, the grief I'd held in gave way and I erupted into tears. Somehow I managed to tell her that his father had been buried the day before.

The truth of Henry's death completely engulfed me. I lost all control over my emotions and the flood of misery would not be held back.

The look on the doctor's face showed her concern and she understood that I'd gone through more than I could handle. She took it upon herself to give me an injection that put me instantly to sleep.

For the next two days, each time I awoke I was given another needle and put back to sleep.

Finally, on the third day, I was allowed to stay awake and meet my son—and we were released from the hospital. Before leaving, I found out that I had been the talk of the maternity ward because of what had happened. It's a weird feeling to know that strangers are looking at you with pity and sympathy, that they're talking about you. I was more than happy to go home.

My boys were excited to meet their baby brother, Eugene. Here I was once again, left to repair my broken family.

Mentally, I wasn't doing at all well. My spirit had plummeted into a great sadness and my days consisted of little more than waking up and feeding and caring for my fatherless children. My friends and family couldn't fill the vacant place in my heart, although they tried. I felt like such a failure. A loser.

I was so unsettled. Everything I did seemed to turn out wrong. I wanted to scream. I wanted to punch. I wanted to smash everything around me. Nothing made sense. The hurt wouldn't let go. I just wanted to check out, but instead I put on a courageous front for everyone's benefit. After all, someone had it worse than I did.

Not long after leaving the hospital, the letter finally came from Ontario. I picked up the envelope, my hands shaking, and I stared at it. Tears flooded my eyes and began to trickle down my cheeks. I was afraid to open it because of what I'd find, yet I was afraid not to, just in case this had all been some kind of weird mistake. Until now, I'd held onto a last small ray of hope that Henry wasn't really dead.

Ever so carefully, I opened the seal and pulled out several pages of beautiful handwriting from Terri. Slowly unfolding the paper, I began to read.

I can't remember everything the letter had said, but I was led to believe that Henry had been at a party at a friend's place and learned too much about a drug deal. Later, he'd been shot in the head while sleeping on the couch.

Knowing Henry's nature, this manner of death didn't surprise me.

But after discussing this situation more recently with my daughter-in-law, who had met Terri and Terri's mother, I was given more information about what really happened. There were parts of the story I hadn't been informed about.

Apparently Henry had been talking to his mother and sister about me, a woman back in Thompson who claimed to be pregnant with his kid, which he said was impossible. They suggested that he go back to his doctor and get re-examined. He then discovered that he could have children, which was when he'd written me a letter asking for forgiveness.

Henry was on his way back to Thompson when he stopped for a layover at a friend's house. That night, there was a party, and sometime during the evening a guy involved in organized crime came into the house with the intent of going after Henry's friend for some reason. Henry was asleep on the couch at the time and was shot.

We'll never understand what really happened, but he was shot in the head, taken to the hospital, and remained in a coma until the next day when the doctors began operating to remove the bullet. During the surgery, Henry died.

I was told the letter I'd written to Henry, prior to the accident, had arrived in his mother's mail at the same time he was in the coma. His mother and sister had opened it and read it to him, in the hopes that it would spark something in him to wake him up. That letter was how Terri had found my address. I was also informed that the guy who shot Henry received two years in jail.

After finally facing the truth about Henry's death, time droned on. Little by little, life settled into an everyday routine and the ache gradually began to recede. Small rays of light pierced the darkness that hung heavily over my soul. My children, the centre of my world, gave me a purpose to carry on until I could walk out of the darkness and once again embrace life.

Later in life, after becoming a Christian and learning the many benefits of forgiveness, I decided that I wanted to meet the guy who shot Henry. I wanted to know what he looked like. I wanted to know what had really happened that tragic night. Most of all, I wanted to stand face to face with him, look him in the eyes, and say, "I forgive you for shooting the man I loved and the father of our child."

I thought about this many times through the years as I watched Eugene grow into a man. Who knows? If the guy is still alive, maybe one day I will meet him and have my opportunity. It's just a thought, but it's important to me.

On the Brighter Side

Up until this time, I'd had eight siblings. But approximately seven months after I gave birth to Eugene, a new sibling made her grand debut into our dysfunctional family unit. Mom had been pregnant the same time I was.

Mom named her Loretta, and I called her Ducky, because she was absolutely adorable. She's almost twenty and a half years younger than I am and she grew up being an only child at home, since the rest of us had our own homes and families by that time.

According to Mom's doctor, she was past her child-bearing years, so he had told her she no longer needed to take birth control. Well, that just goes to show you that doctors don't know everything. Some may call Loretta an accident, but it isn't so. Every child is a beautiful gift from God. I, for one, couldn't imagine our family without Loretta.

Did she have an easier life growing up with our parents than the rest of us did? No! In many ways, I believe she had it worse. At least when Mom and Dad were getting into their squabbles during my childhood, me and my siblings had each other. There had been a sort of weird comfort in knowing we weren't alone. Loretta was totally on her own, and so she became Dad's main target when she got older; he wanted to pick on someone else besides Mom.

It's also sad to think that she never had the opportunity to get to know us as her brothers and sisters. She ended up playing with our children, and because they were older than she was, they didn't call her Auntie Loretta, just Loretta.

Eighteen
Clay

I'm not sure where I first met Clay, but I think it might have been at the pool hall. He was a handsome young man, blond, blue-eyed, and built rock solid. He got on well with my kids and it didn't take long before he moved in with us.

He was a member of a motorcycle club, and I rode with him. Mostly he rode with his club members, though, because my kids were babies and they needed me at home. He also bought one of the first Harley Davidson FXS Low Riders that were brought to town. For what it cost him, he could have put a nice down-payment on a classy house, but what a sweet ride!

Clay taught me that a motorcycle came before any woman. He'd say, "You can kick the dog and screw the wife, but don't touch the bike." Nice to know one's place![13]

He wasn't a tall man, but he held himself like a giant and no one messed with him. He also had his black belt in judo and participated in tournaments. I was proud to be with him and we had a lot of fun.

When we were around the other club members, I felt slightly out of place, but I always felt like that. Some of them scared me, but I never let on. The women were hard and mouthy, so I kept my distance. It helped that one of my brothers was friends with some of the members, although he never joined. Overall, I was respected.

On a busy Friday night at a local tavern, Clay and I sat at a large table with some of the club members. The place was packed wall to wall and people were waiting at the door to get in. We were all having a good time dancing, joking around, and visiting other tables.

---

[13] A little sarcasm there.

That is, until the fight broke out. We didn't know the cause of it, but someone from the club came charging overtop our table to attack someone on the other side, sending all our drinks flying. Fists started swinging and the whole place erupted into a free-for-all.

When we heard that the police had been called, Clay told me to go outside and wait. He joined me a few minutes later, then helped put his and the other member's chain belts[14] around my tiny waist, under my coat, and told me to walk away. He said we'd meet later.

To say I was weighed down would be putting it lightly. The belts pressed heavily into my hips, causing a great deal of discomfort. I walked over to a nearby building and waited in the shadows so no one could see me. From here, I could still watch what was happening in the tavern.

Sometime later, Clay caught up with me and relieved me of my burden. He said if the police had found these on them, they might have charged them with carrying weapons.

Another night, Clay invited a few of his friends over after a night at the bar. They were all pretty wasted. Because I had to get up early with the boys, I only visited for a short time, then headed off to bed.

Clay came into the bedroom at some point during the night and crashed.

The next morning, I woke up to find a young woman wandering around my apartment looking for her makeup. I asked Clay about her and he said that she had passed out, so they'd left her there. One of my two older boys had gotten into her purse, took her makeup case, and gone back into his room and coloured an abstract mural on my newly painted wall. I had to repaint that bedroom; the mural just wouldn't do.

She was irate when she found out what had happened to her makeup and left in a huff. We never saw her again.

First Love Came Calling

At the age of thirteen, I had a gigantic crush on an ex-boarder's son, Reece, who was several years older than me.

Reece became good friends with my brother Garrett and came over to our house quite often. On one occasion, he visited while Garrett was painting the upstairs bathroom. While this was going on, Reece said something rude to me and I up and booted him in his privates. He dropped to the floor and rolled around in excruciating pain.

I knew I was in big trouble, so I went downstairs and commenced drying the dishes I had already washed. By the time Reece came down, I was painstakingly drying the blade of a very long and sharp butcher's knife, prepared to defend myself at any cost.

He came into the kitchen with such a pained expression on his face and said through clenched teeth, "If you want to practice your kicks, practice on some other dummy, please. Don't use this dummy to practice on."

I was truly sorry I'd done that, but I must have felt threatened by him.

After that, I saw Reece at the skating rink and would watch him hanging around with the teenage girls. I felt I didn't have a chance. Sometimes I felt heartsick, because the crush was real, but I couldn't have gotten involved with him anyway. His father was Bert the paedophile.

---

[14] These are belts made out of chains instead of leather.

Years later, after I had married, separated, had three kids, and moved in with Clay, Reece of all people came knocking on my apartment one day carrying a bottle of my very favourite wine. He'd been out of town for a long time and was back visiting friends.

On this day, Clay was working outside of Thompson, so I nervously invited him in. My heart skipped a beat as we shared the wine and got more comfortable with each other.

Then Reece began to share his feelings about me. He proceeded to tell me that he'd wanted to date me since even before I had married Steve. He had just been too shy to ask me out. It turned out he had almost gotten the nerve to do it one day, but then Steve walked into the room and we left to go on a date. I was none the wiser and Reece never tried again.

How ironic is that? I thought he hadn't cared about me other than for being Garrett's little sister.

Before Reese left that night, he asked if he could kiss me just once. Because I was living with Clay, I had to say no. That was so hard, because I really wanted to. My relationship with Clay was rocky at the time.

I haven't seen Reece since. But when I ran across a picture of him taken at a fortieth high school reunion back in 2002, he still looked great!

Introduced to Drugs

One night after the boys were in bed, Clay and my brother James smoked up in the living room. Clay came up with the brilliant idea that it was time for me to get high with him. With the kids being so young, I hadn't wanted to be put in the position of not being able to care for them if they needed me. I didn't know what the affects of pot would be and didn't want to find out. By this point, he'd asked several times and I'd always turned him down.

Since James was with us this night, and I knew he'd take care of the kids if he had to, I finally gave in.

"But if I can't handle this," I told them, "you'd better be able to care for the boys."

They readily agreed.

So, to shut them up, I took a couple of tokes and within minutes I was no longer in control of my movement, speech, or thinking. I sat as stiff as a board on the couch next to Clay and watched the picture on the TV fall over and over into itself, like something from *The Twilight Zone*. It was freaky.

To get away from the TV, I carefully got up to get a glass of water from the kitchen. To get there, I had to walk sideways between two kitchen chairs facing back to back. In my mind, their backs were almost touching one another, so I had to turn sideways and very carefully manoeuvre my way through them; in actuality, they here a fair distance apart from each other, if they were really there at all.

When I finally made it to the sink, I reached out to turn on the tap, but the hand didn't look like my own. Then I noticed the butcher knife nestled between the taps and the wall and I began to imagine what would happen if this unfamiliar hand reached for the knife to slit my wrist. I was truly scared.[15]

I couldn't even speak to ask for help, because my mind was playing perverted tricks on me. I was walking around in Wonderland and thought Clay and my brother were laughing at me.

---

[15] That became a constant fear every time I did drugs. I had to stay clear of all knives after that.

Completely paranoid, I turned to Clay and managed somehow to communicate to him that I had to go to bed, that I couldn't handle this. Awkwardly, I made my way to my dark bedroom and thankfully lay face down on the bed and tried to regroup.

Clay followed me and lay down beside me. Placing his arm across my back, he calmly asked if I was okay. When I looked at his face, I was shocked by what I saw. I could see his face changing over and over into the faces of the other guys I had been with before him. I didn't know who he was until his own face came into focus—and even then I wasn't sure if it was really Clay. That really shook me up.

In confusion, I buried my head into my pillow and didn't say anything in case I called him by the wrong name.

We must've woken up Eugene because he started crying. When I turned my head, I saw him holding onto the bars of his crib, crying for me to hold him, except the crib bars touched the ceiling, and so did he.

Now I was *really* freaked out. My baby needed me and I couldn't take care of him.

Feeling desperate, I pleaded with Clay to take care of Eugene until I could get myself under control. Instead of arguing, he got up and carefully took Eugene out of his crib, cradled him in his arms, and began talking to him as they left the room.

That was my introduction to drugs. The only thing I can figure out is that the weed must have been dusted with PCP or angel dust. The dealers were known to do that in those days.

You'd think that experience would have turned me off from taking drugs ever again, but sadly it didn't.

Not long after that experience, Clay and I broke up. He was out of town so much, so we decided to go our separate ways after just a few months together.

Nineteen
Rick

I met Rick at a bar. We talked, danced, laughed, and got along great. Even more importantly, he wasn't deterred when I told him that I had three very young children at home. He said he'd like to meet them, and I was only too happy to introduce them to him.

On one of our dates, he invited me over to his place. After a few drinks, we stopped by the venders and he picked up a case of beer. After putting it in his truck, he told me that a young couple shared the duplex he rented; he figured they would probably be out for the night.

But upon entering his place, we found them still home. They seemed friendly and Rick asked if they wanted to join us for a drink. We went into his living room and I sat quietly as Rick talked with his friends. After a few more drinks, I found myself relaxing and enjoying their company.

Rick told me he had fought in the Vietnam War, and to prove it he took out his photo album and showed me pictures of himself with his comrades in army fatigues holding their weapons. He shared some of his experiences of how the war had dramatically affected him.

At that time, Vietnam seemed so very far away, but after meeting him and hearing some of his story the war felt closer to home. I found what he had to say most interesting.

After a few more drinks and getting very drunk, it seemed only natural that we would end up in his bed. At first I felt awkward because of the other couple, but he assured me there was nothing to worry about and of course I believed him.

We dated about three weeks and spent a lot of time together. He enjoyed my kids and they liked him in return. Rick adopted the habit of coming over to my place during his dinner breaks from work and the boys and I looked forward to seeing him. I was once again starting to enjoy life and the feeling of being cared for.

But once again the inevitable happened.

Mid-morning one day, the boys were fed and playing peacefully in their room while I sat at the kitchen table drinking a hot cup of coffee and enjoying the bright sunlight through the windows. All seemed perfect in my minuscule world.

Until the telephone startled me out of my daydreaming.

Thinking it could be Rick calling, I cheerfully answered and heard a strange woman's voice on the other end.

"Is your name Barbra?" she asked.

"Yes."

She tactfully informed me that she was Rick's fiancée, who had been out of town for a month attending a teacher's learning seminar. She was wondering if Rick might be there with me.

What was she talking about? Rick's fiancée? He didn't have a fiancée… did he?

I was stunned. This was like a replay of the phone call I'd received from Terri, informing me about Henry's death. I was using the same phone, the same TV table, and the same apartment all these two years later.

This simply wasn't funny. I was taken completely off-guard.

In answer to her question, I told her that Rick wasn't there. She then asked if I was expecting him anytime soon.

"Yes," I said. "He'll be stopping by at lunch time."

She went on to inform me that he had cheated on her once before, but this time she was eight months pregnant and engaged to be married to him.

I couldn't believe what I was hearing. She went on to ask if she could come over and talk with me. She wanted to surprise Rick with her presence when he came in for dinner.

If she really was his fiancée, I figured the least I could do was let her have her say and do what was right, allowing him to be caught at his own game.

For the next half-hour, my brain was in utter shambles. I sat dumbfounded at my kitchen table, wondering if this woman was on the level. Thankfully, the boys were still content to play by themselves and didn't need my attention. I didn't have any to give them. Even the sunshine from my living room windows had lost its magic.

What was happening? And what about that couple who had lived with them? They hadn't said a thing about Rick living with someone else. Not one word. If this was true, then what had that couple been thinking about me? I felt so ashamed, so dirty, so humiliated, so very used. I had slept in this poor woman's bed… and now I had to face her.

The more I thought about the situation, the more distraught I became.

On and on the thoughts hammered at my brain until I was jolted into the present by a soft knock on my door. Resigning myself to the fact that I had to face her, I slowly got up from my chair and walked solemnly to the door.

Standing before me was a young pregnant woman, very pretty, and not much older or taller than myself. She looked so delicate and her eyes were kind and pleading. I immediately liked her and felt sorry for her. It had to have been hard on her to come home and discover that her man was cheating on her. I knew that feeling only too well.

Sadly, I opened the door wide for her to come in. I also offered her a cup of coffee, which she gratefully took. The kids were still busy, so we had time to talk before Rick showed up. I explained to her that I hadn't had any idea he was involved with someone else. If I had known, I wouldn't have given him a second look. I apologized and she received it well.

In this moment, I wasn't thinking about myself. Those thoughts were overridden by what I knew she was going through. If her story was true, Rick didn't deserve her or the child she carried.

We didn't have long to wait before there was a knock at the door. I got up to answer it, knowing full well who it was.

When I opened the door, Rick stood there with a big smile on his handsome face. "Hello, honey!"

I didn't answer, but his fiancée did. His smile instantly disappeared when he heard the woman's voice. I stepped back and allowed him to come in and look around the corner in astonishment. His fiancée had gotten up on her feet.

This was going to be a faceoff, so I walked away to stand in front of the living room window.

With my back turned, my mind flashed back to the trailer in Nova Scotia when Steve and his father had fought over who was going to get rid of me and Joey. Now I could hear Rick defending himself to his fiancée, telling her that I meant nothing to him, right in front of me. And in my own kitchen, to boot.

I turned to watch them just as they came to some kind of conclusion and prepared to leave together. Despondently, I watched the door close behind them. He didn't so much as say goodbye. It was over. Rick's fiancée got what she'd come for and I was left alone, hurting, ashamed, and empty.

A gloomy silence filled the room. Neither one of them had considered the condition of my heart or how I was feeling. Tears rolled down my cheeks as I looked out the window as they walked to Rick's waiting truck.

Feeling completely and utterly spent, I went to the kitchen to prepare the kids' lunch.

Several weeks passed when one delightful evening, while I was walking home, a truck came up behind me and blew its horn, causing me to nearly jump out of my skin. I turned to see who it was.

Of all the nerve! It was Rick.

He rolled down his passenger window and asked if he could drive me home.

You've got to be kidding, I thought, shaking my head.

In a stern voice that left no room for argument, I told him. "No. Go away and leave me alone."

And with that, he drove off. Who in their right mind would want a guy like that anyway? I never saw him again. Nor did I miss him. Another one bites the dust!

Twenty
Michael

I t took me a while to recover from the hard blow I took from Rick, so I didn't go out often—that is, until my sister Darlene talked me into going to a nightclub. Because it was a new place, I figured I'd check it out. We had a good time listening to the live band and watching the couples on the dance floor.

As the evening progressed and the bar became crowded, a good-looking guy named Michael approached me and asked if I'd like to dance. I accepted. When I stood up to walk to the dance floor with him I felt small. He was quite a bit taller than I was.

After the dance, Michael and his friend Denny joined us at our table, and sometime during our conversation Michael told us that he and his ex-girlfriend had recently split up. He was staying at Denny's until he found a place to live.

I don't remember the details of how it came about that Michael moved in with the boys and I, nor do I recall how long I'd known him before this happened. It probably wasn't too long. What I do remember is him asking me to go with him to his ex's place to pick up his belongings while she was at work. I agreed, but I wish I hadn't. If the shoe were on the other foot, I wouldn't have liked her coming into my home that way.

Not too long into our relationship, which had been a wonderful, Michael's ex caught up with him and he decided to go back and give it another try with her. This once again rocked my world. I felt lost as I watched him pack up and move out. I cried, trying to understand how he must be feeling. After all, he had been with her before me.

We agreed to remain friends and to keep in contact.

After some months, I received a phone call from Michael. It turned out that they'd split again and he had moved back to his home town in Williams Lake, British Columbia. He asked if I'd join him there for a visit, all expenses paid. By then my sister Darlene had moved in with me and she encouraged me to go while she watched the boys for me. She also figured I could use the holiday.

So, with a lot of humming and hawing, I finally gave in. I didn't like the idea of leaving the boys behind, but Darlene insisted they would be fine.

I didn't expect Michael to keep his word about paying all my expenses, but much to my surprise within a week or so he mailed me a round-trip airline ticket. I was really going to B.C. to be with Michael again! I was every bit as nervous as I was excited.

The trip over the Rocky Mountains was absolutely breathtaking. I never in all my life thought I'd ever see them with my own eyes, yet alone fly over them. They truly are magnificent! And being on a plane by myself with no crying kids was truthfully enjoyable.

Arriving at my destination in Prince George, I left the plane on very shaky legs. I was as nervous as could be, not knowing what to expect. Had I done the right thing? Up to this point, I hadn't felt very sure of myself and I almost turned around and got back on the plane.

While I contemplated my retreat, Michael arrived. Lifting my face to look him in the eyes, all the old feelings gushed forth. It was as though we'd never been apart. Throwing caution to the wind, we embraced and enjoyed a wonderful reunion.

When we drew apart, I noticed that one of his arms was in a cast. He shrugged it off by saying he'd broken it while playing hockey. He insisted it would be fine once it mended.

We spent our first night in Prince Gorge, and the next day Michael took me to meet his parents. I felt very much at home and accepted there. The evening meal was filled with stimulating conversation, followed by an excellent piano solo by his father. I felt so at peace, like I had been wrapped in a protective blanket of love. I never wanted it to end.

Later that night, Michael led me out of his parents' home and down a short path leading into the bush where a small cabin was nestled amongst the trees on their property. I was amazed that his parents had no objection to us sharing a room.

In the blissful week I spent with Michael, he proudly showed me the town where he's grown up. He introduced me to his closest friend and his girlfriend, both of whom I immediately liked. It was as if we'd know each other forever. We had a blast together.

The week was filled with travel and activity, and before we were ready for it, sadly the last night descended upon us.

Michael's friend invited us to spend the evening at a bar where he was part of the band. We had a fun time listening to the band and watching couples dance.

And at some point in the evening Michael knocked me off my feet and asked me to marry him. I honestly didn't know how to reply. I was torn! Tears stung my eyes, because I truly wanted to say yes. But after the way he'd left me back in Thompson, there was nothing to reassure me that it couldn't happen again. The thought of bringing my children out here only for him to decide he didn't want us anymore...

well, it was just too big of a chance for me to take. I still had all those memories and fear from being left alone in the trailer in Nova Scotia. Then there was Henry's death and Rick's betrayal.

I didn't have much in the way of trust left.

Turning him down was so hard because I truly loved him and couldn't bear to leave him. He was such a wonderful person and I knew he cared for me, but I wasn't stable enough to trust him—or anyone, for that matter. Not only that, but I worried about what would happen if his arm didn't heal well enough for him to get a good-paying job. How would he support us? The last thing I wanted was to be a burden to him.

In the end, I told him that I couldn't marry him, but I couldn't tell him why. I probably should have, but I was too messed up in fear.

We tried hard not to waste the rest of the night in regret, because we only had a few more precious hours before morning arrived and I had to catch a plane back to Manitoba.

Just before closing, I watched Michael get up from our table and walk over to the band. He and one of the members spoke for a few moments, and then he came back and asked me to dance a waltz with him. Only too happy to, I allowed him to take my hand and lead me onto the nearly empty dance floor.

Ever so gently, he placed his good arm around my waist and pulled me close, then whispered, "This song is for you." I felt shy yet flattered.

As the short musical introduction to the song began to work its magic, I relaxed against him. It was so beautiful. I'd never before heard this song—"Silver Wings," by Merle Haggard—but I was ready to enjoy it.

Then I heard the lyrics. They were about a guy standing at an airport watching as the plane departed that held the love of his life. It flew away into the sun and he knew she wasn't returning. His heart was broken.

Tears burned my eyes as those words became branded on my heart. I was so shaken by the truth of them that all I could do was bury my face into his shoulder and cry silently. It took everything I had to hold myself together to complete the dance. I wanted to hold onto him and never let him go. I knew he hurt, too, and I knew I was the cause of it.

This was his final gift to me that night. The song said everything I was about to do. If ever I wanted to change my mind, it would have been that heartbreaking moment.

The next day, in great hardship, I said my goodbyes, knowing it would be the last time I saw him. I wished with all my heart that I could have said yes to his proposal.

As the plane left the ground, the words of the song replayed in my mind. Was he thinking about the song, too? To justify my decision, I convinced myself that I had done him a favour by not sticking him with an already-made family. It was the only way I could console myself.

Even during my next relationship, Michael and I had kept in contact by letter for quite some time. Then one day he phoned and told me that he had met someone special and they were going to be married. I even had the opportunity to talk with her. She sounded very nice and I wished them all the best and really meant it. I was happy for him, yet again I wondered for the millionth time if I had made the gravest of mistakes by not trusting him.

Not long after, our correspondence came to an end. I felt it best that the ex-girlfriend not remain in the picture.

Even to this day, hearing "Silver Wings" always reminds me of Michael. It throws me back into the past to relive that remarkable time we shared. I still hold on to that special love I had for him.

Twenty-One

Dewayne

Quite a while after returning home, new neighbours moved into the apartment just below mine. Their music was excellent but loud. I didn't mind it during the day, but at night it was a little tough to get my boys to sleep. But they liked to party, which happened in the evening and on the weekends. I couldn't really complain, because I liked my music loud, too!

To add a little drama to the situation, this happened to be during a summer heat wave. I opened my living room windows, hoping to let in a breeze. That's when I discovered that they liked drugs. With their open window just below mine, I smelled the pungent odour of rancid marijuana.

My apartment was like a vacuum, sucking up all the odours from their apartment. Most times I even knew what they were cooking. There were times when the smell of pot was so strong that I had to close the windows. Who were these people?

A short time later, I finally met my party hardy neighbours. Their apartment was right across the hall from the laundry room, which I was scheduled to use two times a week. One day, while my kids were down for their afternoon nap, I took a basket of clothes downstairs to put in the washing machine and found their door wide open.

The sound of the latest pop song played on their stereo. Trying not to be nosy, I went straight into the laundry room and began loading up the washing machine. But I looked up when I caught some movement in my peripheral vision. That was my first glimpse of Dewayne, a powerfully built man who stood over six feet tall. He was standing in his kitchen with his bare muscular back turned towards me, wearing only a pair of cut-off jean shorts and tall black rubber boots.

He was mopping one of the dirtiest floors I'd ever seen, smeared with spilled booze, cigarette ash, and dirt. The kitchen table was cluttered with empty beer bottles from his company he had the night before.

Oh yeah, he caught my attention.

When he heard me in the laundry room, he turned to see who was behind him. After he said hi, he smiled and his face just seemed to light up. This guy was hot! I mean, *really* hot.

I shyly returned the smile and said hi back. He asked where I lived and I told him he was my downstairs neighbour. Then I quickly turned back to putting my laundry into the machine and headed upstairs.

So that was the new neighbour. Interesting!

I found out later that he was sharing his apartment with a guy named Leon, who I later met and liked. I also discovered that Dewayne was the owner of the shiny black Harley Davidson that was parked out back every night. He didn't belong to a biker club, but he enjoyed riding with his many friends. He also drove a very sporty black and chrome 1970 Camaro SS.

We met several times in and around the building before he asked me if I'd go out with him. Of course I said yes. After that, when he saw me with the boys he'd stop what he was doing and talk to them.

In the first couple of months that I went out with Dewayne, I introduced him to my parents, which I didn't usually do. They seemed to take a liking to him, and he them.

One Easter, I got an unexpected invitation. During this period, Mom had had enough of Dad's unbearable treatment and left him, taking Loretta with her. But Dad wanted me and Dewayne to come over for dinner. He just asked that we bring one thing—a bag of pot, since he knew that Dewayne both used and sold. I really didn't want to go, but it was Easter and I didn't want him to be alone. I got a babysitter for my sons.

When we arrived at the house, Dad led us to the kitchen and offered us a drink. The fridge was well stocked with beer, whisky, and mix. Dewayne accepted a beer while I chose a coffee. Looking around the kitchen, I could tell that he'd already been hard at work because whatever was on the menu was already in the oven while pots simmered on the stove.

After Dad paid for the pot Dewayne had brought him, we headed to the living room with Dad leading the way.

So far, so good, I thought.

Until we reached the living room. Never in all my life, and I mean *never*, had I expected to see a strange woman sitting quietly on the couch with a drink in her hand while music played softly from the stereo. She looked quite at home sitting there, and she smiled at me as I entered the room.

If that wasn't enough, Dad walked right over the couch, sat down, and put his arm around her shoulders, like he'd used to do to Mom. She looked as though this was a natural occurrence, like she belonged there.

Millions of shockwaves exploded my mind. Hidden tears stung my eyes. The urge was strong for me to walk out and never return. What the hell was he doing with this woman, and in Mom's house? How dare he?

But I didn't say any of this. Of course not. Not me. I convinced myself that there was nothing out of the ordinary happening here. I didn't want to make a scene.

Instinctively, I followed Dewayne's lead and sat down on the other couch next to him, trying to avoid looking across the room at Dad and the woman.

It didn't take Dad long to introduce us to this undesirable person. She, as it turned out, was my aunt—or rather, my dad's brother's wife. To make it worse, she just so happened to have the same name as my mother.

Everything inside me wanted to scream every kind of obscenity at them. *Traitors! You f—ing traitors! You rotten bastard!*

All the while, he sat there with a pleased smirk on his face. I felt as though he was rubbing this in my face, as though to tell me that he didn't need my mother. After all, he knew Mom and I were close.

Instead of allowing him to see how this affected me, I put on the same mask I had used for years to pretend that nothing was out of the ordinary. Pretence shifted into gear. Simulating a smile, I greeted my aunt as if it was the most natural thing to do, and Dewayne did much the same. I had heard about her and felt sorry for her situation, since my uncle had been said to treat his wife the same way Dad treated Mom, but this was our first time meeting each other.

I immediately disliked her. I hated her almost as much as I hated him.

Dewayne casually pulled out a joint, lit it, then pulled on it a couple of times. He passed it over to Dad, who took a couple of drags before passing it back.

Out of my great fear of Dad, I had to stay and play the whole scene out. I felt like I had to endure this in silence, so afterward I didn't tell any of my brothers or sisters. I especially didn't tell my mother.

I felt like such a traitor myself, but that's what happens when you're fearful and under the control of a lifetime dominator.

My aunt didn't stay with Dad too long before returning to her home in Prince Albert. Eventually Mom came back and they tried again.

Common Law

After a few short months of enjoying each other's company, Dewayne asked if the kids and I would move in with him. I said yes, enthusiastically, and he immediately went on an apartment hunt.

It didn't take him long to find a two-story three-bedroom townhouse unit for us at 10 Yale Place, built on the edge of town almost next to the Burntwood River. It boasted grassy backyards and had its own playground where the kids could hang out. It was a nice, clean place to live. The house even had a basement for the kids to play on rainy days and during the winter.

If our relationship were to be tested, it would have been the first day we moved in. Dewayne had a stereo system that was to be envied, with a set of heavy black speakers that could blast the windows out of any place if it was turned on high enough. I'm generally a strong person for my size, but I couldn't lift or even put my arms around them.

Somehow, during the move, one of the kids had put his foot through one of the woofers. I was horrified and waited for the bomb to drop. But Dewayne calmly took the kids aside and explained to them why they shouldn't play near or touch his stereo system.

What can I say? I was impressed! And they didn't go near his stereo again.

They, like me, loved music. My mom and dad had sung, but mostly Mom. All of us kids had sung, too, with music being a big part of our survival. Singing is where I still go when my world feels like it's crumbling down around me. Somehow it's the glue that holds me together.

Dewayne also had a love for music. He had two hundred or more LPs, placed up against the living room wall on the floor next to the stereo system in rows of fifty. The biggest problem with all that music was trying to figure out what I should play next. There was so much of it and it was all good!

Anyway, we found the people in that area to be friendly and we fit in nicely. We met several new couples and it didn't take long before we were partying at their houses or ours. The fact that they had kids my sons' ages made it even better. By this time Joey was five years old, Blayne was three, and Eugene was two.

Now that the boys were a little older, I didn't mind getting a babysitter so I could ride along with Dewayne. I loved to sit behind him as we cruised the town's main streets. We generally ended up in a bar with other bikers. What I really enjoyed was when we were riding and other bikers joined us. It looked good and sounded even better. I loved the throbbing sound of a Harley. It's a heartbeat like no other. When several of us rode together, the bikes emanated power.

Cruising the highway was the best. I wore my hair just below my shoulders, and when we rode it would whip around in the wind. In those days you didn't wear a helmet and I didn't like elastic bands. It would take a lot of yanking to get the knots out, but it was worth every bit of pain. I just loved to ride!

I heard it said once that riding in a car was like riding in a cage. I fully agreed!

In the winter, the bike was brought into the house and parked in front of the living room window because we didn't have a garage. The boys knew not to touch it. Dewayne explained that if it were to fall on them, they could get badly hurt or killed. And because they loved and respected Dewayne, they listened to him. He didn't need to speak to them twice.

As for me, I had no problem with it being parked there. It made for a great conversation piece and another piece of furniture to dust, which I didn't mind at all.

Dewayne wasn't the type to sit around twiddling his thumbs. He wanted to show us things and take us places.

One day, he came up with the idea to take us camping for a weekend at Paint Lake. The only camping experience I'd had until now was when my father had taken us when I was little, and we all know how that turned out. Eugene was still going through diaper training, so this was going to prove to be an interesting experience for me.

Dewayne borrowed a large tent with camping gear and found us a fairly private spot surrounded with trees. We were close to the bathrooms, which really helped. The weather was peaceful and didn't rain! The boys took to it immediately. There were plenty of campers all around and lots of activity. I also found out I was a natural girl guide. I would get up in the morning before anyone else, get a good fire going, and have bacon, eggs, and hashbrowns ready for the first ones who crawled out of their sleeping bags. I also enjoyed chopping wood and keeping camp.

One morning, Joey and Blayne had been out exploring the camps close by, and on their return they shouted excitedly that they'd found marbles lying all over the ground. Curious, I asked to see them and they proudly dug into their bulging pant pockets and pulled their marbles out and held them out for inspection. Dewayne and I could hardly keep from laughing. They had found rabbit droppings and filled their pockets with them.

Although I didn't drink much or smoke marijuana, we were party people and it didn't take long before the other campers joined us at night around our campfire. They brought their own drinks and pot was passed around freely. There was no trouble, just relaxing, enjoyment, lots of conversation, and making new friends.

The boys enjoyed themselves immensely. We would definitely do this again.

Dewayne worked down in the nickel mine, INCO—drilling holes, packing them with dynamite, and setting them off. Rather dangerous, but that described his personality. He was generally laidback, but if a good scrap came his way he'd be only too happy to oblige the instigator. He worked Monday to Friday, and when the weekend came it was time to play.

INCO had bowling teams every Friday night, and the men liked to bring their wives along. They were also allowed to bring their own bottles of liquor into the bowling alley, and Dewayne's beverage of choice was whisky. It was always a good time until someone started a fight. It was nothing to see Dewayne go up and overtop tables or chairs to get at someone who wanted his face rearranged. Twice the police were called in and Dewayne was hauled off to jail for the night, leaving me to find my way home carrying his boots and jacket. That usually made for a short and disappointing night.

After getting out of jail the next morning, we'd return the bowling shoes the police had hauled him away in and pick up our car.

He was tough and usually only scrapped when someone provoked him. I'd never seen him back down to anyone. He also had a lot of friends who would back him up, but he didn't depend on them; he'd just go for it.

After we'd been together for a while, Dewayne asked if it would be all right if he invited his parents for a visit, and I didn't see a problem with it. I hadn't met them yet. It turned out that only his mom was able to make the trip from their home in Winnipeg, and she stayed about a week. I really liked her. She seemed friendly. She talked easily with the boys and I felt we were accepted.

Not long after her visit, Dewayne and I decided to go to Winnipeg for a football game, along with my brother James. We stayed with Dewayne's parents, and I met his father for the first time. He turned out out to be really nice guy.

But I wasn't allowed to share Dewayne's room. I was given my own room while James and Dewayne shared his. I was angry about this, because Dewayne hadn't warned me beforehand that this would happen. We'd already been living together for more than a year, and his mother hadn't had a problem with it when she had come to visit.

When Dewayne didn't fight for us, I felt betrayed. I said nothing to his parents, but I didn't make things easy for Dewayne.

It took many years later, after finding God, for me to understand why they hadn't let me share Dewayne's room. His parents had good morals and had stood on them. Later in life, I was ashamed over my behaviour and wish I could apologize for it. But as often happens, it's too late.

Dewayne's parents owned a cabin in Ontario, somewhere around Kenora. For a holiday, Dewayne took us there for a week. That year, *Jaws* came out, as well as a movie about a bear that went around mauling campers. Dewayne wanted to see the movies and insisted I go with him, even though I loathe those kinds of movies. I went with him, but most of the time I sat there with my hands over my eyes or looking away from the screen. They scared me so badly that I didn't want to go swimming or hiking—and here we were, surrounded by woods and the lake! And it didn't help that part of the bear movie's plot was about to come true; just after we arrived, I heard on the radio that a bear *had* badly mauled someone outside of Kenora.

We made good use of our time and painted the cabin. On the backside, we only needed a small ladder, but on the sides and front, where the hill slopped towards the lake, extension ladders were needed. It wasn't an easy job, but in those days I loved to paint and heights didn't bother me; I took to the ladder like ducks to water.

But what I enjoyed most was fishing and canoeing. It was so beautiful lying on the dock, soaking up the sun—as long as Jaws stayed in the water. But it wasn't Jaws that ultimately got me, oh no! It was a miserable wasp. The sucker stung me on the right foot, causing it to swell and burn with pain. I could barely walk on it for two days. That was a nasty piece of business.

After the boys were in bed for the night, Dewayne and I would take our coffee and go down to the dock and sit quietly, listening to the sounds of the wilderness, gazing up at the starry sky. He'd blow a joint while I smoked a cigarette. It was so peaceful. The calm lake looked like black velvet. Every so often, we'd hear a fish jump in the distance. Those moments made the trip worthwhile, even with sharks and bears lurking about in my overactive imagination.

Because my foot was in so much pain, I decided to stay at the cabin with Eugene and Blayne while Dewayne took Joey fishing. They were gone for a few hours and came back around suppertime. Dewayne walked into the cabin with a very drunk child under his arm and a very apologetic look on his face. As it turned out, Dewayne had forgotten to take water with them and so all Joey had had to drink was 99 proof alcohol that had been left in his tacklebox from their last fishing trip.

"Since you got him drunk, you can take care of him," I insisted.

Dewayne carefully set him down on his feet and the poor little guy could hardly walk, but he had a smile on his face. Five years old and he was on his first drunk.

Dewayne managed to get some supper into him then put him to bed, but the supper didn't stay down for long and his sheets and blanket were soon covered with it. I felt so sorry for the little guy, who felt miserable.

As I stripped the bed of its sheets and blanket, I was getting madder and madder. I took them down to the lake to rinse them off while Dewayne picked Joey up and brought him down too. He dunked the kid in the cool water to clean him off and hoped that would help sober him up. Dewayne was truly sorry for what he had done to Joey and took good care of him the rest of that night.

Marriage Proposal

The life we shared was good. Dewayne was great with the kids and they adored him. He treated them as if they were his own. They looked up to him and wanted to be like him, tough and strong. They sat with him while watching TV and waited for him to come home after work. He'd discipline them when needed, but he also talked to them when they wanted something or just wanted to be with him. He'd get down on the floor and wrestle with them, picking them up, one by one, and tossing them across the room onto the couch; they'd bounce off of it and come back for more.

Sometimes when company was over, we'd sit around the living room listening to tunes, talking, and having a few beers and tokes. Then Joey and Blayne would disappear and come back dressed only in shorts. With Dewayne's permission, they would put on a kickboxing show for us. They made for good entertainment and everyone would get into it, even little Eugene. He was about three and he'd climb up on the back of whoever was on top. He didn't want to be left out. Sometimes we had to remove him or he'd get hurt because his older brothers would get serious. Then the kicks would really fly. If they got too rambunctious, Dewayne would have to break them up and calm them down.

After being together over a year and a half, Dewayne surprised me one day by asking me to marry him. He wanted to make our relationship permanent. He loved my sons and wanted to make them his own. It was what I truly wanted, but I was still married to Steve and needed to get a divorce, which I hadn't even thought to look into before this. Living common law was fine for me, because if it didn't work out I didn't have much to lose. Who needs a piece of paper, right?

Dewayne had never been married, though, so I applied for my divorce.

Twenty-Two
Such Sweet Sorrow

The day inevitably came when my first child was ready to spread his wings and fly off to school. I remember that first day as I stood at the door of our home and kissed my little man goodbye as he made his way to the bus that would take him off on his own for the first time.

I wasn't ready to let Joey go and I had to hide the tears as I released him to take his next big step into society. I handed him the first of many lunches I had packed for him.

It was hard—a major milestone in motherhood. No one ever said it was easy being a parent.

Not long after starting the divorce procedure, I noticed that Dewayne's need for more and more drugs was growing rapidly. He would come home from his dangerous job every day and fire up a joint or whatever other kind of drug he had on him, almost as soon as he walked through the door.

It just seemed to me that he was always stoned. Don't get me wrong, he was a content man, but after a while it became personal to me. I felt like he was living in another world, which didn't include me—not that he didn't spend time with me, but it felt like he was never really *with* me. Drugs were becoming an important part of his life.

When we'd first met, he had been satisfied with only getting stoned on the weekends, but it subtly became an every night occurrence. I didn't have any problem with it on the weekends, but his lifestyle was changing, and changing fast.

One weekend, Dewayne suggested we take a trip into Winnipeg, so we packed up the family and headed off on what I understood to be a little holiday. What I didn't know was that the purpose of the trip was to pick up five or six pounds of marijuana, which he then planned to sell.

When we arrived home after the trip, Dewayne walked through the front door and shoved the bulky brown paper package on a shelf next to the front door and left it there in full view.

The next morning, while Dewayne was at work, a rather tall and imposing police officer came knocking on the front door. When I came around the corner from the kitchen and saw the officer standing on the other side of the screen door, I went into panic mode. I knew the officer could see the package on the shelf.

Throwing my damp dishtowel over my shoulder, I walked up to the door on wobbly legs and opened it. Politely, I asked him what he wanted, all the while my heart hammering inside my chest. I expected the worst.

The officer produced some legal paperwork and asked if I knew the whereabouts of our friend Leon. By this time, my brain went blank. It must have looked like I was trying to think of where Leon might be, but what I was really doing was trying to clear my head of fear.

In a weak, trembling voice, I told him that I hadn't seen Leon for some time. With that, the officer turned and walked away.

A flood of relief washed over me. It took quite a while before my heart settled down to a normal rhythm again.

To say I wasn't happy about what just happened would be putting it mildly. When I told Dewayne about the visit, the package was immediately removed out of the house and there were no other pickups, to my knowledge.

Medical Mystery

When I was twenty-four, I was very active and worked hard, not only at home but also for my parents, who owned and operated a small food concession in one of the local bars. By evening, I consistently found that I was getting to be short of breath. At first I ignored it, but as the symptom persisted I did what any wise woman would do: I went to my doctor to find out the cause.

The doctor thought I had a lung infection, so he prescribed penicillin. Happy with that, I went home and took the medication.

But instead of getting better, I felt worse. When the pills ran out, I went back to the same doctor and he decided to get an X-ray of my lungs. He found inflammation and gave me a different set of pills, which was still a type of penicillin.

My condition kept getting worse, even with the new medication. I was finding it harder and harder to breathe when I lay down at night. Several nights I had to gasp for air, and I would hyperventilate. I told Dewayne what was going on, but he thought it was all in my head. I was also starting to feel a great deal of pain in my chest as well. What was going on?

I began to think that if I went to sleep at night, I wouldn't wake up in the morning—and the thought of leaving my children motherless gave me the will to fight through this.

On the worst night yet, I remembered a little Bible that my brother James had given me when we were kids. I had put it in the headboard of my bed a long time ago and forgot it there. I wasn't a believer, and I didn't know much about God, but the book was sacred to me nonetheless.

Suddenly I felt an urge to read it. So while Dewayne was asleep, I pulled out the pocket-sized book and carefully opened it to a random page and began to read. I had no idea what I was reading and the fact that it was the King James Version didn't help my understanding of it. With all the thees and thous, it was like reading Portuguese, but somehow it helped quiet my mind. My laboured breathing began to even out and a calm came over my body, enough that I could drift off to sleep. I began to read the Bible every night, and every night I found that same peace.

I went back to the doctor and he scanned my lungs again. This went on for several months, with him giving me more and more penicillin. I gradually worsened until I felt extremely lightheaded. Several times while working with Dad, I felt faint and nearly blacked out. My condition was making it difficult to cook and serve his customers, but I didn't say anything. I as really scared!

When I couldn't pretend everything was okay anymore, I finally told Mom what was going on and she told me about a new doctor who had just come to town and suggested I go see him. Taking her advice, I made an appointment and, surprisingly enough, got to see him right away. I told him about all the tests and medications I'd taken. He was honest with me and said he didn't know what was wrong. Then he picked up his phone and made an appointment for me in Winnipeg to get tested for allergies.

I took the bus five hundred miles south to Winnipeg in the hopes of finding an answer to my medical mystery. I had no idea what I was in for. During the testing process, I was injected with some fifty needles, in line formation, under the skin on each arm. In no time, almost ever puncture hole swelled up and turned angry red. My arms looked like puffy red pincushions. I didn't know what any of it meant and no one told me anything. Growing up, I'd learned not to ask questions, just to do what I was told and keep quiet.

A week later, the results were in. Upon walking into the doctor's office, he looked at me gravely and told me I was very fortunate to have come to see him when I did. The results showed that I was allergic to just about everything, including penicillin. No wonder I was getting sicker! If I hadn't come to see this new doctor, I probably would have died within the month. So much for Dewayne's diagnoses that it was all in my head!

Immediately, I was given a list of foods I was allowed to eat, which didn't amount to much, and a list of things I needed to remove from my house. I was advised to remove all carpets and anything else that collected dust. Fortunately, we didn't have any carpets, so we didn't have to move.

The next step was for me to take allergy needles, which I would have to take for the rest of my life. When I went in for my first needle, the doctor injected me in the upper arm then told me to wait in the waiting room for ten minutes in case I had a reaction. Should I have a reaction, they had the antidote to counteract it. If I didn't have a reaction, I could go home.

To say the least, this was a very distressing ten minutes. I'd been told I could lose consciousness or even die from the injection.

This became my weekly routine. Each week I traded off which arm to take the shot in, because the needles caused the skin to swell in a two-inch diameter circle. It hurt to the touch for several days after, and of course that's the very place my children would touch me.

After a year of trading off arms, the muscles in my arms started to pull in my hands, causing much pain, so I had to start taking the needles in my thighs. I took them for close to two years, and to the doctor's amazement all my allergy symptoms disappeared.

Although I outgrew the allergies, I still stay clear of penicillin. The whole episode was stressful and painful. What we figured out was that this was a byproduct of the eczema I'd endured as a child.

What I didn't get at the time is that the Lord had begun to call me while I was reading His word, but I wasn't ready to listen. I stopped reading the Bible and put it away. Yet today, I have no doubt that it was His word that gave me the peace I needed in order to sleep. God knew that one day I would look back on that time and know with certainty that He had been with me.

Losing Dewayne

Dewayne and I had been together two years when our relationship began to show serious signs of trouble. I wasn't happy with Dewayne being stoned all the time. I didn't understand why he needed it. I felt like he was escaping into his world of music and drugs because he didn't want to be with me. He seemed to need the drugs more than he needed me.

For him, drugs, booze, and dealing had become the focal point of our parties. I remained straight, because I had the kids to care for. After my first experience with drugs, I wasn't too willing to risk a repeat performance. I'd have a beer or two, but that was it.

Dewayne and I drifted apart and argued a lot. On those occasions, I sometimes left the house in the night hurt and crying. There was no place to be alone in our house, no place where I could shed my pain, so I found my refuge outside. With all my heart, I would wish for him to come after me and take me home and tell me everything was going to be all right, but he didn't. He'd go to sleep as I sat up late in the night, feeling sorry for myself. I was so insecure and lonely, and I knew I was losing him.

It finally did come to the point where we couldn't live together anymore. He liked his new life, and my immaturity and constant complaining got to him. So he finally moved out and left the house to me.

Twenty-Three
Devin

It didn't take long until depression became my full-time companion once again. My closest and dearest friend had left me after two years—another failure added to the list of failures I'd already accumulated. During this time, the doctor put me on a strong dose of Valium to level out my anxiety.

Some of my single girlfriends had started going to the bars and asked if I wanted to come along. What did I have to lose? Dewayne was gone. And so the bars became my new life. I couldn't stand to stay home alone.

I was also back on welfare, abusing the system by using the money they gave me for babysitters and alcohol. All I understood at the time was that I hurt and couldn't handle the long, lonely nights. And because I was still so naïve, I fell into other relationships. Some of them truly disgusted me.

Drunk and out for revenge against Dewayne, I met one of his biker friends at a bar and invited him home with me. We had a one-night affair, and that was the last I ever wanted to see of him. I felt totally disgusted with myself.

It took me seven long, agonizing years for me to get over Dewayne, because we ran in the same circles and kept running into each other.

Several months and a few men after our breakup, I met Devin, a good-looking, hard-working man who was genuinely interested in me. He worked as a hairdresser and barber. He had a large clientele and made good money. Sometimes after his shop closed for the day, he'd take me to the shop and try different hairstyles out on me, and then we'd go out for the evening.

We dated for a while, and after a while he got a place that was big enough for us all to move in together.

We got along very well at first, but somewhere along the line he began to act strange.

One night he didn't come home until late, so I went to bed and waited for him. I figured he had gone to the bar after work, and I had no problem with that.

When he finally came home, though, I heard him banging around in the kitchen. I figured he was making himself something to eat. He then came downstairs to the basement, where our bedroom was located, carrying a piece of toast.

While he stood by the bed, a large gob of honey dripped onto the carpet, and it looked to me as though he had it smeared all over himself. He just seemed to be sticky everywhere.

I went upstairs to the kitchen to get a wet cloth to clean it up—and when I entered the kitchen, I found the honey jar still open with its contents covering the whole jar, along with the knife he'd used. The honey was also smeared over the kitchen counter, down the cupboards, and onto the floor. He had even managed to coat the hairbrush I had left sitting on the counter.

He followed me into the kitchen and I had a few choice words for him. In response, he stepped over to the wall that divided the kitchen from the dining room and began smashing his forehead into the corner where the metal plating joined the walls together under the paint.

Horror-struck, I pleaded for him to stop. It was as though he didn't hear me. He kept bashing his head, almost knocking himself out. Afterward he had a glazed look in his eyes, as though he were out of his mind. Several red welts were forming on his forehead.

Somehow I managed to pull him away from the wall and got him to sit at the table. He wasn't at all himself, but I could tell he wasn't all that drunk. Something else was bothering him.

When I asked what was wrong, he told me he was jealous of any man who looked at me. I didn't know what to say to that; he was afraid I would leave him for someone else. I assured him that I wasn't looking for anyone else, nor was I going to leave. That seemed to settle him down enough for me to get him cleaned up and put to bed.

After cleaning the kitchen and bedroom carpet, I lay awake beside him, examining the many large welts on his forehead and pondering the events of the evening. It had been really freaky.

Some months later, Devin came home from work long after supper was over and the kids were in bed. It wasn't unusual for him to be late, because his hours fluctuated. As I cleaned the kitchen and prepared him something to eat, he went into the bathroom to wash up. He was taking longer than usual. I called to him several times that his supper was ready, and when he finally came out I noticed that he had changed into a dark blue T-shirt. This was unusual, since he never changed after he came home from work.

Instead of coming to the dining room table to eat, he sat on the couch and padded the seat beside him. He wanted me to sit with him and talk. So I covered his dinner to keep it warm and sat beside him. While he was talking about nothing in particular, I noticed that his shirt was developing wet black blotches across the chest. He continued to talk about nothing of importance and seemed to act perfectly normal, but each time I looked at the front of his shirt the blotches got bigger and bigger.

When I asked what was going on, he calmly looked me straight in the eyes and told me it was nothing. Then he changed the subject.

More wet spots began to appear, so on impulse I grabbed the bottom of his shirt and yanked it upward. In horror, I saw that his chest had been sliced open in deep, long lines, either by a razorblade or knife. The cuts crisscrossed his chest as if a lion or tiger had raked its claws over him.

I got up and stepped away, studying his facial expression. There wasn't any emotion there. Frightened, I asked him why he had done it. I can't remember what he said, but obviously he needed help. I'd never seen anything like this before and I feared for my children.

Leaving me standing in the living room, he calmly stood up and walked back downstairs to our bedroom to clean up and change.

While Devin was downstairs, as quickly and quietly as I could, I rushed to the phone and called James. In whispers, I told him what had happened and then begged him to come and get us out of there before Devin did something else. He said he'd be right over.

I tiptoed to the front door and unlocked it, so James wouldn't have any problem coming in to help. By this time, my insides were shaking violently and I frantically grabbed a suitcase from the hallway closet. I went into the boy's room and threw enough clothes into it for the kids to wear for a day or two. Then I woke them up, one at a time, and warned them to be very quiet. They sensed something was wrong, but they listened and didn't make any noise.

When they were ready, I had them sit on their beds. I told them to stay in their room until I came for them, then quietly closed their door. I went back to the living room and waited for either Devin or James to show up.

After what seemed like an eternity, James came for us. It was actually only about five minutes. He had either been very close to where I lived or he drove like a madman.

Just as I opened the door to let James inside, Devin came up the basement stairs. Devin was surprised to see James at this time of night, but I didn't stick around to hear what they had to say to each another. I went to the kids' room, picked Eugene up in one arm, and grabbed the suitcase with my other hand. I told Joey and Blayne to follow and stay close behind me.

With James there, I knew Devin wouldn't put up a fuss.

My head felt like it was going to explode from all the pressure. I could hardly think.

My brother stood protectively in the doorway, watching Devin until the boys and I were safely out of the house. I left without saying anything to Devin, because I couldn't handle any more than what I already had on my mind—escape.

I just didn't understand what had happened. I had never seen anything like that before, and God willing I never will again.

James took us to my sister Darlene's apartment. To say she was surprised to see us is an understatement. I explained what had happened and she gladly welcomed us in. James then left us in her very capable hands and went home.

By this time, the boys were fully awake and asking questions I couldn't answer. Darlene and I made up makeshift beds for the boys and got them settled down for the night. I had to share her bed, and that was very strange for me. I had never shared a bed with a full-grown woman before and I was very uncomfortable, but I was grateful to have had a place to go. She even invited us to stay as long as we needed.

We stayed with her for a couple of days, until I got us back on welfare. With the help of others, and Devin agreeing to stay away from the house while I was there, I was able to retrieve all our belongings.

I didn't see him again for nearly a year, but when I did, he was still working as a hairdresser and had a new girlfriend. He said he had gone to get help and that it was a good thing I moved when I did because he didn't know what he would have done next in the condition he'd been in. He was truly sorry for what he put us through and we parted as friends.

Twenty-Four
Return to Fox Bay

We didn't take long to settle into our new apartment, which was located once again on Fox Bay. Strangely enough, we moved in right across the back alley from the apartment building we'd lived in before. Not only that, but we had the exact same apartment number and location in the building, since all twenty or so buildings here were built identically. When I looked out of my living room window, I could see the back of my old apartment. It was like coming home.

About a week after we'd moved in, I was sitting on the front steps of my building watching the kids play when I looked across the road and spotted a woman who looked familiar, but I couldn't quite put my finger on where I'd seen her before. She had just come out of the building where I used to live, and she had two daughters who were about the same ages as Joey and Blayne.

She recognized me, too, and came over to say hi. Her name was Jeannette and she and her husband Cole had come over to Dewayne's and my place a couple of times. Cole was one of Dewayne's suppliers. I told her that Dewayne and I had split a while back and the boys and I had just moved in.

I hadn't talked much to Jeannette before, because she was usually stoned and talking with the men about drugs, a subject I wasn't educated in; I didn't have much to add to their conversations.

Jeannette and I started inviting each other over for coffee and our kids got on well together. We discovered that we actually had a lot in common. She came from a rough background and was going through some tough times with her man, so she could relate to me.

When I was at Jeannette's place, she'd fire up a joint, even if it was early in the morning, and then offer me a toke. Careful not to offend her, I'd politely decline and she'd smoke the whole thing herself. After several weeks of unconsciously breathing in the smoke from her joints, I found that I was getting a little high.

In the guy department, I was getting more and more screwed up all the time. I carried a lot of heartache and loneliness that just wouldn't go away. With all that hurt, anger, and resentment stored up in me, it wasn't long until I accepted the joint that was passed my way while we griped and complained about the men in our lives.

Jeannette wanted someone to go with her to do a drug pickup at the airport. She didn't want to go alone. I guess I was going to lend "moral support." So, without thinking through the consequence of my actions, I went along with her like the good little friend I was.

I found the pickup to be a nerve-wracking experience. It was scary and exciting all at the same time. I'd heard a few stories about how the police used sniffer dogs and I anxiously looked around to see if I could spot one.

My nerves were about stretched to the limit by the time Jeannette walked up to the window and claimed her package. We then made a beeline to the exit and jumped into the first available taxi.

I kept thinking the police were close behind us and expected to be busted any minute, but it didn't happen. Instead we made it home undetected and were ecstatic that we had so easily gotten away with it. Of course, that experience was meant to set me up for the next pickup, and this time I'd be doing it on my own.

The next package was coming in on the bus in the next day or two. I was to wait for the call that would tell me what time it was coming in.

On the day when the call came in, the kids were in school and I had decided to paint my bathroom while I had the place to myself. I was up on a ladder with paint smears on my hands, arms, and old shirt when Jeannette called: the parcel would be arriving in an hour. My heart raced with uncertainty and fear, but I said I'd do it.

I quickly washed up, changed my clothes, and grabbed a taxi to the bus depot. So much for painting!

By the time I retrieved the precious cargo, my mind was fried. My imagination had played through all the different scenarios of what could go wrong. In my heart, I knew what I was doing was wrong and I wasn't one bit proud of it. I couldn't get into the taxi fast enough to deliver this package to its owner.

When the job was done, with shaky hands and tattered nerves I returned to painting the bathroom, but not without being totally disgusted with myself. I said to myself, *That's it. Never again.* I think the real reason I did it was to gain approval, trust, and respect, as well as to supply my own needs. But do you think it stopped there? No.

I allowed Jeannette to leave different kinds of drugs at my place in case her customers needed anything while she was out. So they'd come by my apartment and she wouldn't lose a sale. In return for selling them, my highs were free. That was my launchpad into drug-dealing, and every now and then the thought crossed my mind that if I got caught I could go to jail and even lose my kids. I quickly brushed these thought away by having another toke. That would solve the problem for another day.

Jeannette, seeing that she could trust me, arrived at my place one night after our kids were in bed carrying a set of scales, a small box of baggies, and a brown paper parcel. She taught me how to weigh and bag weed; later it would be hash and magic mushrooms. Then she taught me how to cheat on the weight in order to keep some aside for our own personal use. Honour amongst thieves.

In the years after moving back to the Fox Bay apartment, I began to drink more. I also got stoned almost every day. I'd been visiting the bar on the weekend, but eventually that escalated to include weekdays. My values had changed and I became proud of it. Dewayne and others came to me to buy their dope and I felt important. What I couldn't see is that I was doing the same thing to my children that Dewayne had done to us. I wasn't the parent to them that I should have been.

That's just the way it is with addiction. We become selfish and self-centred. It's all about us and we don't see beyond our own needs and wants. We know we're hurting the ones we love, but those short-lived regrets get shoved aside when drugs and booze take over. It's a nasty cycle, a never-ending emotional roller-coaster ride for the addict as well as their family.

So there I was, starting a whole new different life.

I still cared about Dewayne. The only reason I probably got caught up with Devin and the other guys had been to stop the hurt I felt after Dewayne and I separated. Each time I heard the sound of a Harley on the street, I'd look out my front window to see if he was driving by, which he did quite often. But I'm sure it wasn't for my benefit.

I looked for him everywhere I went, and I even went to places just to be seen by him or to see him riding his bike. It became an obsession. I would sit on my stereo with the music playing sad songs of love gone bad and watch out my front window, waiting for him. The kids and I walked miles around our area just to see if I could catch a glimpse of him.

There were times when I did run into him while I was out doing errands. He'd stop and ask if he could give me a lift on his bike to wherever I was going. Sometimes we ended up going to his place, making out, and then I wouldn't see him again for a couple of weeks. I'd feel used, betrayed, and rejected in the fullest sense. But I put myself in that position. Whatever morals I'd had when I lived with him had vanished into thin air.

Many nights, after the boys were in bed, I'd shut off all the lights, burn candles and incense, blow a joint, then play my favourite tunes on the big wooden stereo under the living room window. Sometimes I'd sit on the stereo, look out the window, and get lost singing my favourite songs. These songs usually matched the condition of my heart. If I felt low, they'd be love songs. If I was in a I-don't-give-a-rat's-behind mood, then it was rock, so loud that I could feel the base pounding in my chest: Bob Seger, The Eagles, Fleetwood Mac, CCR, Bob Dylon, J. Giels Band, Styx, Alice Cooper, Pink Floyd, Meatloaf, Deep Purple, April Wine, and on and on. I was usually trying to lose myself in another world. I really liked the rock music of the 70s. There was so much good talent.

Even though I was only small fry and didn't account for much in the dealing world, I had my own customers, and sometimes one of them was Dewayne. There was a time when I wouldn't even get drunk, yet alone smoke up, when we lived together. Now I had become one of his suppliers. How ironic.

Late one evening, after the boys were in bed, I smoked a joint and sat in my favourite highboy chair with the lights out, candles burning and rock music playing low on the stereo. It felt so good to mellow out after a long hard day.

As I was on the verge of falling into a much-needed sleep, a soft rap on the door interrupted me. Begrudgingly, I dragged myself out of my cozy chair to answer the door.

Much to my amazement, Dewayne was standing there. He'd stopped by to pick up a bag of pot. I invited him in and offered him a chair at the kitchen table, then gave him a beer and went to retrieve a bag of pot and some magic mushrooms from my stash. I already had a joint rolled, so I fired it up so he could see that it was good.

We sat talking for a bit, and then I offered him a teaspoon of the magic mushrooms. I also took some myself. By this time we were both getting pretty wasted. After he'd decided to buy a bag of pot, I suggested he roll one of his own for us. While he did that, I got us another beer. Then it was my turn to roll, and before too long I had managed to drink and smoke him under the table, so to speak. He couldn't handle any more, but I kept toking.

In my crazy thinking, I felt like I had shown him! I felt smug and self-righteous. I don't think he knew quite what to make of me. I was becoming a not-so-very-nice person and I don't think he liked that.

Coolly, I saw him to the door and we said our polite goodnights. With great sadness, I went back to my favourite chair and cried. I had thought he would be proud of me because I finally understood what he had liked so much about drugs. But the reality is that my demeanour was becoming hard. I was building some seriously thick walls that pushed people away.

I loved him and wanted him back, but that wasn't going to happen.

Family Moves In

When my sister Darlene needed a place to stay, I invited her to move in with me. It was good to have her there, since I hated being alone. For a little excitement, we'd grab a sitter, go to the bar, smoke whatever we had on us, then get into her car and drive around town until we found another car with a couple of good-looking guys in it. We'd follow close enough behind so they couldn't see our faces. When they figured out what we were doing, they would turn their vehicle around and chase us. Laughing hard, we'd take all the roads Darlene knew and eventually lose them. It was a lot of fun, and also scary. I really don't recommend it. Who knows what could have happened if they'd caught up with us?

One night, Darlene and I went to a bar and she got chatting with a member of the band. At the end of the evening, she invited the whole band back to my place. They'd recently cut their first recording in the United States and received their first single; they needed a stereo to play it on. They all seemed extremely excited to hear it, so it must have been true.

I think she was interested in one of the guys, but I couldn't be bothered with any of them. I never considered myself a groupie.

While I sent the babysitter home, Darlene got a beer for each of us. We then settled the guys on the couches. I went in to check on the boys and found them sound asleep, but they probably didn't stay that way for long because when I played the stereo it was usually fairly loud.

I found a vacant spot at the end of one of my couches and settled down to listen to what the band was so excited about. As we listened to their new song, I did what I always did: I sat cross-legged, shut my eyes, and got lost in the music. I began to sing their song almost word for word. I'd never heard it before, but many times I can hear a song I've never heard and know the lyrics.

The lead singer got slightly miffed with me. "You don't know this song. It hasn't been released yet."

But I sang most of it anyway. I wasn't showing off; I just loved music and singing.

Someone put on Jeannie C. Riley's song "D.I.V.O.R.C.E." and again I forgot everyone in the room. I sang it from start to finish with all the passion of one who had lived it. At the end of the song, I was jolted back to reality by the lead singer placing his hand on my arm. He asked if I'd ever considered singing, as in a band, and I abruptly told him no. But he said I should consider it. I figured he was just jacking me around and trying to put the move on me.

The problem was I truly wanted to believe him, I just didn't have any self-worth or confidence. So I blew him off.

Today, so many years later, I believe that he was serious.

Anyway, the band heard their song, had a couple more beers, and left. I never saw them again, nor did I ever hear their song play.

Darlene stayed with us for a couple of months before happily moving out on her own.

My home was always open to my family if they needed a place to stay. It really irked me that so many of them couldn't go home because Dad either kicked them out or just plain didn't want them there. Sharing my home was always a pleasure, even though they had to sleep on one of the couches. Coming from such a crowded home of brothers, sisters, and boarders, I didn't get to know my brothers or sisters well until they took turns moving in.

My brother Andrew was only thirteen years old when he came to my door asking if he could stay. Dad had kicked him out for good this time and Mom had already sent him to other places to live, like our aunts or her friends. In Andrew's words, he was passed around like a rag. That was just so wrong.

Without hesitation, I welcomed him in. I can't remember how long he was with us, but it was probably for only a month or two.

One afternoon Andrew came home really drunk. Although the details of what happened escape me, for some reason I ended up locking him out of my apartment, leaving him to stand in the hall where he did a lot of yelling and making threats. I gave it back to him every bit as good as he gave me. Because he was so angry and determined to get in, he booted my door open, which really frightened us. No doubt the other renters were shaken up as well.

So now it was my turn to kick him out. It always bummed me out that I felt the need to do this. Andrew was so special to me and my boys really loved him, but that was just the way of it. We were all so hot-headed, so screwed up and clueless when it came to dealing with problems. We only knew how to vent through anger and destruction.

I didn't handle this situation at all well. In fact, I managed to make things much worse, blowing everything way out of proportion. We became unforgivingly angry at one another, which caused us to go our separate ways.

He went to the streets until he could find a place to stay. Because of my own anger and self-right-eousness, I never once considered his safety, being out there by himself in the streets of such a hostile and dangerous town. Some sister I was.

Twenty-Five
Overdoses

Not long after moving back to Fox Bay, I started having serious abdominal pains. The doctor had a hunch about what was wrong, but he wasn't sure, so he sent me to Winnipeg. When I went south to the big city, I was usually gone overnight and had to leave my boys with a babysitter. This trip proved to be extremely devastating. It was for a biopsy of my cervix.

Later that evening, after having the biopsy, I caught the bus for home. I was to arrive in Thompson at about 6:30 in the morning.

I was okay for most of the twenty-four-hour trip, until the last few hours. By the time we reached Thompson, I needed to go straight to the hospital. My abdominal pain was so bad that it felt like my insides were going to fall out.

My doctor examined me, but he couldn't diagnose the problem. He ordered several days of total bedrest in the hospital, with more tests. Then he gave me a shot of Demerol to kill the pain. Since I liked my drugs, the Demerol was the only nice thing to come out of all this.

My new concern was to get a babysitter to watch the boys. Jeannette had been watching them until now, but she couldn't keep watching them; she had her own things to do. The only person I could think of was Mom, but I couldn't arrange anything until after I was settled in my room.

With the rails on each side of the bed lifted up and the lights on low, I asked the nurse if I could use the phone. She wheeled in a large payphone and parked it beside my bed. In desperation, I made my call for help.

While talking to Mom, I heard someone at her front door talking urgently, but I couldn't make out what was being said.

"Oh my God," Mom gasped.

When I asked what was wrong, she told me that Joey had been taken to the emergency room and he was there right now. I hung up, then pressed my emergency button for the nurse. I was in the process of climbing down from the foot of the bed when two nurses came rushing in and asked me what I was doing. I told them where my son was and that I was on my way to him. They tried to detain me, but I wasn't having any of it. Eventually they agreed to get me a wheelchair.

When I entered the emergency room, I could see my son's small body sitting up with his head flopping from side to side while a nurse held him up. I rushed to his side before my nurses could stop me. The doctor who was in charge told me they'd just pumped his stomach for Valium, but couldn't determine if they had gotten it all or how much damage had already been done. Holding his body against me, the doctor went on to say that he didn't know if Joey would live through the day—and if he did, he might have brain damage.

"I want to go to heaven and be with my mommy," Joey kept slurring. And then he would call for me. "Mommy, Mommy, Mommy."

He couldn't see me or feel me touching him.

He had taken what was left of my prescription of Valium. I kept my medications hidden in the top drawer of my tallest dresser, which was too high for my children to reach—or so I thought. I didn't know he knew they were in there.

My mind was in turmoil. Between the little bits of sleep I'd gotten on the bus, the pain in my stomach, the effects of the Demerol, and what was happening with my son, I was very close to losing it.

What did the doctor mean he might die? Anxiously, I reassured Joey that I was there with him, but his head kept wobbling from side to side. He had no control over his movements.

I was terrified of losing him. I felt so helpless and blamed myself for my negligence. I held him close to me and kept repeating over and over again that Mommy was with him and that he was going to be okay.

The doctor told me they were going to keep a close watch on him day and night. The nurse gently took him from me to put him on a gurney, so she could take him up to the children's ward. They wanted him settled in so they could give him whatever he needed to survive.

The Demerol fortunately wasn't as effective as it was supposed to be. Its purpose had been to stop the pain and anxiety and help me sleep, but sleep was the furthest thing from my mind. Despite my need for bedrest, I told them I wasn't leaving my baby; I was going to be by his side the whole time he was in danger. They didn't argue with me, but I had to agree to get back in the wheelchair so a nurse could push me alongside Joey's gurney.

Joey was placed in a single room right across from the nurse's station. After they had him settled in bed with his rails up, my nurse wheeled me in beside him—and that's where I stayed for the rest of that day and throughout the long night.

Joey kept asking me if we were in heaven yet, and I kept reassuring him I was with him. He kept calling out to me, "Mommy, where are you?" I'd tell him I was right beside him as his head tossed back and forth across his pillow. He told me why he'd taken my medication. He had thought I wasn't coming home, that I had gone to heaven because I was always sick and going away to see doctors.

I slept in my chair with a blanket wrapped around me. The nurses were so good. They encouraged me and brought food and drink. I broke a lot of rules, but I wasn't leaving him no matter what. They understood that.

It was a hard couple of days, but I believe God spared Joey's life, because he got better and better. There were no signs of brain damage.

As for myself, the doctor told me he wanted to keep me under observation in case they needed to perform an emergency surgery on my stomach. In the end, they came to the conclusion that I had a cyst on my ovary that made it feel as though I was giving birth to a baby. That's exactly what it felt like. I still hadn't received the report on the biopsy.

Joey and I left the hospital to recover together. Although I drank and did drugs, when it came to my three sons there was no mom prouder than me. I loved them with every bit of love I was capable of giving. It was my sons who brought me home at night. It was my sons who gave me a reason to live, because there were so many times when I wanted to give up and die. Sometimes it was just too hard to go from day to day.

To myself, I was a failure and not worth anything, but my kids loved me and that was all I had to hold on to. They needed me and I needed them.

One evening, at the kids' bath time, something happened that I will never forget, although I don't remember exactly what led up to it. Maybe the boys were fooling around, but at some point I took Blayne out of the tub and yelled at him. He was five years old at the time.

Suddenly, my hands were around his neck and I began choking him. Fortunately, something snapped in my brain and told me to let go. Shocked back to my senses, I removed my hands from around his little neck.

His face was filled with fear.

Oh my god, why had I done that? I was completely sober. I hadn't drunk anything nor done drugs. It never happened again, but I never told anyone about it either. Like my other two sons, I kept it to myself.

Although I don't know why I did this, it probably didn't take much on my part. So many things had gone wrong in my life by that time that I was an explosion waiting to happen. Unfortunately, the explosion was unleashed on my innocent little boy that day.

It grieves me to know I was capable of committing such horrendous acts against my children. When these things happened, I wasn't in my right mind. It was as though something would take me over.

While writing this, it has occurred to me that I was no different than my father. My dad tried multiple times to kill his kids.

The Bible talks about curses being passed down from one generation to another, and this is a prime example of that. These curses can be broken through forgiveness and the shed blood of Jesus.

When I took this matter up with the Lord, I forgave my forefathers, then my father, then myself, and finally I asked God to forgive me. When I did that, I felt something horrible leave me. I then prayed and broke the curse off my own children and my children's children in Jesus's name.

You shall not bow down to them or worship them; for I, the Lord your God, am a jealous
God, punishing the children for the sin of the parents to the third and fourth generation of

those who hate me, but showing love to a thousand generations of those who love me and keep my commandments. (Exodus 20:5–6)

...he punishes the children for the sin of the parents to the third and fourth generation. (Numbers 14:18)

Brain Explosion

Sanity on the verge of leaving
Massive lights exploding my brain
A moment's reality of dying
I vowed I'd never do it again

All drugs and booze ever gave me was a false illusion of enjoyment and destruction. I thought I was normal! Yeah right.

There came a day when I nearly died of an overdose. It was the weirdest experience I'd ever had and I remember it plainly. My girlfriend Elaine came for a visit and I asked her if she wanted to get high. Without hesitation, she agreed.

I stuck a pair of table knives through a burner on the stove and heated them until they were red hot. I had a little bit of hash oil, and with a needle I managed to scrape out enough oil for the both of us to have a few good tokes. The oil was potent and it should have been enough for us to enjoy for an hour.

But no, I wasn't satisfied with just a few hoots. The little piece of tinfoil I had used as a lid to cover the bottlecap of hash oil had lots of oil on it, so I bent it in half and, like the pig I had become, I hot-knifed the whole thing and got a rip-roaring blast. There must have been six or seven hits of oil in the tinfoil. It hit me so hard that I could barely stand. I staggered my way to the living room, dropped down on the couch, and waited to see what was going to happen.

Elaine sat in the highboy chair across from me, looking wasted on what little I had given her. With the stereo playing, we tried to carry on a conversation, but after a short time we gave up and went into our own little worlds.

All of a sudden, I found that if I moved my pinkie finger ever so slightly, my whole body would charge with electricity to the point that I could hardly stand it. When the first shockwaves subsided, out of curiosity I tried to move it again and an even greater wave rippled through me. I realized I had to sit perfectly still to prevent it from happening again.

Frantic, I looked to Elaine for help, but her attention was elsewhere. I didn't know what was happening to me and I needed her to talk me down, so I wouldn't freak myself out. I knew I was in trouble!

To add to the situation, a knock on my apartment door startled me, setting off a whole new set of violent tremors from head to toe. I thought I was going to explode. I couldn't turn my head, but I sensed the door opening and then heard it slam shut. Every sound was magnified a hundred times its natural volume.

I could just barely make out the person standing in front of me. She looked down at me and proceeded to tell me something. I could see her mouth moving while her hands waved in the air to emphasize what she was saying, only I couldn't hear a word of it. With each movement of her hands, more shockwaves tore me apart.

I wanted to plead with her for help, but I couldn't get a word out of my mouth. I could only stare while shockwave after shockwave exploded inside me. I felt like I was dying.

Then, as suddenly as she'd come in, I heard the door slam again and she was gone.

What had just happened here? Elaine sat there and looked at me as if to ask what that had been all about. Now that I had her attention, I desperately wanted her help, but suddenly everything in my head went black. Bolts of lightning flashed in my brain.

Now I was really scared and tried to cry for help, but I couldn't make a sound. The top of my head was about to blow off.

Was I dying or going insane?

I have no idea how long I sat like that, but it was terrifying. I kept thinking, *If I live through this, I'll never do it again.*

Years later, while talking to someone about what had happened, it was explained to me that my experience had a name: "went down." It's a kind of overdose that resembles an epileptic fit.

That wasn't the only time I almost died of an overdose. On a warm summer evening, perfect for a bike ride, James called and asked if I wanted to go to the bar with him. I got a babysitter for the night, knowing I wouldn't be home until late.

James picked me up on his chopped Kawasaki, but just before leaving we shared a joint. The ride to the tavern was short, which disappointed me because what I really wanted to do was ride around for a while just for the sake of riding around. We also arrived during the supper hour and the place was lit up with hardly anyone there.

He picked a table next to the bar and ordered a couple of beers. As soon as we sat down, I started to feel the effects of the joint and felt paranoid. My back was to the room, and I didn't like the feeling this gave me. I always preferred to have my back to the wall. I liked to know who was behind me.

I didn't mention anything to James about how the drugs were affecting me, because I didn't want him to think I was some kind of pansy who couldn't hold her drugs. Instead I suffered it out and concentrated on the stupid wall in front of me. I'm sure if he'd known what I was going through, he would have taken care of me. But I was too full of pride to say anything.

After a bit, he caught sight of someone he knew and so he got up and said he'd be right back. To fill the time as I waited for my brother to come back, I decided to do the next best thing: take a trip to the washroom. I carefully got up and hoped I was walking normally towards the back of the bar, crossing the front of the dance floor on the way.

By the time I was returning to our table, the drug hit me hard. I felt frozen to the spot, which made my situation very awkward. With great determination, I forced one foot in front of the other, then did the same with the other foot. It felt like everyone in the place was watching me, but I couldn't let them see that I had a problem.

Actually, no one was watching; it was just my paranoia at work.

I figured I was doing okay, because I managed to get as far as the dance floor. I kept telling myself to just be cool, but my insides were acting strange and I felt like I was about to black out. All I could think about was, *Where's James?* I needed to get back to my table as nonchalantly as possible without making a fool of myself.

As I approached our table, I suddenly found myself staring down at myself. I was hovering up on the ceiling, looking down at myself. How on earth was I doing this? I looked around and could see the whole bar. I felt peaceful and in full control of my mind.

Watching myself, I felt no connection to my body whatsoever, but I could see that I had almost made my way back to the table.

Then, just as quickly as I'd left my body, I found myself back inside it. And I wasn't stoned anymore either.

I never told James or anyone else about that experience, because I didn't want them to think I was nuts. It was definitely a bad trip. James almost had a dead sister on his hands. Imagine what that would have done to him!

I know without a doubt that I had an out-of-body experience and no one can convince me otherwise.

It wasn't until I became a Christian many years later that I finally understood what happened to me that night. I know for certain that God spared my life by sending me back into my body and that He had a purpose for doing so. I'm truly grateful.

I know firsthand that when you die, you really do leave your body while remaining very much aware of what's going on around you. And I know for sure that there is life after death.

I spoke to a young friend of mine about what happened and he shared with me something he saw on a television documentary. It's said that the body sometimes will try to accomplish the mind's last thoughts before the body dies. That may very well have been what happened in my case, because I saw my body still walking in the direction I desperately intended for it to go, and before I reached the table I was back inside of it.

I believe that God sent me back because it wasn't my time. He gave me another chance to change my ways.

Did I quit drugs and drinking after that, though? No! As a matter of fact, I got worse.

Twenty-Six
Moving Again

I soon got back the test results from the biopsy that had been done of my cervix. It turned out that the walls of my cervix and uterus were full of cancer cells that could become active at any time, so a hysterectomy was highly recommended. I would be left with only two ovaries.

I felt the agony of being slowly and deliberately crushed. My childbearing days were over and I was only twenty-five years old.

While waiting on a date for surgery, Jeannette eagerly introduced me to two of her male friends who had purchased an apartment building just down the street from me. There had been a fire there, and the former owners hadn't wanted to invest their time or money into restoring it and so they'd put the building up for sale. These guys bought it for a steal, renovated it, and now were looking for the right people to fill it. Jeannette and Cole took a bottom suite, and Jeannette wanted me to move there, too. She talked me into taking a look at the apartment just above hers.

I was shown a beautifully remodelled two-bedroom suite that appealed to my taste and my pocketbook. Every room had been freshly painted and the bedrooms were spacious and bright. But it was the combined living room and kitchen that won me over. The living room boasted a new carpet, accompanied with natural-looking stone panelling which ran about three feet up the wall and was bordered by stained lumber. The rest of the walls were finished with coarse white stucco. It was tastefully done and looked rich.

The kitchen counters were done in blond butcher block and the sink was stainless steel. At one end of the counter stood a brand-new fridge, and on the other end was a matching stove. On the wall between the counter and top cupboards, I imagined what it would look like if I replaced the wall with lightly smoked mirrors to give it depth and elegance.

The owners told me I could do all the decorating I wanted as long as it improved the appearance of the apartment and I paid for it. So I immediately accepted their offer.

Because of the many times I had moved thus far, I wasn't in any hurry to begin packing until the day before. On moving day, I only needed to take a couple of uppers, and just like that I could empty the apartment, have it cleaned, and be partly set up at the new apartment the same night. And that's what I did.

If I'd known what I was in for when I moved into that apartment, I would have taken my boys and run as fast from there as our feet would take us. This place was beautiful to look at, but as time passed it became like a ghetto. All seven units were being rented out to drug addicts, dealers, and potential alcoholics, myself included. People were coming and going at all hours buying and selling drugs. There was always a party, always music playing. And if I ran out of dope, I only had to go to someone's apartment and borrow a joint or whatever there was to be had. So much for borrowing an egg or cup of sugar… we took it to a whole new level.

My choice to move there enabled me to continue on my road to destruction, one which I hadn't intended to take when I'd decided to join Jeannette in having that first joint. It wasn't her fault. The decision was all mine.

Shortly after getting settled in, I was notified about my impending hysterectomy. Today, the surgery is basically simple—a couple of small incisions is all one has to recover from, or so I'm told. But back in the 70s, they sliced you from one side of your abdomen to the other in the shape of a smile and you had to stay in hospital for a week. If that wasn't bad enough, each day all the stitches had to be cleansed and the bandages changed. And whatever you do, you can't cough because it felts like someone is ripping your guts out.

Before I could leave the hospital, the stitches had to be removed. So in came a nurse with her tray of surgical tools: a small scissor, pair of tweezers, gauze, and alcohol rubs and bandages. The tweezers were used to pull each stitch away from the incision, so she could cut it and pull the stitch out. No problem, right? After trying several stitches without any success and seeing the pain I was in, she gave up and sought the help of another nurse.

How was it that these stitches weren't coming out? A new nurse quickly surmised the problem: someone had sprayed a plastic coating over the stitches which had to be dissolved before the stitches could be removed. The poor nurse apologized over and over for the pain she caused me, but I assured her it wasn't her fault. I was just glad to get this over and done with. I wanted to go home to my kids.

During my stay in the hospital, a friend of mine named Don came to visit wearing a large bandage on his left hand. He had come to the emergency room to get his hand patched up and had figured he might as well come up and see how I was doing. He had been at my place doing some renovations to surprise me when I came home from the hospital. He had removed one of the panels off my living room wall because it was covering a wall socket, which had been mistakenly covered over by my landlords. While wielding a jigsaw, he had hit something hard in the panel and the blade jumped and badly cut his other hand. I felt terrible for him, yet I was also touched by his thoughtfulness.

He then noticed that I was in a lot of pain myself, so he offered to rub my lower back to alleviate some of the pain. How could I turn down such an offer? He came back on several occasions to keep me company. Fortunately, his hand repaired nicely.

I'd first seen Don at the bar heading to the dance floor with a different girl on his arm almost every other dance. I figured he was quite the popular guy, and he danced very much like John Travolta. No wonder the girls all wanted to dance with him. This was, after all, the era of disco.

When we'd finally met, I had found out he was a dance instructor. That explained all the dance partners. I also discovered that he only lived a couple of apartment buildings down from my place.

We began to spend a lot of time together. He liked to cook exotic dishes, and I became his taste-tester. He often did little jobs to help me out. We'd meet at one of our places and talk about anything as we drank coffee. He never joined me when I smoked up. More for me! I thought he had been involved with one of my sisters, so I never encouraged anything between us except friendship.

When I was finally released from the hospital, I went straight for the drugs and stayed stoned as much as possible throughout the three-month recovery period. I just didn't want to face the reality that I couldn't have any more children. I'd tell myself it didn't matter. Well, at least I didn't have the monthly menstrual cycle anymore and all the pain that went with it.

My life was constantly falling apart and I couldn't handle it without the aid of drugs. It was my way of checking out.

My doctor gave me instructions on how to care for myself once I was home, but I didn't follow them. I wasn't supposed to wash dishes. I wasn't supposed to vacuum the carpet. There were many things I wasn't supposed to do, but I did it all because I didn't know how to ask anyone for help. I couldn't show weakness. I had to stay strong. Plus, I didn't want to be a bother to anyone.

Pride! Yes, I was full of pride and stupidity.

Since I had to stay home and heal, my world was made up of the people from my building. We'd bought and sold drugs from one another. Soon we started meeting at each other's places where we'd share a few beers and get wasted. All the children mingled together and in only a few months we were all one big happy family, holding loud noisy parties, dealing drugs, and fighting.

Gordon and Millie, a couple of heavy drinkers in their late thirties, moved into the bachelor suite downstairs with their five kids. Their only furnishings were wall-to-wall mattresses on the floor. Because they had such little money, they couldn't afford to wash clothes in the laundry room and also drink. So there was always a pile of stinking clothes soaking in their bathtub. Clothes were hung on makeshift lines wherever possible. Their bathroom was so dirty that I'd make an excuse to go up to my place to get something, just so I could use my own bathroom. Even though their place wasn't clean, it didn't stop any of us from partying with them.

At first, it would take me a painful two to three minutes to slowly and carefully walk down the hallway stairs to get to their place. I'd be bent over from the pain in my abdomen and could only take baby steps. Once there, I'd sit on one of their unkempt smelly mattresses and get stoned with whomever else was there. Their apartment door was usually left open for anyone to walk in.

After a month or so, Jeannette discovered that our kids had acquired lice from Gordon and Millie's kids. Why Jeannette and I never got lice ourselves is beyond me, but we did the special shampooing and combing anyway. It took quite a while to get the lice under control. Jeannette washed our kids' hair and comb out every louse, then squish it with her thumbnail. I believe she found a certain amount of pleasure in it. It was a good thing she knew how to deal with them, because I didn't.

As for Gordon and Millie, they didn't stay long after that. They just up and disappeared one night.

Gambling and Fighting

Seeing as how I wasn't going anywhere due to my recovery, I started holding poker games at my place, much like my parents had. At first we started with just a few friends playing for nickels and dimes, but it didn't take long to escalate into something bigger. Sometimes the game started after supper and by midnight the table and counter would be cluttered with empty liquor bottles and overflowing ashtrays. The smoke, mixed with the loud, filthy language, hung thickly in the air while our kids played around us to the music blaring from the stereo.

Gambling got inside me, much like the craving for my next high. A couple of hours just wasn't enough time to play. I hated it when these evenings ended. It was like coming down from a great stone and feeling depressed, empty, and lost. I needed to stay high.

When I lost all my money, I found that watching the game wasn't an option. I had to borrow money, even if I couldn't afford to pay it back if I lost it, in order to stay in the game. All I knew was that I had to play.

Realistically, I had no money to gamble, buy drugs, go to the bars, and pay babysitters. I used the money I got from selling drugs and the money welfare entrusted to me to pay our rent, buy our food and clothes, and pay the bills. I did pay the rent and the bills, but the clothes and food money ended up being spent on my addictions.

As a result, my children wore clothes much the same as I had while growing up: second-hand and full of holes. Even my own weren't much to look at. Food wasn't plentiful either. I'm ashamed to say that I stole from my kids, but at the time I couldn't see that truth, nor did I associate myself with being one of the many who abused the welfare system.

On any given day or night, a fight could break out in the hallways between different tenants or their friends. Many nights I stood spreadeagle with one hand and foot on the door and the other hand and foot on the wall behind me to keep people from breaking down my door.

Instead of street brawls, we had hallway brawls. Until the fighters were finished, neither my sons nor I could leave our apartment. These fights were extremely distressing. We never knew what to expect when it was over. Would there be blood on the walls and floors? Or a body?

One particular fight comes to mind and it took place in the middle of the day. The couple who lived across the hall started the fight inside their apartment, then brought it out into the hall. The yelling and screaming was hard to take, but much worse was when the man started to slap the woman. I could hear his hand connecting with her skin. Then she'd scream and retaliate. Her body hit the walls a few times, and at one point it hit my door with a heavy thud.

Eventually I'd heard enough and angrily swung my door open to tell them to get away from my door. When I did, she fell flat on the floor at my feet, with her shirt ripped wide open, exposing her bare breasts. He was coming down on her with his arm pulled back as far as he could; with a clenched fist, he was going to drive it home into her face.

I angrily screamed at him to stop—and much to my surprise, he did. He looked up at me in shock as I told him to get the hell out of my apartment or I was going to call the police.

She lay on the floor crying and tried to cover her top as best she could with what was left of her shirt. With a final hateful glare at her, he got up and went back into his place, slamming the door behind him.

When I helped her up, I could tell she'd been drinking heavily. Who knows who was to blame for that fight? Soon she was stable enough to walk, and she staggered back across the hall, flung open her door, and started yelling all over again.

The fight was on again. It was like watching my mom and dad all over.

Sometimes after a night of partying, someone would end up passed out on one of the stairwells or hallways in the morning. You had to walk carefully around their bodies to get by them without waking them up. You never knew what kind of mood they'd be in. They could come up fighting and hit you before they knew what was happening.

It saddens me to be reminded that I sent my kids off to school without first making sure the coast was clear for them to walk safely out the door. This building was like a warzone.

Not only did we have to watch out for our fellow humans, two of the tenants owned dogs that occasionally got loose. One was a German shepherd and the other a Doberman pincher. They weren't all that friendly, but I suspect they were there to warn their owners when strangers or the police were walking in. I was concerned where it came to all the kids in the building. The dogs were just as unpredictable as were their owners.

The boys and I had a dog, too. He was no more than a half-grown pup—and a mutt, to boot. But he was friendly as can be and liked to be outdoors on our front lawn. There was a large area for him to run around out there, and it was a long way from the main road.

And then it happened. Jeannette and I were sitting on the front step watching our kids playing with him one day when I guess he got overly excited. He just took off running for the main road, and before we could stop him he ran right in front of a car. We heard the squeal of tires as the driver tried to brake, and then the dull thud sound of the puppy's body connecting with metal.

Jeannette and I took off running across the lawn to see if he was okay. By the time we got there, the terrified driver was standing over our dog, apologizing profusely. The pup's body lay quivering on the side of the road. Blood trickled from his mouth.

It was not the driver's fault. It was mine. The pup should have been on a leash, but in those days nobody really used them.

I so desperately wanted to pick him up and take him home, but his insides were busted up and there was nothing we could do but watch his life slowly seep out of him.

The kids and I were so shook up that Jeannette told us to go back to the steps while she stayed with him. I'd never had to deal with death that way, so I didn't know what to do. I watched at a distance and felt exceedingly helpless. The kids were crying and filled with remorse because they thought it was their fault. It was just one of those dreadful things. They'd never seen death before and I couldn't fix this.

Someone phoned the city pound and they came and took his body away. This was a hard pill for us to swallow.

Twenty-Seven

Brent

I met Brent one night at a bar and found him easy to talk to. Surprisingly, he called the next day and asked if I'd go out with him. For the next couple of months, the boys and I saw quite a bit of him, and from there it didn't take long before he was ready to move in.

But before he did, he had something important to do. He was a member of the Outlaws Motorcycle Club in Ontario, so he went back home to say his goodbyes. He had been a member for some time and now claimed to be finished with that way of life. He wanted to start fresh.

I have no idea how he was able to walk away without some kind of retribution. Once you were in, you didn't just up and quit these clubs. But apparently he could, or at least that's what he told me.

Brent never talked about what he had done in the past and I didn't want to know. He had also competed in a motorcycle race in the U.S. that was aired on TV. I was impressed, because the show he'd appeared on was one that my dad watched all the time.

He also took a trip to B.C. before he moved in, to pick up his dog, which was a fat, snorting, nose-licking, pigtailed pug named Chewy. The kids and I took to the dog right off; he was quite a remarkable little guy. He liked when I smoked up. He'd come and sit next to me and we would get stoned together, him leaning on me for support.

The dog also liked his beer. He would snort and carry on until I gave him what he figured was his share. Obviously he and Brent had gotten wired together quite a bit. Brent had owned him since he was a wee pup, so for him to bring his dog to live with us meant he planned to stay.

Brent said that he had given up doing drugs and the drug trade a little while before he met me. It was a shame he had settled for me, because I'd been in this lifestyle for a few years and wasn't about to give it up.

He also didn't smoke and he asked me not to smoke in the bedroom, because it stunk. I honestly didn't know what he was talking about. I'd been around cigarette smoke all my life, so I didn't really know how much it stunk. I was used to having a cigarette before going to sleep and before I got out of bed in the morning.

How he put up with me, I really don't know.

Dad and Mom took me and the boys, along with Brent, on a fishing trip to an unknown lake. There was a small secluded beach where the boys could play in the water. One of them found a large piece of styrofoam and they discovered it worked quite well as a raft. They had a great time taking turns with it. Eugene, the youngest, floating around on it.

I turned my back for a minute to talk to my parents, and when I looked in on Eugene again I found that he and his makeshift raft had drifted a long ways from shore in the twinkling of an eye. I panicked and screamed for someone to help him because he couldn't swim and we were losing him to the current that was sweeping by.

Brent sprang into action. He ran across the beach, kicked off his shoes, then dove into the water and with experienced smooth strokes he caught up to Eugene, who was scared and crying. Brent calmed him down and assured him he was all right. He then pulled Eugene into shore, where I was more than ready to hold on to him for dear life. I had been terrified that I would lose my baby.

Brent was only with us a few months before he started looking for a different type of work that would pay better wages. It didn't take long before he successfully landed a job working for the rigs in Alberta. I wasn't happy about it, but he was excited, so off he went.

He was gone three weeks at a time and came home for three or four days at the end of each month. The rest of his time was spent traveling by bus to and from his rig.

While he was gone, I continued much as my life had been before he came, only I didn't go out as much. And when he came home we didn't go out, which disappointed me. It was a dilemma.

The one thing that really bothered me is that while he was at the rigs, he ate steak and we ate porridge. I was still on welfare and don't recall him giving me any money to support us, or his dog. However, he did come home with piles of new biker shirts, jeans, and magazines. To add insult to injury, one time he informed me that he had decided to build his own motorcycle from the ground up. He would tell me which part he had purchased and sent it to the U.S. to be sandblasted or chromed.

Another time, Brent came home with the idea of collecting the logo decals of as many oilrigs and oil companies as he could get. The idea was to handwrite each company and request their logo and enclose a self-addressed stamped envelope. It sounded like a great idea, and when he saw I had caught the vision he produced a very large and heavy advertisement book containing a few hundred company addresses. This book was about half the size of a thick city phonebook. I'm sure my eyes bulged when I saw it.

Because my handwriting was neater than his, he generously volunteered me to do the job, after he drew up the sample letter he wanted to send. All I had to do was rewrite the letter and change the name of the company each time. I agreed, like the soft touch I was, so Brent bought large writing pads, boxes of envelopes, and books of stamps.

I spent hours carefully handwriting and personalizing each letter and envelope. If I made even one mistake, I'd tear them up and start over, which I did a lot.

At first it didn't seem like anything would come of all my labour, but after a month of impatient waiting, envelopes began trickling back. Excitedly, I'd rip open the envelope to find a neatly typed letter with the company letterhead and logo at the top of the page, along with their decal.

My hard work had paid off! We got so many responses that I bought a thick photo album so I wouldn't lose any of them. Every decal was so very different—some shiny, some small, while others were big. Many companies even went so far as to enclose information about their company. I'd really hit paydirt and Brent was pleased.

About six months after Brent left to work on the rigs, he came home and surprised me with the most beautiful engagement ring I'd ever seen. It had a large cluster of diamonds with a stunning ruby in the centre. He asked me to marry him, to which I immediately answered yes.[16]

Around this time, Brent invited his friend Jake from Ontario to come and stay with us. He and his wife Shelly had split up and he wanted to start over somewhere new. Since it was such a small apartment, Jake was given the couch to sleep on. He was fun to have around and we enjoyed each other's company. We'd sit around in the evenings and get wasted. Because he was frustrated with his life, he would complain about Shelly a great deal, but he really missed his kids.

It didn't take Jake long to find a job and his own place, but he still didn't know very many people in town so he visited often. He was usually the last to leave after a party. I was lonely too, with Brent out of town for work so often. I guess that's what made us so vulnerable.

One night Jake asked me to massage his aching back. Only too happy to help a friend, I said okay. He took off his shirt and lay down on his stomach on the living room carpet. On my knees beside him, I began messaging his shoulders. The kids were in bed, the music was playing softly, and the lights were low. Slowly I made my way down his back, rubbing and massaging, all the while keeping up a steady flow of conversation about nothing in particular.

I don't know how it happened, but suddenly Jake was sitting up facing me, and the next thing I knew he was drawing me into his arms and was about to kiss me. Caught up in the moment, I almost gave in.

Then I came to my senses and pulled back in dismay.

"No," I said, "What are you doing? You've got a wife and I'm with Brent. We can't do this."

And yet at the same time I wanted to.

I got up fast and walked to the kitchen, putting space between us. I was pretty shaken, unable to believe what had been about to happen.

I told him he'd better leave. He, too, was shaken by the evening and apologized over and over again as he retrieved his shirt and coat.

I never told Brent about that night, because I didn't want to hurt his friendship with Jake. After that, Jake only came over when Brent was home and we were polite to one another.

Not long after, Jake's wife and kids moved to town. When I first met her, I felt ashamed and didn't feel that I had the right to be her friend. But as I got to know her, we became close friends, and over time Jake and I healed our friendship.

---

[16] It escapes my memory just when I had acquired my divorce from Steve.

One thing I'm sure of is that if we'd kissed, we would have gone all the way. It's amazing what loneliness can cause one to do. That night provided the perfect setup: no kids, low lighting, soft music, being stoned, touching a half-naked body, all the while longing for our spouses. No matter how innocently things start, that sort of situation can take you to a place you never dreamt of going to… and it can destroy everything if you give in for just a moment's pleasure. It would have destroyed Brent and me, Brent's friendship with Jake, and the friendship between me and Jake. I could never have lived with myself.

The Unexpected

Within that same year, following my hysterectomy, I found a large lump in one of my breasts. I was once again full of fear of that dreaded word: cancer.

I had it checked out immediately, and my doctor didn't want to take any chances. He wanted it out as soon a possible. I was to have the surgery done in Winnipeg, but it would take a few months before they could schedule me in. In the meantime, I was to sit and wait patiently.

Easier said than done.

While I waited for that ominous day to arrive, another surprise hit me right between the eyes. During a doctor's visit, he noticed that my right eyeball seemed to be shrinking in its socket. So after the fork damage, the cataract, and the two failed surgeries to try and remove that cataract, I now had to contend with a shrinking eyeball.[17]

As we talked more about the shrinking eye, I mentioned to the doctor that I often banged my head on corner shelves and cupboard doors. Walls even jumped out and hit me sometimes because I couldn't see them. That's when the doctor advised me to have the eye completely removed, in case one of those knocks to the head caused my good eye to go blind. After all, the two eyes were connected.

Disbelief gripped me. He was kidding, right? By the look on his face, though, I could tell he was extremely serious.

I was lost for words, unable to give him a definite answer. I wanted to scream and scream and scream… punch walls, break something, anything to express the misery I felt.

Instead I went home, got stoned, and lost myself in some of the hardest and loudest rock music I could find. No matter what I tried, I couldn't escape reality. I couldn't even tell my kids. They would probably think their mom was out to lunch again.

Brent was out of town, so I couldn't talk to him about either of these suggested surgeries. I had no way of contacting him for moral support because I never knew where in Alberta he was. Sometimes he'd call from a payphone, otherwise I didn't hear from him.

My parents and my friends didn't know what to say or do to alleviate the turmoil I was facing. My world was crumbling, and so was my body.

With the fear of losing my sight, I began to practice walking around in the dark when no one was around. I'd shut off all the lights, blindfold myself with a towel, and then try to find my way around. I

---

[17] Over the years, I'd also had two other eye surgeries which I haven't mentioned. Twice the eye began to wander to the right side of the eye socket, a condition which is called being "wall-eyed," and I needed surgery to correct the problem. I was very self-conscious about this. After each surgery, I had to wear an eyepatch for more than a week.

found that I became disoriented very easily. Many times I ended up with stubbed toes. I even tried to pour water in a glass to see if I could hear when it was full. Not an easy task. The smallest jobs I took for granted suddenly became enormous and difficult.

I tried putting on a good front for everyone's benefit because I couldn't handle their looks of sympathy, but that only resulted in wearing another mask to cover up what I was really feeling. My moods began to shift fearfully. One minute, "I can do this!" The next, "No, I can't and don't want to!"

How was Brent going to react to all this? When he came back from work, I finally got my answer. While the boys were in bed, he asked me if I'd seen the doctor about the lump. I told him that the doctor was setting a date for surgery. He was fine with that; there was compassion in his eyes.

Then I sprung on him what the doctor had said about my eye. That must have really rocked him because he blurted out, "I don't know how I'll take you with an artificial eye."

I felt like I had just been sucker-punched. Gone was the compassion, and in its place was doubt and confusion. If ever I needed him to take me in his arms and hold me, it was then, but he didn't. My guts were wrung out like a twisted dishrag.

Well, at least he was honest about it. After all, I didn't want the eyes taken out either. I'd seen some of the glass eyes out there and they didn't look at all normal to me. I mean, you could tell they weren't real.

I didn't know what to do or say. Would he be able look at me with just one eye? Would he be embarrassed? Wouldn't I have any worth? Would I be a freak?

Thinking I would lose him, I put off making any decision. But I knew I would have to do it eventually.

If that wasn't enough, another health crisis was to come my way.

One day I was invited to go to a coffee house and listen to my friend's sister play guitar and sing. I'd never been to the place, nor had I ever heard her sing, so I got a sitter for the boys and waited outside on the front step for my friend to pick me up. While waiting, I somehow twisted my knee and heard a loud popping sound from the kneecap. I instantly felt excruciating pain. I could hardly stand, yet alone walk.

Hopping on one leg, I made my way back into the apartment, taking each step up the stairway on my backside. By the time I made it, the knee had swollen to twice its size. I knew I wasn't going anywhere that night, so I paid the babysitter for coming and sent her home. Taking a couple of painkillers, I sat on my couch with the leg elevated, hoping the pain would subside.

By the next morning the knee was still swollen. So there I was, off once again to the doctor. He figured the cartilage under the kneecap had slipped out of place. If it didn't go back into place in the next few days, I could expect surgery.

That was it. I'd had it. Just kill me. Someone put me out of my misery. This was more than I could take.

"When you get me on that table, let's just get everything over and done with," I suggested when I saw the doctor next.

Unfortunately, he told me that wasn't medically possible.

If my mood swings hadn't been bad enough before, the worst was yet to come. The knee did eventually heal on its own, but by then I was really angry, full of fear and resentment, and afflicted with paranoia. In other words, I was on the verge of a total breakdown. I began building invisible walls inside so nothing and no one could hurt me anymore.

Darkness continued to settle over my world. Different masks flew on and off my face with every different person I encountered. I didn't know how to handle my emotions. One minute I'd be laughing and smiling and having a great time. Then suddenly I'd be angry, full of anxiety, and pull away from everyone.

After Brent's remark about my eye, I stopped confiding in him. I dreaded how he would respond.

About the only time my true pain showed was when I drank, and then my tongue could slice a person to bits. My vocabulary was so foul. I hardened my heart and couldn't even cry.

The only place I felt secure was in the world of music. Music expressed my feelings, longings, and dreams—that is, those I had left. It was a world of fantasy, and no one could cut that out of me.

I soon couldn't get up in the morning without firing up a joint to go along with the cigarette. Loneliness ate up my insides and I paced like a caged animal. I became a recluse.

Before too long, I was needing more and more drugs. I couldn't get stoned enough to silence the torment that hammered at my brain. I didn't go out unless it was absolutely necessary, and when I did I'd shake like an earthquake inside. Overtaken with paranoia, I would rush home afterward to fire up another joint to calm my shredded nerves.

The apartment building became my refuge, and gradually I was suffering from cabin fever. I didn't want to go out into the real world. It wasn't safe anymore.

Twenty-Eight
All Too Familiar

Things were getting pretty hot in the drug trade, so much so that the police put up two stakeouts to watch our apartment. Although it was scary, Jeannette and I laughed it off in order to keep what little sanity we still possessed. After all, there wasn't a thing we could do to stop it from happening.

One of the stakeouts was in a hotel just down the street. They rented a room facing the front door of our apartment. At the same time, they rented an apartment across the street that faced our back door. They could see how many people were coming and going and everyone who lived there.

Another time, a plainclothes cop was discovered walking around our apartment lawn. Jeannette and I were sitting on the front steps with coffee in one hand and a cigarette in the other, talking about nothing in particular, when suddenly a strangely dressed person came around the corner of our apartment. Immediately we recognized him as an undercover narcotic officer. He was dressed in denim overalls, a plaid shirt, with a silly-looking straw hat on his head. He looked like a farmer off the show *Hee Haw*. He was as phoney as a three-dollar bill, considering we lived a long ways up north where there wasn't any farming.

Jeannette couldn't help herself. "What are you looking for, narc?" she called out to him.

Realizing he'd been recognized, he picked up his pace. We never saw him again, but that didn't mean there weren't others to take his place.

Finally the appointed time came for my dreaded breast surgery. I managed to straighten up long enough to take the bus to Winnipeg. Sadly, there was no one to accompany me, which made it a long and lonely twenty-four-hour ride. My imagination wreaked havoc on me. The very idea that I had to once again expose my breast was bad enough, but they were going to cut into it. What were they going to find? Cancer? I really didn't want to find out.

There was only one bright spot in all this. When I booked into the hospital, at least I was given my own private room.

The lump that was to be removed was on the top part of the breast, but during the surgery they examined the breast closer and discovered a second lump. They made two very large incisions to get at both lumps.

When I awoke and felt my breast, fear instantly gripped me. A huge bandage started over my right arm and came down across my ribcage under my left arm, flattening the whole left side of my chest. My first thought was that they had performed a mastectomy. I lay there in utter horror.

When the nurse noticed I was awake, she rushed over to my bedside to calmly assure me that they hadn't remove the breast, but that they had found yet another lump. A biopsy of each lump showed that they weren't cancerous, however. That was a great relief.

A few days later, the large bandage was removed and smaller ones replaced it. With this done, I was allowed to go home.

More than a week after the surgery, the swelling from the incisions were so ugly-looking that I had to talk to my sister Darlene about it. If Brent had felt unsure about the prospect of me losing an eye, what would he say when he saw my breast?

When it comes to my anatomy, I am very private. For me to say anything about my fears to Darlene, it was no small matter. She lovingly assured me that the swelling would go down and everything would look normal again once they healed. I grabbed her words and held on to them for dear life—and over a long period of time, her words proved to be true.

On a day much like any other, an unexpected visitor almost turned my life upside-down. The boys were either watching TV or playing in their room, and thankfully no one had come over to visit. I had a gram of hash and felt the need to get high, so I turned on a burner, got ready what I needed, then went in search of my toking pen.

While I was doing that, I heard a knock on the door. I quickly went to see who it was and, to my dismay, there stood a police officer. He was the very last person I would ever want to see at my door, especially with my drugs sitting out on the kitchen counter in full view. If the officer took even one step into my apartment, he would see what I was up to.

Fortunately, it turned out he was looking for someone and wanted to know if I knew his whereabouts. Forging calmness, I told him I didn't. And much to my relief, he left.

Quickly I closed the door and leaned against it in a full-blown panic attack, my heart pounding a mile a minute. Man, that had been way too close.

When I could function again, I returned to the kitchen. Joey was standing next to the counter with a scared look on his face. The stove was shut off and there was no sign of the two knives or my drugs. Joey pointed to the cupboard next to him and explained that he'd put it all away so I wouldn't get caught.

That should never have happened. I had put my son's life in danger. Joey could have been horribly burned, but thankfully he wasn't. He had protected me instead of me protecting him.

It's amazing the situation didn't turn out worse. I often had people over to smoke up or buy drugs. We all could have been sitting at the table getting high when the officer knocked. I would have opened it, thinking it was just another customer. I could have been busted and my boys would have witnessed it. They would have seen their mother handcuffed and dragged off to jail, and they would have ended up in foster care. As an addict, these thoughts didn't cross my mind until many years later. Instead I was just relieved not to have been caught and felt thankful for what Joey had done.

Only a short time later, I asked Joey what he wanted to be when he grew up. His answer staggered me and I'll never forget it.

He looked me straight in the eye. "I want to be a policeman," he said confidently.

"Why?"

Without hesitation, he replied, "So I can bust you, Mommy."

That threw me for a loop. Not long before, a friend of mine had asked me what my sons would do when they grew up, and I'd answered, "Oh, I'll probably sell them their first bag, then sit down and smoke their first joint with them." I'd thought that was a pretty cool answer. I wanted to be a cool mom. Instead I was a pathetic excuse for a mother.

Emotional Breakdown

With violent rock and roll blaring
Kids were removed to their beds
Trying in vain to sleep
Pillows jammed over their heads

The pulsating tunes had me mesmerized
Strobe and black lights hypnotized
Drugs and booze near paralysed
And people pleasing I'd not realized

Should my children need attention
Who would see to their needs
In anguish I realized my failure
While fear and self-pity breeds

Around this time, I started stuttering when I talked. When people spoke to me, I had to think of my answer first in my head, to make sure it made sense, then stutter out my reply. By the time people heard what I had to say, they'd be looking at me like I was nuts. So it got to the point where I spoke less and less. What was the point anyway?

When I was angry, which was quite often, I started putting my small fist into brick walls, gyprock walls, and even mirrors. I would take one look at myself and hate what I saw. After shattering a mirror, I would walk away feeling even worse because now my hand was cut, bleeding, and bruised.

In some ways, I wanted people to know how much I hurt, but in others I was ashamed and embarrassed of my actions. My life wasn't normal and I knew it. I was so full of hurt and self-hatred that I just needed to vent it somehow without hurting anyone.

I spent about one full year stoned and drunk from morning to night. There were times when I would lie in the middle of my bed in the fetal position with tears in my eyes, yet I couldn't cry—because there was someone out there who had it worse than I did. And so I'd hold myself really tight, afraid that I would fly apart into a million pieces.

Whenever anything good came my way, it was like I had a huge cankerworm inside me that ate it all up and left me with nothing but defeat and failure. I would think to myself, *No one can hurt me anymore. The only thing they can do to me is kill me, and then they'd be doing me a favour.* I just didn't care.

With the surgeries, fighting in the hallways, police watching our building, and Brent always gone, I couldn't get out of bed without reaching for a joint. I needed it just to level off, so I could perform the duties of a mother by feeding and dressing my children and sending them off to school.

The rest of the day was then spent cleaning my apartment and socializing with the other drug-dealers in the building. We partied day and night.

When I managed to get over the cabin fever, I became a regular bargoer once again and wouldn't come home until the bar closed—and I usually brought people with me, which meant the kids didn't get much sleep before going to school the next day.

I hated what I was doing to my boys, because my dad had done the same thing to me, but I didn't have the will or desire to change it. After five years of this lifestyle I didn't think it could get much worse. I was destroying my life and ruining my kids' lives, too.

How often did they hear their mother coming home after an all-nighter and end up in the bathroom puking her guts out? I'd be hanging onto the sink, trying to steady myself as the room swam around and around, all the while my guts protesting to relinquish all the alcohol I'd consumed. I'd then humble myself before the great white porcelain throne, bending knee for a close encounter. I'd bow in adoration and complete submission, just inches above the royal seat, grasping the bowl with all my might as I made my nightly offering.

As a mother, I was a waste of skin. The kids saw me drunk and stoned all the time. It was the opposite of what they deserved from their mother. Sure, I washed their clothes, fed them, and kept a clean apartment, but they had to put up with mood swings, endless parties, and strangers standing around to buy dope. They never knew who or what they were coming home to. In the mornings, they'd be woken up by a stoned, quick-tempered, foul-mouthed mother and I didn't even know what they did outside the home or at school the rest of the day. I didn't partake in any of their school activities.

At some point, I found out that they went to church. I didn't know when, where, or how that had started.

The only thing that seemed to matter in my distorted world was my need for love. I needed a man to make me happy. I loved my kids, but I was so damaged emotionally and mentally that I wasn't capable of giving them the love they deserved. I gave them much the same as my father gave me—nothing.

How many fights did they witness? How many of those men I brought home did they get attached to and have to say goodbye when I ran out on them, or when they'd had enough of me? How many of those men did they dislike? How many times did I withhold my love from them and give it to some stranger for a night because I was so hungry for love myself? How many promises did I make and break? Too many, that's how many.

When it comes to my children, I hold many regrets. I feel the remorse whenever I think about the unstable life I put them through. But through all this drama, they managed to survive. I did a lot of stupid things, but I loved them, even if it was warped.

One of the things I constantly felt guilty about was how seldom I attended their parent-teacher meetings. I had performed so poorly in school myself that I felt completely out of my depth talking with their teachers. Just walking into the school caused me enough panic to want to turn around and run back out. And when I did try attending a meeting, I mostly didn't understand what the teacher was saying; I'd nod my head at what I thought was the right cue and answer yes or no, guessing what they wanted to hear. Teachers intimidated me, as did most authority figures.

Truthfully, I hated myself when I missed something special the kids were doing in school, but if I had of gone I would have felt alone, shrivelled up, and filled with anxiety. Panic overtook me when I was out among the "proper people," of which I was not one. I resigned myself to the fact that my children would survive my lack of participation, just as I had survived when I was younger.

Deep down, I did care that I had failed my kids, but that was just another reason to smoke a joint.

There is so much I don't remember about my kids' childhoods. They joined various clubs, and I don't remember how any of it happened. I didn't know where they were or what they learned.

So Long, Fox Bay

The day started like any other, having a quick toke from the roach[18] I'd left in the ashtray beside the bed the night before. Catching the buzz, I groaned and forced myself to get out of bed. The apartment block was quiet this morning. It was one of the rare times when it was really silent.

It was Friday and the boys had to be fed and sent to school. They had their usual chatter and disagreements, then finally headed out the door. The apartment needed cleaning and clothes needed washing, so I found my bag of pot and smoked a nice big fat joint to motivate myself.

During the afternoon, Jeannette came to visit and share a beer and joint. Cole had been out of town on drug business and was returning sometime that afternoon, so she was going to surprise him by making a special dinner, with a tablecloth, candles, and a nice bottle of wine. She was excited and didn't stay long.

The day passed nicely and I managed to accomplish all the tasks I set for myself, without interruptions.

Then, while the boys and I were enjoying our supper, we heard a thunderous crash that scared the bejeepers out of us. The door to Jeannette's apartment below us slammed shut, causing the ornaments on my shelf to rattle. The apartments weren't soundproof, so we could hear Jeannette screaming at Cole as objects shattered in the background.

It seemed their supper wasn't such a hit.

---

[18] A roach is the butt of a marijuana joint.

The boys and I were shaken, but we managed to finish our meal. The boys got up and went to their room to play while the fight remained in full swing. I was concerned for Jeannette's little girls, who had to watch and hear all this. How well I remembered what that was like.

After another slam of their door, silence reigned. I figured that Cole had left and I felt relieved, since their argument had triggered an anxiety attack brought on by my childhood memories.

I went downstairs to see if Jeannette was okay, but on the way I had to walk around broken supper dishes and a stained tablecloth. That explained the loud crash. She had literally cleared her kitchen table by wrapping everything up in the tablecloth and tossing it out onto the hallway floor.

Proceeding carefully around the debris, I entered her apartment and was shocked to see all the destruction. It looked as though a tornado had ripped through the place. Sure enough, there was a whisky bottle. Her ornaments were smashed, along with books and albums strewn in every direction.

When I found her, she was smashing more of her dishes against the walls. Earlier she had curled her hair and dressed specially for the occasion of her husband's return, but her hair was now a total disaster and her face was streaked with mascara and tears. I tried to reason with her to stop, but she wouldn't, so I went back upstairs and called her sister, who said she'd be right over.

Pretty soon I heard a loud pounding on my door. Upon opening it, there stood Jeannette in total disarray. She brushed past me and began yelling about what Cole had done, her eyes wild with rage. I could tell she'd been drinking heavily. Her arms were flaying wildly as she moved further into my apartment.

As she recounted her story, the fire in her was being rekindled. She headed toward my shelf dividers and was about to demolish them. No way. I shoved her up against the wall beside the open door she'd just come through and pinned her there. I kept telling her to settle down, but she either wouldn't or couldn't comprehend who I was and what I was saying.

To keep her from getting away, I managed to get a hand around her throat to pin her. With my other hand, I forced her arm down by her side. She was squirming and screaming obscenities at whatever it was that seemed to be coming at her, which made it really difficult to hold on, since she was taller and heavier than me.

Somehow, she grabbed my little finger and twisted it until it felt like it had broke, but I still wouldn't release her. Ever so slowly, I managed to wrestle her to the floor and sit on her.

It was at that moment that her sister showed up, backed up by her husband. Several people came out of their apartments to see what was going on. When I was able to look up, I saw my boys watching us. They were very frightened, but I had my hands full keeping Jeannette from hurting herself any more than she already had.

After what seemed an eternity, a paramedic finally knelt beside me to take over, so I could get off of her. He then asked if Jeannette had done any drugs. I knew she'd gotten into the whisky and was stoned on whatever drug Cole had brought back with him, but I had to lie to him and tell him I didn't know. That was the way of it in the drug world; you didn't rat on anyone, even if it meant their death. At least that was the way I understood it.

Once she was calmed down enough to be examined, the paramedics put her on a stretcher and took her to the hospital. She was in the worst condition I'd ever seen her in. Come to think of it, everyone I hung out with was becoming more and more agitated, easily angered, fighting and screwed up. Nothing was fun anymore.

I managed to settle my boys down and reassure them that everything was going to be okay with Jeannette because she was going to the hospital. Jeannette's brother-in-law must have taken Jeannette's girls. Meanwhile, someone stayed and watched my boys while Jeannette's sister and I went to the hospital to see her.

At the hospital, I found her sitting alone on an examination table in the emergency room, smoking a cigarette. So I lit one of my own, defiant of hospital rules.

At one point, Jeannette's sister and I were talking to her assigned doctor. We only had our backs turned for a moment, but when we looked back Jeannette had up and disappeared. We looked everywhere in the hospital for her, and then we hit the streets. We searched every street between the hospital and home before giving up and going back to my place, where we sat for a moment and talked in the car.

During the conversation, I happened to glance up and see the curtain in the upstairs apartment move. I knew immediately where she was. Jeannette had been given the key to a friend's suite, kitty-corner to mine, while he was out of town.

We thought it was best to leave her alone. I'd had enough for one day. I was completely drained, not just with what had happened, but also with life in general. Besides, my finger hurt.

After yesterday's episode, and it being the weekend, I felt an urgency to get away from all the people in my building. It seemed like everybody was fighting, and on top of that I was worried that the police had the place under surveillance.

My nerves were beyond frayed. If I'd had any money, I would have moved out, but instead I phoned a couple I knew who lived in an apartment building on the other side of town. They both had the day off and invited us over.

With a throbbing finger, I packed up the boys, grabbed a taxi, and escaped for the day. We were greeted with smiling faces and the boys gladly went off to play with their kids.

Sitting at the kitchen table, with a steaming cup of coffee in front of me, I finally felt relaxed enough to unwind. Of course, it wasn't long before I pulled out a large chunk of hash and her husband and I proceeded to get stoned. And of course, with the drugs, the stereo got turned on. And of course, the stereo was too loud according to their neighbours, who banged on their door to complain. As it turned out, my friends already had issues with those wonderful complaining neighbours, so that meant a fight, which ended up with a lot of angry words and threats to call the police.

It was starting all over again. I simply couldn't take another fight, so I phoned Mom to see if the kids and I could head over there. I was so close to losing my sanity. It felt like my world was spinning out of orbit.

Finally someone picked up the phone and James answered it. He was supposed to be in Winnipeg! What was he doing here? Hearing his voice was all it took for me to break. I literally begged him to get us out of here. There were no questions asked; he was on his way after I gave him the address.

Again, James to the rescue! What would I have done without him?

I apologized to my friends and quickly got the boys ready to leave.

When we arrived at my parents' house, I went straight downstairs to the basement and locked myself in the bathroom. I sank to the floor and violently shook. I was about to slip over the edge. It felt like the hordes of hell had been loosed to destroy me.

When I finally pulled myself together and reluctantly left the safety of the bathroom, I found James patiently waiting for me just outside the door. He demanded to know what was going on. I told him about everything that had happened, all the miseries of my life.

"It's settled then," he said. "I'm coming to your apartment first thing in the morning and you had better be up and ready to move."

He didn't say where we were going or how we'd get there. We just had to be ready to go because he was moving us out.

This only added to the emotional rollercoaster I was riding on. It just seemed to get worse and worse. I should have been grateful to him, but instead I felt overwhelmed by the fact that I would have to pack up my apartment and move to who knew where. All I could see was more pressure.

I was mentally and emotionally drained. Actually, I was ready for the psychiatric ward.

Before James dropped us off at home, we collected newspapers and boxes to start packing. Feeling anxious and confused, I did whatever James told me. I was barely holding on by a thread and he was the only one I could trust.

True to his word, he showed up the next morning. He brought three helpers along with him and they hauled out my furniture and packed up the truck. To speed things up, he dropped some of my smaller items out of my second-story window to someone who was standing in the back of James's truck below, which was parked on the front lawn.

I never saw an apartment packed up and cleared out as fast as mine was. As I took my last look around, I felt utterly defeated. We were homeless and we never got to say goodbye to anyone.

This was all too familiar.

Twenty-Nine
Winnipeg

Apparently James had talked to Mom and they decided it was best for us to stay with her and Dad. But as soon as James found us all a ride, we would be heading back with him to Winnipeg. The idea of living in Winnipeg just sickened me, but I no longer had the right to make my own decisions. I'd already proved how incapable I was at caring for my kids and myself. At the time, though, I blamed my problems on everyone else. I couldn't see the role I played in all this.

A few things happened back at my old apartment building while we stayed at Mom's. The first day, a girl was badly beaten up out on the front lawn by three other girls. The next night, a guy who had been staying at a friend's place in the apartment was picked up by the police while carrying a .22 rifle; his intention had been to shoot some guy who had beaten up his sister, and he spent the night in jail only to be released because the gun hadn't been loaded. The woman who lived next door to me then tried suicide by popping a bunch of pills. An ambulance was called and her life spared.

What a place. The apartment should have been burnt to the ground.

Three days later, a friend came and loaded us all into his truck and drove us to Winnipeg. I had visited the city a number of times, but while driving in I was freshly reminded why I was none too thrilled at the prospect of living here. It was way too big and overpowering for me. Just walking across a street seemed like a mammoth accomplishment. There were just too many cars and people. I was a small-town kind of girl and felt way out of my league.

And now it was to become our new home. I didn't think it was possible for my spirit to sink any lower than it already had, but it did. I felt trapped.

I was completely dependent upon James. This was the third time he had rescued me out of a bad situation. My mind was whirling from how fast everything had happened. My house of cards had toppled.

Yet I'm sure if I had been left living in Thompson, I would've eventually been put in the psychiatric ward.

James took me out to a restaurant, and soon after we were joined by my brother Lawrence. Apparently James had previously talked to Lawrence about getting the boys and me out of Thompson. He'd had a pretty good idea about the people I was hanging out with, and since I had last seen James my situation had grown progressively worse.

Lawrence explained that he had plenty of room at his place in Ste. Anne, a small town just outside the city, so we could live there instead of in the city. He had a son named Troy who was in foster care. Because Lawrence was a long-haul truck driver, he had no one to take care of his son while he was on the road. If I moved in, chances were he could get Troy back under his care.

Troy was the same age as my boys. All I would be required to do was take care of Troy, pay rent, and keep the house clean in exchange for a place to live. How could I say no to that? It was so simple and straightforward. Even I could handle this!

During this time, I had no way of contacting Brent to let him know where we were and that we were all right.

Several years later, I was told by Jeannette that three days after James moved us out, the anticipated police raid took place. They hit every apartment except mine. They were looking for Thompson's main dealers. Jeannette and Cole had moved upstairs into my suite, so they didn't get caught.

When I think of what might have taken place during the raid, I thank God for how He protected us from experiencing it. I can only imagine the terror the boys and I would have endured while police, possibly with dogs, busted in doors and took the tenants by surprise. If it were anything like what one sees on TV, the atmosphere would have been electrifying—police shouting orders, telling people to stay put while they trashed and raided their homes in search of weapons and drugs… only those who were there that day know for sure.

For the longest time, I found it rather strange that the police had hit every apartment except mine. The explanation I could think of was that I must have kept a remarkably low profile. Perhaps they hadn't suspected me of dealing, or perhaps I was only small time.

However, more recently it's occurred to me that the surveillance teams must have watched me move out, so they assumed my apartment was empty and didn't see Jeannette and Cole move in.

I'm just really grateful we weren't there to find out. I believe God had His hand on us. He knew what was coming and got us out in time.

Thirty

Ste. Anne

I don't remember the ride to Ste. Anne, but I remember how relieved I was that we wouldn't have to live in Winnipeg. The idea of living with Lawrence and Troy greatly appealed to me. I'd always felt safe with Lawrence, and the fact that he was offering his home made me feel wanted.

We pulled into his driveway and drove around into the backyard. Lawrence parked the car on a large cement pad and then welcomed us to our new home.

Stepping out of the vehicle, I looked up at the house with mixed feelings. I knew there was no going back. I had no money, my furniture and belongs were elsewhere, and we didn't have anywhere to go back to. I felt completely and utterly trapped.

I was, however, greatly impressed with the size of the house. It had two stories, lots of windows, and a large closed-in back porch which ran the length of the house. Grabbing as much of the luggage as we could carry, we entered through the dimly lit porch into a brightly lit and spacious kitchen that boasted many top and bottom cupboards and a good-sized window over the sink. A part of the counter extended out from the wall beside the back door, making it a peninsula.

The main floor held three rooms—the kitchen, dining room, and living room, each connected with one another. The kitchen and dinning room ran along one half of the house, with the living room taking up the other half.

I wasn't at all impressed with the view from the dining room and living room windows, though. Each provided a perfect view of the big old neighbouring church and its graveyard with sprouting headstones. It was absolutely grotesque as far as I was concerned!

The upstairs contained three bedrooms and a bathroom. The four boys were to share two rooms while Lawrence had his own. I would have the living room couch, which contained a foldaway bed. So I got the stereo and the TV! Not a bad exchange for my own room.

Ste. Anne wasn't a very big place, so it would be easy for me to get around. There wasn't even a taxi. To shop for groceries, we had to drive eleven miles to nearby Steinbach.

Lawrence was able to get Troy out of foster care. I was accepted on welfare and we got the four boys enrolled in school.

How did my children feel about all this? Shamefully, it never occurred to me to ask them. I just dragged them through the mud with me. I had taken them away from all that was familiar, their grandparents, friends, and school. Really, how should they feel? I assumed it wouldn't take them long to settle in and find new friends while I remained in my own selfish little world.

Come to think of it, no one ever asked how I had dealt with all the moves when I was a kid, so I guess that was why it never occurred to me to ask how they were doing now. That's really sad.

Thinking back on it now, we were constantly starting over. New town, new people, trying to fit in somewhere. And just when we thought we'd arrived, *bam!* Time to go. Adios, amigos!

Lawrence took me to the Ste. Anne bar, which was about a mile straight down the road from where we lived. It was a long walk, but at least I wouldn't get lost coming home as long as I kept heading in a straight line. He introduced me to some of his friends and they just happened to be bargoers like myself, which appealed to my taste in people.

I began meeting more people on my own, and of course it didn't take long to navigate my way to Keira, a young woman who liked her drugs as much as I did mine. She became my new supplier. Even with a geographical move, we always gravitate to like-minded people. We're like magnets. Keira became my closest friend and we spent a significant amount of time together.

Somewhere in all this, Brent found us. He could only stay a couple of days, though, and then he was off once again to Alberta for another three-week stint working on the rigs. At least he knew the whereabouts of his dog.

On one of his visits, we went into Winnipeg on a new Harley Davidson. Where and when he got it, I don't recall. Maybe he was trying it out to see how well it handled before buying it. Well, as far as I remember, it handled quite well because we were downtown Winnipeg and heading to Portage La Prairie when Brent said to me, "Watch this." He put both his hands in his coat pockets and we began to weave in and out of traffic with no hands on the handlebars. I have no idea how many miles we travelled like that, and in those days we didn't wear helmets. It was a thrilling and completely insane ride.

As the summer passed, my desire to return to Thompson began to fade. The boys went to school, then spent their summer holidays mostly outdoors. I rarely knew where they were. Lawrence was on the road much of the time while I took care of the boys and kept house. It was a full-time job, so when I had extra money I'd buy a bag of weed and party. If I didn't have money, but my friends did, we'd get together and smoke either at their place or mine. But most times I just got stoned by myself, cleaning the house with my favourite tunes blasting on the stereo.

Around fall, Lawrence surprised us by bringing home a lady friend from Ontario named Ellen and her five-year-old daughter Sherry to live with us. This was becoming a very full house, but because I was used to having people around I didn't have any trouble accepting them. Now I had company during the days and someone to help with the cleaning.

However, it was quite the adjustment to have a little girl in the house. Although she wanted to be with the boys, they had no use for her. They were too busy doing their boy things and she was a pest as far as they were concerned. They were outside kids and didn't want a little girl tagging along. I felt kind of sorry for Sherry, but there wasn't anything I could do about that.

Brent still came by for a couple of days each month, but when he visited at Christmas we had a hard time getting along. We didn't do anything but fight, which was my fault. I wanted to be out celebrating with my friends, to introduce them to this common-law husband I'd told them about. They probably thought he was a figment of my imagination, because we never went out when he was home.

Because I was so stubborn, I walked the cold snowy mile down the street to the bar on New Year's Eve, picked up a case of beer, and headed home to party on my own if I had to. When I was drunk enough, in justified anger I said my piece and told Brent where he could go. He left right after New Year's, giving me no address or phone number. What a strange relationship.

On another of his visits, he and I went into Winnipeg. He mentioned something about getting a new truck and it didn't take long for him to find the one he wanted. He got all excited when a shiny black and chrome pickup truck met him face to face. Without any hesitation or discussion with me, he ordered it to his specifications with all the bells and whistles. Beaming with excitement, he was told he could pick it up in a few months. Just like that, it was a done deal. Yet here I was on welfare with barely enough money to buy food! Wasn't I the stupid one to allow that? But I had gotten used to being prioritized behind cars, motorcycles, and any other object that took a man's fancy.

On one of those days when the boys were out, the house was clean and I found myself bored to tears. I don't know where Ellen and Sherry were, but I needed to get out before I went stark raving mad. Knowing I had two dollars in my bank account, which was enough to buy a beer, I put on my winter coat and high-heeled boots and made the mile-long trek through the crusty snow to the bar.

There were a few people sitting about, but no one I knew, so I picked a table near the pool table and wrote out a two-dollar cheque for a beer.

I'd barely touched the beer before a guy came to my table and challenged me to a game of pool. If I lost, I'd owe him. So yeah, why not? I was halfway through the game when Lawrence walked in and told me I had two minutes to finish up and get into the car if I didn't want to be locked out of the house while he and the rest of the family went to Winnipeg. I tried to reason with him that it would take a little longer to finish the game, that I was winning, but he wouldn't listen.

"Two minutes," he repeated.

And then he was gone.

In anger, I grabbed my beer and downed what I could before shrugging my shoulders at my opponent. Throwing on my coat, I rushed out the door into the cold evening air. While searching the parking lot for

Lawrence, I slipped on a patch of ice and went down in between two parked cars. I felt a searing pain shoot through my right ankle and up into my leg.

Now I was really mad. I tried to struggle to my feet, only to find I couldn't place any weight on my foot. I'd seriously hurt my ankle. I looked around for Lawrence, but his car wasn't even there. Where the hell was he? He'd left me! The jerk hadn't even given me the two minutes. I felt the deep need to kill him the next time I saw him.

Struggling to keep my footing, I carefully climbed back to my feet and stumbled to the door of the bar. I limped back to the table and found the rest of my beer gone and the table wiped clean. Things definitely weren't getting any better. I didn't have enough money for another drink.

While I was pondering my next move, a woman of my acquaintance came in with her husband. They rescued me by coming over and sitting with me. I told them what had happened and explained that, for whatever reason, I didn't have a key to my house. My foot was throbbing so much that I unzipped my boot and made the mistake of opening it all the way. Instantly my foot swelled and I couldn't put the boot back on. What next?

My friends bought me a beer and I sat with them with my foot on the seat across from me. When we finished, the woman said she'd take me to her place so I could wait for my brother's return. Saying goodbye to her husband, she helped me out of the building and into her car.

I apologized for being such a nuisance, yet thanked her for her kindness. When I finally got hold of Lawrence several hours later, he was already home. So my friend drove me home.

Hobbling into the house and as mad as a hornet, I wouldn't let on to Lawrence just how much pain I was in. It was his house and I didn't want to get into a fight with him. I had to grin and bare it, pretending everything was just ducky. I wanted to kill him more than ever, because he was wearing one of his arrogant I-told-you-so smirks.

During the night, the pain was so severe that I hardly slept. The next day, I wrapped my ankle in a tenser bandage, not wanting anyone to see my injury, least of all Lawrence. The foot was killing me, though.

Later that afternoon a couple dropped by to visit, so I served coffee and anything else they wanted while Lawrence sat with them. At one point, I needed to go down to the basement to do the laundry, so when no one was looking I sat on the top stair and made my way down on my bottom, holding my wounded foot out in front of me. On my way back up, I did the same thing.

I was so glad when they left, so I could sit down and elevate the foot.

That night and the next day went much the same. I walked three days on that foot, and by the third night I lay on my bed in agony. The foot had the ugliest bluish-black colour I'd even seen and it was swollen so tight I thought the skin would pop. Tears streamed down my face and I felt like screaming and crying.

Lawrence picked that moment to come downstairs, as he was getting ready to head back on the road. He stopped long enough to ask if I was ready to go to the hospital and have my foot checked out yet. He had known all along I had injured myself but hadn't said anything until then. Even the smug look on his face didn't bother me at that point. I was more than ready.

I quickly got dressed and pulled on my boot, carefully covering the wounded foot with a thick sock. It was dark out and he had to be in Winnipeg to start his run, so he dropped me off at the hospital and left me there. I had no idea how I was to return home.

X-rays were taken and it was discovered that I had fractured the ankle. A cast was put on, starting under my knee and going right down to my toes. I was to come back in a week so the doctor could take it off and put me in a walking cast. In total, I'd be in a cast for six weeks.

I was then given a pair of crutches and told I could go home. Without a ride, I got a crash course in learning how to walk on crutches by myself.

Never having had the need to use crutches before, it took a while to learn to walk on ice and snow. It was a good thing I'd put on that heavy sock to cover my toes or I would have been going back to the hospital with frostbite.

After the truth was exposed and I got over being angry, Ellen thought it would be interesting if she drew something on the bottom of the cast, so when I put my foot up on a chair people would see the drawing. I gave her the okay and was shocked, to say the least, when I saw what she drew. It wasn't the sort of picture you'd want to see on the bottom of anything. It was a male's private parts, drawn in the shape of a man's face, all drawn in bright-coloured felt pens. And when I put a rolled-up woollen sock over my toes, it looked like a betoqued Frenchman. Not wanting to be a prude, I kept it. It just goes to show how twisted our minds were. She even drew a dotted line to show the doctor how to cut the cast off so we could save the picture.

With my leg in a cast, you'd think I wouldn't go walking by myself through slushy snow to get to the bar just for some bar action, but you'd be wrong. As soon as I figured out how to navigate the crutches, off I went. The walk just took a little longer than usual. Most times I'd get a ride home, because by then I'd be pretty well wasted.

If memory serves, it was early spring and I still had the cast when I met up with James in Winnipeg. We sat in his living room with music playing and had a few tokes and a beer, just like the good ole days. We were catching up on how we were doing when Dewayne suddenly walked in.

James hadn't told me he was sharing the house with Dewayne! Although he was surprised to see me, he seemed pleased that I was there. He grabbed a beer, lit a joint, and joined us. I felt the same. All the old feelings I still had for him resurfaced, although I put on my mask of indifference.

As the afternoon wore on into evening, we all became pretty intoxicated. The music was blaring our favourite tunes and one of the last things I remember is sitting on the couch enjoying the company.

Then I found myself standing in front of the open fridge, my whole body shuddering with live electricity. I didn't know what was happening to me. I must have been in the process of grabbing a fresh beer, but how had I gotten there?

James entered the dimly lit kitchen and made his way over to me with an angry scowl. He looked as though he wanted to strike me. Confused, I asked him what was wrong and he informed me that Dewayne and I had been dancing and flirting with each other for more than an hour—and if I thought I was going to bed with him, I was pretty much mistaken.

I was dumbstruck. Never in my right mind would I do such a thing. I had no recall of any of it, but if my brother accused me of having done this, then I must have done it. He wouldn't lie to me. I was mortified.

It suddenly occurred to me that I had been in a blackout, and that shook me hard. I wanted to tell James, but I didn't think he would believe me as he disgustedly turned away and left the room.

Filled with shame, I returned to the living room and sat on the other end of the couch from Dewayne. He gave me an odd look as if to ask, *What are you doing over there?* I was totally screwed up and didn't know what to do. My brother was still scowling at me, as though daring me to defy him.

I'd never experienced this reaction from him before. When James told me to do something, I did it— not out of fear, but because I knew he cared about me.

Dewayne, not knowing what had gone on in the kitchen, approached me and asked if I was ready to go to bed with him. Awkwardly, I shook my head and turned away. I couldn't believe this. How could I have done this with Dewayne when I was still with Brent?

Angrily, Dewayne stormed off to his room and James took over the couch. I guess that was his bed.

I couldn't go home now, because James wasn't about to drive me. So where was I to sleep? In the end, I lay on the bare floor in the coatroom with a coat that barely covered me.

It was a long night, with sleep kept at bay as I shivered from the cold and nerves. The fact that both these men were mad at me only added to my misery.

That was the last time I encountered Dewayne.

Shortly after that episode, Brent and I had a king-sized blow-up which put an end to our engagement. The relationship couldn't last, couldn't be healthy, when the two of us were never together. He was a stranger to me and I needed more that just three days a month with him.

He left shortly after. I packed up all his belongings—which were few—and locked them away in the truck he had parked out back. He was going to come back for that truck, along with his dog Chewy. It would be hard to part with the dog. I knew Chewy better than I knew his master.

Well, the decision was taken out of my hands. One day, Chewy didn't come home. The kids and I searched for him, but he wasn't to be found. He always stuck close to home when he was let outdoors to do his business, so the only answer we could come up with is that someone took him.

I was heartsick, and I couldn't tell Brent since I had no way of contacting him. I felt terrible and afraid. He'd had that dog since he was a pup. They had been through thick and thin together. I felt like I'd lost one of my children and let down Brent at the same time. What was he going to say, or do, when he found out?

Not long after, Lawrence took me into Winnipeg for a night out on the town. There, he introduced me to a casino. I liked to gamble, so this place was right up my alley. The place was booming with customers and the music was loud and got inside me. I tried a few tables, but had no luck.

Not long into the night, I met a good-looking guy who started up a conversation with me and asked if he could buy me a drink. Sure, why not? After a few drinks, Lawrence said he needed to get home. I was disappointed that we had to go so soon, but Lawrence talked to the guy and he agreed to drive me home later.

We stayed at the casino for a few more drinks, then ended up at his trailer where I spent the night. In the morning, he dropped me off at my friend's home in Winnipeg. I didn't give him my address or phone number. We said our goodbyes and I never saw him again.

When I arrived home, I found out that Brent had stopped by the night before with his new truck and had given the boys a ride in it. While they were together, the boys had told Brent about Chewy's disappearance. After returning the boys, Brent left. I never saw him again.

In just six short weeks, I'd managed to fracture an ankle, end an engagement, lose a dog, and sleep with a total stranger. None of this made me the sharpest crayon in the box.

Thirty-One
Greg

Spring had arrived and the cast was removed. My foot was as good as new. So good, in fact, that one afternoon I came up with the brilliant idea of walking down to the bar and bringing home a case of beer. It wasn't often that Ellen joined me, but today she decided to come along. Off we went.

By the time the boys were let out of school, Ellen and I had a pretty good buzz happening. I was so immersed in dancing to the stereo that I didn't hear Lawrence drive by and park his car behind the house.

When the song was finally over, I opened my eyes to see Ellen standing next to Lawrence, and next to him stood a stranger. At least I had the grace to blush. How long he had stood and watched, I don't know, but he had a big grin on his face and a case of beer in his hand. It looked as though we were in for a party tonight, only we girls had gotten a head start on them.

When Lawrence introduced us to our visitor, with great joy I suddenly recognized him. I'd first met Greg at his parents' farm at Churchbridge, Saskatchewan. He was our first cousin. He had an identical twin brother, Ron, as well as an older sister.

At the time, I had been ten and he, twelve. Mom had been on one of her runaways and had taken several of us with her. We'd been stuffed into two small bedrooms and pretty much had the run of the farm. I'd spent as much time with the boys as I could, because they were friendly. I always had a hard time telling them apart, though.

I had met Greg again when I was nineteen and pregnant with Eugene. He'd had shoulder-length blond hair, incredible blue eyes, and was clean-shaven in blue jeans and a T-shirt. Overall, very good-looking. We had taken an instant liking to one another, but he had only stayed in town for a day or two.

Greg looked tired, sickly, and in bad need of a shower, so I took him upstairs, gave him towels and shaving gear, then showed him to the bathroom.

Lawrence explained that Greg had been on a week's drinking binge and was very hungover—not to mention, broke.

When he came down, he looked a lot healthier and was every bit as good-looking as I remembered. I introduced him to all our kids. He definitely became the focal point of our once boring day.

At one point, I remember going into the dining room to get something and finding the boys crowded around Greg. Curious, I walked over to see what they were doing. Greg was drawing hockey logos for the boys and explaining what they were all about, as he himself was a hockey player. The boys seemed to hang onto his every word. They really liked him.

When I told the boys it was time for bed, they turned to Greg and hugged him goodnight, which I'd never seen them do with anyone else. Greg hugged each one in turn and told them that he loved him.

I was totally taken aback. I didn't even say that to my kids. In all my childhood years, I don't recall being told by my parents that they loved me, so naturally it never occurred to me to say it to my sons.

Greg really captivated my heart when he did that. Without him realizing it, he taught me how to say "I love you" to my sons. For that, I'll be forever grateful to him.

Later in the evening, after the kids were settled for the night and Lawrence and Ellen were off by themselves, Greg and I settled ourselves on the living room carpet, each holding a fresh beer, and lay face to face on our stomachs talking about the two times we had met. Greg had often asked our other relatives if they'd ever heard how I was doing. He said that out of all his relatives, he had always thought about me the most.

Greg only stayed a few days before Lawrence took him home to Churchbridge, about a five-and-a-half-hour drive. Greg found it hard to leave, as did we all. He promised to return as soon as he could afford to.

With great reluctance, we all hugged and said our goodbyes. I didn't think I'd see him again and life went back to being boring.

Some time after Greg had left, Lawrence and Ellen broke up and she and Sherry went back to Ontario. In some ways it was hard to see her go, yet it had been a crowded house.

Greg did end up coming back, several times. The first time was when my sister Ann came to visit. We celebrated by taking Ann and Greg to the bar. Another time I remember Greg and me sitting in the back seat of Lawrence's car with two other people, heading up to Thompson to visit family and friends. Of course we drank most of the way there and back.

Out of the blue, Greg and his brother Ron once showed up for a couple of days without telling us they were coming. They drove up in an old junker called a car, bright orange with dents all over. They must have been sideswiped at some point, because the driver's side door had to be tied shut with a rope; cardboard and tape were used to cover the window on the passenger's side. How the police hadn't stopped them is anyone's guess.

As it happened, Lawrence was home for that visit. Michael, who also had moved to Winnipeg, came out to Ste. Anne to join us, which of course meant it was party time. We started early in the afternoon, and by midnight we were all pretty much wasted and tired.

Lawrence and the kids had already gone to bed, so it was up to me to get our cousins settled and Michael on his way home. Michael argued about having to leave, and he insisted that he would only go if Lawrence told him to. For some reason, this angered me. In fact, I got so mad that if someone were to have told me what I was about to do next, I wouldn't have believed them.

Picture this: Michael and I stood by the dining room door, with the stairway in view, having our disagreement while Greg and Ron remained in the living room, probably wondering what all the fuss was about.

Without thinking, I pulled off the jacket I'd been wearing and slapped him across the face with it. Then I drew back my right arm and drove my fist up under his jaw. The unexpected contact threw him off-balance and set him on his butt in a dining room chair with a stunned look on his face.

When I realized what I had done, I knew I'd just signed my death warrant. I was so terrified that I turned to the wall next to me and punched two holes through the gyprock.

"Now look at what you made me do!" I screamed.

Suddenly, it registered what I'd just done to the wall. I looked up just in time to see Lawrence coming down the stairs, demanding to know what the hell was going on. Now I was really in trouble.

Behind me, a mattress was leaning against the wall. I began to punch the mattress over and over again, releasing all the pent-up fury and frustration. I knew I had gone too far.

By this time, Greg and Ron had come into the room to see what the ruckus was about. Michael was still holding his jaw with that shocked look on his face. What a sight we must have been.

Michael told Lawrence that I'd told him to go home, and Lawrence backed me up: "She lives here. If she says you have to go home, then you have to go." So Michael left mad and Lawrence went back to bed.

After cooling down, we all went to bed.

The next morning, I had some explaining to do. I told Lawrence I would repair the wall. Examining the holes, I realized how lucky I was to have missed the stud. That could have been detrimental to my hand.

I could hardly believe what I'd done. When we were kids, Michael had sometimes beat on me, and a couple of times he'd bent me over and pounded his fist into my back. He could be very mean and was by far stronger than I was, so for me to punch him in the face like was a sure sign of insanity on my part. For more than a week, I walked about in constant fear of his retaliation.

A week after Greg and Ron had gone home, the boys were in school and Lawrence was out on the road. I was in the kitchen washing up the breakfast dishes when I heard a car driving up. Looking out the front window, I saw that it was Michael's car.

I didn't have enough time to close and lock the front and back doors without him seeing me, so I was trapped. With no one to protect me, I did the next best thing: I went to one of the cupboard drawers and grabbed a towel and one of the biggest butcher knives we had. I stood by the sink, with the island counter between me and the back door, pretending to wipe the knife.

I heard the car door shut and his footsteps coming towards the back porch. My heart raced at the sound of the squeaking hinges of the porch door open and shut.

As Michael crossed the porch, he called out to whoever was home. Reluctantly, I told him to come in, all the while maintaining my defensive position and trying to look as calm as possible. I readied myself in case I needed to use the knife.

He walked only a short ways into the kitchen and stopped on the other side of the counter, facing me. As calmly as I could, I asked him what he wanted. He grinned, put a hand to his chin, and gently rubbed the place where I'd hit him.

"I'm sorry I took so long to come back and apologize for not going home when you asked me," he said, unexpectedly. "I would have come sooner, but when you punched me in the jaw it swelled up and hurt so bad that I could hardly talk or eat."

Was this a trick?

With an apologetic smile, he commented on my upper cut to the jaw. Said it had been a good one.

Slowly, I released the breath I'd been holding, then carefully put the knife back into the drawer. I also apologized to him for my part in the fight.

What really gets me in all this is that I don't know why Michael couldn't have stayed with us. Why had I thought he had to go home to Winnipeg after partying with us? He had been every bit as drunk and stoned as we were. It's taken me a long time to realize the injustice of that night and how stupid I acted. Although the house had been crowded, surely Michael could have pulled up a piece of rug somewhere.

I was to blame for every bad thing that happened that night. I'm so very sorry for having hurt him like I did.

Greg came back to spend a few weeks with us because he had been talking to the captain of the Ste. Anne's slow-pitch team. He'd gone to a tryout and now they wanted him on their team. He played all positions with skill, but he excelled at pitcher and shortstop. He had some thirty or more trophies and a picture album full of newspaper clippings of some of his achievements in fastball, softball, and hockey. In his early twenties, he had been sent to Ontario to train at a hockey school, but he'd only lasted a few weeks because he drank too much. It's really too bad, because they'd seen something valuable in him.

Anyway, he joined the Ste. Anne team and agreed to play anytime he was in town.

My friendship with him grew tighter. When we were at the bar, we partnered at the pool table. He taught me a few tricks that really helped my game. Since we didn't have much money, we played a lot of pool at five dollars a game, then drank a lot of beer.

One particular night, a guy named Albert came up to our table and challenged us. He had approached me on several occasions and there were times when I'd thought he might be interested in getting to know me better. He was well-mannered and nice-looking, but for whatever reason I had stayed clear of him.

So when Albert and his uncle challenged me and Greg to a game, we had no choice but to take them on. Not far into the game, I started to lose patience with him. Between shots, Albert would go back to his table and talk to his uncle, looking at me while they talked. Also, he and I agreed to share a pool cue, but he kept holding on to it and forcing me to yank it away. This all made me even more determined to win.

I was puzzled that Albert had asked me to play pool with him after what I'd done to him one morning at Keira's place. I had gone to see her early in the morning hoping she would have some drugs because I felt strung out and needed to take the edge off. She didn't have anything, but since I was already there she invited me in and we had coffee.

After a half-hour, Albert and his uncle had dropped by. They made me really uncomfortable and I was feeling rattled. Albert sat next to me, and at one point he reached down with his right hand and slowly raised my pantleg to see how high my boot went. I'd grabbed his wrist and shoved him away, telling him to never touch me again. Then I grabbed the back of his chair and tipped it over sideways, balancing it on two legs. I kept him there a few moments before letting him go. I figured that was my cue to depart.

By the time I got to the kitchen and put my winter coat on, Albert had caught up with me. He backed me into a corner between the fridge and the wall. He may have thought he was being romantic, but it almost got him booted in the family jewels. Since this wasn't my home, I held my temper in check.

He asked me why I'd done that to him and I told him that I didn't like anyone touching me. Then I ducked under his arm and headed for the door.

I figured I'd embarrassed him, but apparently not if he was so willing to play pool.

Anyway, we won the pool game. Just before cut-off, Albert came over to my table and asked if I would go with him to a party.

"Barb, what is this?" Greg jokingly asked. "You came out with me and now this guy comes over and tries to take you away from me? Which is it, him or me?"

Well, I just looked at Greg and burst out laughing. I laughed so hard that my head ended up on the table. It was just too funny.

Albert didn't quite know what to make of this, so he turned around and left.

A little later, Greg and I said goodnight to everyone and started walking home. On the way, I found a can and for the rest of the way home we played kick the can down the middle of the road. It felt so refreshing to be with someone who was every bit as wild and free as I was. We were so much alike, just wanting to enjoy ourselves, even if it meant acting like kids.

Once we were home and found that everyone was already in bed, we finally discovered that we had the same feelings for one another. Instead of Greg sleeping on a mattress on the floor that night, he ended up in my bed and stayed there until he had to go home.

Bedrest

During this time, I had another serious bout of abdominal pain, very much like the pain I'd had back in Thompson after my biopsy. It was so severe that I felt as though I was going to have a baby, only I knew I wasn't pregnant. I could barely walk and it felt as though my insides were falling out.

The doctor didn't know what was wrong, but he ordered complete bedrest. Since Lawrence was out on a road trip, I had the use of his bed to rest. So for the next three days I was pampered and catered to by Greg and all four boys. Greg cooked our meals and served me in bed.

Being served was so new to me. I felt undeserving. I always served others without a thought, but it was hard to receive it.

After three days of rest, I was back to normal. The only thing the doctor could come up with was that I must have had an ovarian cyst. Having gone through all that pain, I should have at least had a baby to show for it, but the greatest blessing was finding out how much Greg cared for me. It moved me to tears.

Of course, the dreaded day arrived when Greg had to return home. There was great sadness amongst us as we said our goodbyes. There was no telling how long it would be until we saw him again, if we ever did.

When it came to my relationships, I'd gotten used to the uncertainty. Here today, gone tomorrow. There were promises of phone calls, but even they faded over time.

Our home felt empty after he was gone, but the love he left behind lingered. I was able to say to my children openly and freely that I truly loved them. We were all the richer for having known him.

Thirty-Two
The Inevitable

I had postponed the inevitable long enough. It was almost two years since the doctor had pronounced it necessary for my right eye to be removed. It had taken that long for me to get past what Brent had said, and I also really didn't want to have my eye cut out, thrown in a garbage can, and replaced with a piece of plastic I would have to carry around in my head for the rest of my life. Man, the thought of that terrified me.

Was I going to become some kind of freak? What man would want to be with a cyclops? Would I no longer have any value?

I couldn't put it off any longer. Day after day, it had weighed heavily on my soul until I couldn't take it anymore. No matter how drunk or stoned I got, I couldn't forget reality. Every time I looked in the mirror, I was reminded that I might soon go blind. The eye was dead and decaying.

It was time to stop procrastinating and do something about it.

The dreaded day soon arrived. With my head held high, Lawrence drove me to Winnipeg and dropped me off at the hospital on his way to work. I made light of going in by myself, because I didn't want to put pressure on anyone.

I didn't feel all that brave once I walked through the front doors of the hospital. It felt like doomsday and I dragged my feet to the admittance desk.

I was given a room with a young woman who was waiting for open-heart surgery. Talking to her took my mind off my own situation. My heart went out to her. Yes, in this case someone had it worse than I did.

The next morning, two nurses came in and prepped me for surgery. I was given a needle to make me drowsy, and then they transferred me onto a gurney. Off we went to the elevator, all the while the nurses chatting soothingly.

When they pulled me out of the elevator, I saw down the long, dimly lit corridor. In my drugged state, I made out the bodies laying on gurneys, much like my own, on both sides. As we passed on our way to the operating room, I realized they were waiting their turn; they seemed to be parked wherever there was empty space. Through open doorways, I peered into other operating rooms at the teams of doctors and nurses handing each other instruments; what affected me most were their blood-stained hands and blood-spattered surgery gowns.

It reminded me of a butcher's shop. As far as I was concerned, the nurses could take me right back upstairs.

No such luck, though. Soon I was parked outside a room with an operation in progress.

What a morbid place, I thought as I went into panic mode. *Are we in Vietnam? Is this a scene from M*A*S*H?*

I was way beyond scared and completely at the mercy of people I didn't even know. I felt really alone. But I'd been alone every other time I'd gone into the hospital, so this was no exception.

Reality had set in. They were going to take my eye. Today.

Nearly overcome by panic, the sound of running water grabbed my attention. I turned my head to look through a window where two doctors were stripping off their surgical gowns to scrub up for another operation. Elsewhere, two nurses were pushing away the person who had been on these doctors' operating table.

I didn't have long to wait before a male nurse came out and cheerfully wheeled me into the operating room. I was transferred onto the operating table and covered in a warm blanket while someone took my left arm and strapped it to a board. The big overhead light nearly blinded me.

Hey listen, I change my mind, I wanted to say. *I don't really want to do this. I was just kidding, right?*

I felt the prick of a needle entering the back of my hand. This was going to happen. Almost immediately, darkness came to my rescue.

Recovery

With a full body shudder that felt like a million prickles exploding over every inch of my body, I suddenly woke up. I felt terribly nauseous and light-headed. My hand went straight to my eye and was met by a thick bandage wrapped around my head. I felt utterly miserable.

They took it. It's lying in a garbage can somewhere inside this building. Oh God, what have I done? I think I'm going to throw up.

Distracted from the misery, I heard a noise coming from the foot of my bed. Moving my head slowly, because I was so disorientated and dizzy, I saw Lawrence and Michael standing at the end of the bed watching me with the saddest expressions I'd ever seen. They seemed so full of sympathy that they didn't know what to say. That was a first.

I wanted to throw up and cry at the same time, and it didn't help that I knew they felt uncomfortable. I felt the need to comfort them. These two big strapping men looked so sad and helpless. They looked in worse condition than I was!

So, like so many times before, I put on my reassuring mask and pretended all was well. I could handle this.

They didn't stay long, probably because they didn't know what to do for me. With great urgency, I wanted to scream after them, "Don't go. Please don't go. I need you. Don't leave me here alone. I don't know what to do. I'm scared. Come back. Please come back." I desperately wanted them to come back and take me up in their strong arms and tell me that everything was going to be okay and that it was all right to cry.

But even if they had come back, I wouldn't have known how to accept that kind of kindness. I had to be tough and strong. Crying was a sign of weakness.

I was so much like a wounded animal, needing to go off on my own and lick my wounds and not let anyone in.

Tears ran down one side of my face as I whispered, "Please come back. I need you."

But they were gone. Tired from all the wild thoughts, emotions, and anaesthetic, I rolled over onto my side, curled up in a fetal position, and gently rocked myself side to side until the blackness came for me.

The next time I awoke, I was alone. I didn't know what to expect once the bandages were removed, but whatever I looked like now, I would have to live with it for the rest of my life. Once again, I suppressed my emotions, shoving them deep inside where I wouldn't have to feel them. I would hold my head high and pretend all was well in my world, no matter what.

The very idea of seeing inside my eye socket sickened me. I had a wild imagination. Would I see my skull? Would the glass eye be a round ball? Was it already in place? I didn't know. No one told me anything and I hadn't asked any questions.

Finally the surgeon came by and informed me that I would have to go to an ocular prosthetics office to get an artificial eye fitted. This surprised me; I guess I'd just figured there would be an eye replacement when I woke up from the operation. He then took off the large bandage and examined his handiwork. Then he covered the socket with a smaller gauze bandage that he taped to my face.

He explained the procedure he had performed. After cutting the eyeball away from the muscles, he'd taken the muscles and wrapped them around a marble-like object and smoothed them out so that an artificial eye would fit snugly overtop. Once the new eye was in, the muscles would move along with my other eye and give it the appearance of being real. That was comforting to hear.

When I left the hospital a day or two later, Michael took me to get fitted for the artificial eye. On our way, we joked about all the things I could do with the eye, like drop it in beer and just generally freak people out. Laughing helped to mask my true feelings. I didn't want anyone to feel sorry for me.

I was grateful for Michael's support as he sat with me in the ocularist's office. The ocularist took the bandage off and looked under the eyelid to see what he had to work with. He then studied my lone eye and walked over to a cabinet that held many thin drawers. We watched as he opened each one, revealing artificial eyes of every colour imaginable. Seeing all those eyes literally freaked me right out. I'd been disturbed by eyeballs ever since I was a kid, and now here I was looking at drawers full of them, lined up perfectly in trays, all of them looking back at me. Panic almost forced me to stumble out of my chair and rush out of the office. It was like my worst nightmares come true.

Oh God, help me get through this.

I had been under the impression that an artificial eye was always round, but that was not the case. Mine was to be shaped like a half-moon.

The doctor chose one out of a drawer, opened my eyelid, placed the eye inside the socket, then stepped back to see what it looked like. That one didn't work, so he took it out and went searching again.

When he found one that worked, he produced a mirror and asked me how it felt. All I knew was that it didn't look like my eye and it felt foreign and extremely uncomfortable. He said I would adjust to it and that the muscles would shrink over time and I'd need a replacement. I took his word for it. I'd had all I could take. I quickly paid for the eye and got out of there.

It wasn't until later that I realized the ocularist hadn't shown me how to take it out or how to put it back in. Nor had he told me how to take care of it. My assumption was that I should just leave it in, like people who wear false teeth. I felt horribly self-conscience in the presence of other people. It was like having a great big zit on my face, something I wanted to hide.

As much as I hated losing my eye, I never thought there would come a day when I'd actually thank God for it.

Recently, I was texting a dear friend of mine. Boomer was lying in the hospital, waiting to be discharged after having had one of his big toes removed due to diabetes. Because of my own amputation, we were able to joke about it.

When I got off the phone with him, he felt better knowing there was someone who understood what he was going through. I cried and actually thanked God for allowing my eye to have been taken so that I could help my friend.

I hadn't ever thought there would come a day when I'd be thankful for that, but it came! It just goes to show that even the ugly things that happen to us can be used to help others.

A couple of days after I got home from the hospital, Lawrence discovered that I'd been holding out on him by saving some of my welfare money. I didn't know why he was angry about it, because I always paid my share while also taking care of the home and his child.

The reason I had been saving is that I'd been thinking it was about time for me and my boys to get our own place. After all, we'd been living with Lawrence for over a year. He, on the other hand, told me in anger that I had two days to get out of his house or else he would throw me out.

I didn't get it. Why was I wrong to want my own place?

It wasn't until years later that I found the real reason, or at least one of them. Lawrence told me that he'd had a lot of bills to pay and needed the help. What I should have done was talk the situation over with him, but I hadn't been mature enough to think about doing something as sensible as that.

So now what was I to do? My circumstances just kept getting worse and worse.

The new eye kept festering with discharge and I didn't know how to properly care for it other than to wash around the eyelids with a warm, wet cloth. In this condition, I didn't want to uproot my boys, but we had no choice in the matter and I didn't have enough money to find a home for us. We were once again homeless.

That night, Greg phoned to see how I was holding up. Just hearing his voice was enough to cause me to break down and tell him everything that had happed since leaving the hospital. He immediately told me to hang on, that he would see what he could do.

When he called back, he told me to pack everything I owned and he'd be there in a day or two to pick us up and take us to Saskatchewan. He had borrowed money and was coming to get us. I'd move whatever belongings I didn't need to Michael's place, where the rest of my furniture was still stored, and then we would come back and get everything once we were settled.

It was unbelievable. One minute we were homeless, the next we were moving to Saskatchewan. The greatest drawback was leaving Troy behind. What was going to happen with him? By this time, he was like one of my own sons.

Thirty - Three
Saskatchewan

Greg's mother agreed that the boys and I should stay on their farm until we could find our own place. His parents were my Aunt Jenna and Uncle Ryan on my mother's side.

We were welcomed with open arms by Aunt Jenna, but Uncle Ryan and his two older brothers weren't all that accommodating. They were in their late seventies, so it was a stretch to have so many young people invading their space.

Right from the beginning, Uncle Ryan didn't like me and I couldn't understand why since I hadn't done anything to him. But I felt his whole-hearted rejection, and it stung. He would literally turn his back on me when I walked into a room. He wouldn't look at or even speak to me. The whole time I knew him, I walked on eggshells around him.

I was told not to pay any attention to him, but that was easier said than done. It bothered me and hurt me deeply.

After several years of this treatment, Greg finally told me the reason his father had treated me that way. One was that his dad had planned for Greg to marry his friend's daughter. When I showed up, I disrupted their plan. The other reason is that Greg had taken and sold a couple of his dad's guns in order to pay to come get me. I was ignorant of all this, but was punished for what Greg had done nonetheless.

The first night at the farm, Greg and I shared a foldout tent trailer which was parked in the driveway. The boys shared a room in the house.

When I awoke in the morning, my eye was glued shut from the discharge. I had an infection and it was getting worse. In frustration, I rubbed the itchy eyelid—and just like that, the artificial eye popped out and fell on the floor. I was mortified. Now what was I supposed to do? The eye had never been out. I felt so embarrassed as Greg bent over to pick it up and hand it back to me. This was no way to start a new relationship!

Greg suggested we go into the house and get some water to clean the eye. Fortunately, it was still too early for anyone to be up. I found a mirror hanging on the wall and headed straight for it. I could see how crusted and sunken my eyelid was.

Greg handed me a damp washcloth and I cleaned away the discharge. When that was done, for the first time I was able to see what the eye socket looked like. With a shaky hand and panicking heart, I spread the lids apart and stared at the socket. I saw angry red tissue smoothed flat over the round ball the doctor had told me about. I let out an immense sigh of relief to discover there was no skull bone visible.

I washed the artificial eye in clean water and got ready for the moment of truth. Would I be able to put it back correctly, without injuring anything inside the socket or causing pain? I didn't even know which way was rightside-up. Taking a guess, I proceeded to gently push it into place. I managed to get it right the first time. What a great relief it was to discover there wasn't much to it.

Weary and ashamed, I looked over at Greg and saw the most compassionate look on his face. He had watched me overcome another one of my life's greatest hurdles. I hadn't known if he would reject me after seeing the reality of the eye, after what I'd gone through with Brent. Instead he took me in his arms, held me tight, and assured me that everything was going to be all right.

For nearly a year, I had to wipe the eye clean every morning and throughout the day. The socket burned and itched constantly, like someone had thrown sand in my eye. Sometimes I'd rub my lower eyelid and the eye would flip upside-down and make it appear as though I were looking at the ceiling. Unless I looked in a mirror or someone told me, the eye would remain that way. It was extremely embarrassing and annoying.

I absolutely hated this thing, but I had to put up with it until someone finally came along and advised me to see an ocularist in Saskatoon. A crack was discovered in the prosthesis, and that's what had caused the infection. Also, the artificial eye was way too big for the socket.

This new ocularist didn't just pull another eye from a drawer. She made a new prosthetic which fit comfortably. It's quite an interesting process to make prosthesis. It's also a full day affair and a very expensive piece of jewellery to wear in one's face.

Recently I asked my new ocularist if the first eye was supposed to have been taken out of a drawer. With disgust, she told me that the first ocularist should have made a new eye that fit my socket right from the beginning—that is, if he'd even known how to do it. Apparently there are many so-called ocularists making easy money by pulling prosthetics out of drawers.

Langenburg

We were at the farm for nearly a month when a two-bedroom house came available in nearby Langenburg, ten miles east of Churchbridge. It was a given that Greg would move in with us. He got us on welfare, and so we were able to move in right away and get the boys settled into school. We also got enough money to return to Winnipeg to pick up all my belongings. It felt great to once again have our own home.

Because Greg didn't have a car, we hadn't gone out much until this, but now that we were in town we had a newfound freedom. Greg had quite a few friends in Langenburg and it didn't take long for me to get to know them. Most of them were drinkers, and of course I found a dealer.

Greg was especially excited for us to meet his best friend Bruce and his wife Dee and their two children. I felt accepted immediately. There were times when I would walk the mile or so down the highway to visit with Dee. When I did that, I carried a knife for protection should anybody driving by decide to harm me. I believe I was crazy enough to use it.

Now, Greg was an avid ball player and it didn't take long for the Langenburg team to recruit him. Of course, this meant partying after their practices, regular games, and during the weekend tournaments. So instead of hanging out at biker gatherings, I was now hanging out with fun-loving ball players. It was quite an adjustment for me.

We were comfortably settled in our new home when Greg got a call from the Ste. Anne ball team to see if he would come back to play for them in the Manitoba provincials. Greg was delighted, but we didn't have the money. Fortunately, the team had already decided to send a small four-seat propeller plane to pick us up in Russell, Manitoba. All we had to do was get to Russell, which was only about fifteen minutes from Langenburg. It was to be an all-expense paid weekend trip. The boys went to the farm, and we were headed back to Ste. Anne.

Neither of us had ever flown in a small plane and we were nervous. I had flown from one end of Canada to the other, but always in jets. This little plane was a whole different ball game!

Two of the team's players were waiting in the plane when we arrived at the airstrip. Greg and I sat in the back seats as we took off. It was awesome, although when we passed through air pockets it felt like our stomachs lurched up into our throats. We couldn't believe our good fortune.

It didn't take long for us to arrive. We were given a hardy welcome back at the bar and Greg was given instructions for what was expected of him during the tournament. He was to pitch. No big surprise there! While they talked strategy, I caught up with some of my old friends, one being my supplier. It was exceptionally good to see her.

For the next two days, I sat through all the games. The team ended up in the playoffs.

At the final game, it was hotter than hell. Most times I sat by myself because I didn't know the other players' wives. Besides, they were far too straight for me. But around the middle of the game, I saw someone I knew who was heading back to town, so I caught a ride with him and had him drop me off at the bar where it was air-conditioned and out of the sun. I had started to get sunburned.

For old time's sake, I headed to the pool table and before long I had a challenger. About an hour later, the whole team burst through the bar's door, ecstatic and loudly announcing that they had won. It was truly a shame that I hadn't been there to see Greg pitch the last inning, and I'm sure he was disappointed I wasn't there as well.

That night, the bar hosted a grand celebration and everyone was in high spirits. Greg was given a gold medallion which he wore proudly. The next day, toting a massive hangover, we managed to board the plane again. The return trip was just as exciting.

Not long after we had moved into our quaint little home, a couple in their late sixties moved into the empty house next door. At first they seemed very friendly. They talked to our boys and said hi to us. Everything appeared normal.

Within a week of meeting them, however, a large truck drove into their backyard and dumped metal poles and link fencing onto their lawn. We figured they were getting a fence, which seemed normal enough. Then we discovered that they were installing barbed-wire along the top and bottom. Now that was really strange. We had to wonder why they did that. Maybe it had something to do with the parties we held? I figure they must have been scared of us. That was reasonable.

One day, we heard that the old man had a .22 rifle sitting by his back door. We also discovered that they raised rabbits in their house for eating. So if we were strange to them, they were definitely strange to us.

We never had any run-ins with them. Why, the old woman even came to our door one day offering me two neatly bagged rabbits. My dad had hunted rabbit when I was a kid, so I couldn't stand the idea of eating those cute little critters. I graciously declined her offer and hoped I didn't offend her.

One afternoon while I was walking past her place, I found the old woman down on her knees weeding along her front sidewalk. I said hi and was about to move on when she returned my greeting and asked, out of the blue, if I knew Jesus.

I stopped just long enough to tell her that I knew who Jesus was. Then I continued on my way. I figured I knew Jesus, because when I was seven I had gone to a Salvation Army church and heard the story of Him being beaten and flogged before dying on a cross. Seeing the cross hanging on the wall had made me want to cry.

I didn't understand then what Jesus's death meant, but I did know what it meant for a person to get beat up—and it broke my heart. I fell in love with Him that day.

I also went to a few other churches with friends. We heard about Jesus and sang beautiful songs, although it was hard for me to comprehend that Jesus could love me when we sang "Jesus Loves Me." Just before I had left Thompson, the Jehovah's Witnesses stopped by my place and left their literature. Jehovah's Witnesses had also visited Aunt Jenna's farm, sharing their faith. Even though I was usually drunk or stoned when they came by, I'd invite them in anyway because they were friends of my aunt.

While I was interested in learning about God and Jesus, I wasn't interested in making any changes in my life. I didn't know I had to.

Not long after my neighbour asked me about Jesus, the pastor from Aunt Jenna's church came by. This man sat with me and explained for more than an hour about the Trinity: God the Father, Jesus the Son, and the Holy Spirit. I argued that there was no such a thing, because that's what the Jehovah's Witnesses had taught me. He was very patient and showed me scripture to back up what he was saying.

Still, I was stubborn and wouldn't back down. I really wanted to believe him, but I was loyal to the Witnesses.

What really stood out to me, though, was that when he finally got up to leave, he wasn't angry. He smiled and thanked me for inviting him in.

Only a few months after this visit, that pastor was in a car accident in British Columbia. I was told that a log came off a logging truck, went right through his windshield, and decapitated him. I never forgot him, and one day I hope to meet him again in heaven, to tell him that he was right, and also to thank him for his patience in sharing the truth.

However, I would not find that truth for several more years.

Therefore go and make disciples of all nations, baptizing them in the name of the Father and of the Son and of the Holy Spirit... (Matthew 28:19)

May the grace of the Lord Jesus Christ, and the love of God, and the fellowship of the Holy Spirit be with you all. (2 Corinthians 13:14)

Thirty-Four
Unleashed Rage

Sometimes when Greg and I were drinking at our one and only local bar and we didn't want the night to end, we'd pay someone to take us to the Russell Inn in Manitoba where we could have an extra hour of drinking. With the time change, Manitoba was an hour behind Saskatchewan.

On one of those visits, a very unfortunate event took place, one that stung me to the core. My reaction to it troubled me long after it was over.

It was Friday night and we were hanging out with our friend Boo along with Greg's twin brother Ron and his girlfriend Marla. Someone came up with the idea of going to Russell and everyone agreed it was a great idea.

Grabbing a case of beer for the road, we headed for Boo's car. As we cruised the highway, we were all in high spirits, sucking back beers, joking, and jostling each other while keeping a close watch for any hidden police patrols.

On entering the bar in Russell, we found it to be packed. We managed to find an empty table somewhere in the middle of the room. A great-sounding band was playing and the crowd was in full swing. Since the waitresses were so busy, we ordered several rounds each to make sure we had enough liquor on the table for last call.

Everything was going great until Marla, who was fairly drunk, made a comment I didn't agree with. It wasn't anything to get bothered about, but she became angry and retaliated by saying something else I didn't agree with.

Then, out of nowhere, she really said the wrong thing to me. She called me a glass-eyed b——. That struck every nerve in my body and my whole demeanour changed. I went from having a good time to wanting to maim her.

Before I realized what I was doing, I was up out of my chair and charging around the table to get at her. She stood up with a shocked and frightened look on her face, knowing she'd gone too far.

In a fit of rage, I grabbed her by the throat and slammed her taller and heavier body up against a square pillar beside our table and glued her there. I looked her straight in the eyes with so much hatred that her began to cry, pleading with me not to hurt her.

The hatred I felt for her at that moment was the same hatred I held for my dad. It was so great that if I'd had that knife I usually carried on me, I would probably have taken it out and plunged it between her ribs.

Instead, with my fingers digging into her throat, I clenched my free hand into a fist and drew it back with every intention of beating her terrified face into a bloody pulp.

That's when Ron grabbed my arm to stop me. In defence of his old lady, he proceeded to threaten me.

Without releasing my hold on Marla, the frightened little parasite, I looked him square on and told him where he could go and how to get there. I wasn't backing down. She had this coming. None of them knew what I'd gone through to get this damned piece of plastic that had been shoved into my skull for the rest of my life. I hated it more than anyone could imagine. For Marla to throw it in my face… it was the most heartless thing anyone could do to me. I hated her for saying it and I hated him for sticking up for her. I would have taken them both on if it had come to that.

Something inside me had snapped. I'd taken everything that had been thrown my way, but I couldn't take anymore. Marla was going to die, and if it took everyone coming down on me, so be it.

That was about the time Greg stepped in and stopped his brother. Someone had to talk me down, and ever so slowly and reluctantly I released my hold on Marla's throat. I looked at her with utter contempt, took my seat, and downed my beer.

Every nerve in my body quivered with rage. I felt eyes on me from all over the bar, but they could all go to hell for all I cared. I had nothing to say to anyone. I wouldn't even allow Greg in.

Like a wounded animal, I went off by myself to lick my wounds.

Marla had no idea how deeply she had injured me and I hadn't realized how capable I was of putting my dangerous emotions into action. Normally I would have let her nasty name-calling ride, but today something had been different. I had wanted to *destroy* her.

It frightened me, but no one would have known it to look at me. Was I sorry for what I had done, for what I would have done? No. I decided that I hated her, and it took a long time for me to let it go.

Let's just say it wasn't a jovial ride home. Marla stayed clear of me for a long time after that, at least until she got up the nerve to approach me and apologize. And I forgave her.

But between her name-calling and what Brent had said to me about not knowing how he could live with someone with only one eye, I became even more conscious and ashamed.

Marla's words had unleashed a rage that had been burning inside of me ever since I'd seen my father first hurt my mother. All those years of injustice were loosed, and after that incident it came to the surface many other times, in the form of angry retorts, defence mechanisms, and acts of self-preservation. I was like a pressure cooker.

Little did I know that I needed serious medical help, not for the body (I'd had my fill of that) but for my very disturbed mind. I thought I was doing okay because I got up every day able to function. I cleaned house, fed Greg and the kids, and grew a great garden. What more could one ask for? So what if I drove my fists into mirrors and walls? I was all right; it was just those stupid people around me who set me off. Why did they have to do that?

In retrospect, Marla's words released something very evil, but I wasn't waging war against her; it was against all the injustices and torment I had faced in my life. I just wanted to put an end to it.

From that one stupid act in Russell, word got around. Because of it, an unwelcome reputation proceeded me in that small Saskatchewan town. Great. And along with this came a misplaced sense of pride. My need to be as hardened as any man was strong. Most women I met turned me off. I couldn't stand their femininity.

Thirty-Five
Life of Danger

Greg took us out to his parents' farm on the weekends to visit his mom and allow the boys to run free. They still had to be careful, though, in case a bull or some cows came grazing too close to the fenced-off farmhouse; my uncle and his brothers didn't raise animals or plant crops anymore because of their age, so they rented out their land for cattle-grazing.

On one occasion, the boys piled into the back of an old truck and Greg drove us far out onto their land, away from any buildings, to do a little target practice. We all stood in the box of the truck and used the roof of the cab as an armrest. I had done this when I was thirteen with my brother and boyfriend. I had proved to be a pretty good shot. Now my boys were proving that they followed in their mother's footsteps. Once they got their feel for the gun, they didn't often miss their targets. It made me proud.

Greg also taught them how to set traps and skin small animals. Joey turned out to be a natural at trapping.

The boys loved it at the farm. During hunting season, Greg sometimes took us with him into the bush. The boys were still too young to get hunting licences, but they got to be a part of the hunts anyway.

One year I decided it was time I got my licence. We stopped by the bar, dressed in our fatigues, to pick up a case of beer before heading out for the day. The regular old coots began to tease me for dressing up in fatigues and carrying my own knife. I bet them I would get a deer and be back to pick up a case of beer for celebration purposes.

Which I did.

But that's not the whole story.

Greg and I were with a dear friend that day who owned a truck that had a skidoo in the back. We'd been out hunting for most of the day, and the sun was already low in the sky before we finally spotted a deer. She was a nice-sized doe in the middle of a big open field. I was sitting next to the rolled-down window, aiming my .303 rifle. I had been drinking and knew I shouldn't have a gun in my hands, never mind shooting it out the window of a truck with the sun going down, but the guys encouraged me to give it a try.

So I stuck the barrel out the window, took aim, and fired. I emptied a full clip at her and missed. I was about to give up when Greg passed me another clip and suggested that I try again.

Bingo. She dropped.

Amazed, we got out of the truck and cautiously walked out to her to make sure she was really dead. If she wasn't, I would have to shoot her in the head.

I looked for any sign of movement, then poked at her with the barrel of my gun. There still didn't seem to be any movement. Next I needed to find out where I'd hit her. My biggest concern was that I'd shot her in the gut, which was one of the worst deaths possible.

Once I confirmed that she was dead, I took out my knife to see if I had what it took to slice her throat. That was when I found out that I had hit her in the jugular. Warm blood covered my hand and knife. Even though she had already bled out, I still had to see if I had what it took to slice her throat.

It felt absolutely appalling, but I said nothing to the guys about how I felt about cutting her. I didn't want to look like a wimp.

Our friend took his skidoo off the truck and drove up to the deer. He and Greg tied her, then hauled her onto the vehicle. Off we went to hang her for skinning in a friend's garage.

By now, it was dark, and before we did anything else I wanted to go back to the bar and pick up a case of beer to celebrate. The old guys were still there, and when they saw me they started teasing me again. I let them know I had gotten my deer, which shut them up real fast.

With immense pride, I walked out carrying a dozen beers. It was time to skin a deer.

For that kill, I won a trophy and had my picture in the paper. But I didn't deserve it. It had been done illegally—while drinking and shooting out a window at dusk—and so my victory didn't taste very good. Breaking the law took all the joy out of the hunt.

But of course I didn't confide that to anyone.

It later turned out that because I'd hit her in the throat, she had bled back into her front legs and the meat was ruined.

Another year, we went out to the farm to hunt. Greg and I were up before the crack of dawn, dressed in bright orange overalls and hunting gear. We grabbed a quick breakfast, then headed out into the cold before the boys were up.

We trudged through about a foot of fresh snow, heading towards the tree line way beyond the house. From there, we moved into another quarter-section of land where there were no farmhouses.

As the morning began to dawn, we were awed by the beauty and stillness of the land. It was so peaceful.

We broke out of the trees and stood partway into an open field, looking for deer tracks. The silence was shattered with a loud bang and the sound of a bullet whizzing over our heads. Greg grabbed me and pulled me to the ground as another shot rang out.

There were other hunters in the area, and they must have been on the other side of the trees and couldn't see our bright orange coveralls.

A couple more shots were taken, and then it grew silent. We hugged the ground long enough to make sure the hunters were gone before we stood up.

Shaken, we got to our feet and decided there was no use continuing. If there had been any deer in the area, they would be gone now. And the chance of us getting shot seemed high. Those hunters had buck fever and seemed to be shooting at anything that moved.

Playing Chicken

Our friend Boo had a sporty little car which was his pride and joy. One afternoon, he came by the house to see if we wanted to go to his girlfriend's place in Bredenbury, which was about twenty miles west.

Greg sat up front while the boys and I listening to the latest hits in the backseat. Boo drove the back roads so he and Greg could drink a beer while we travelled. We spent the afternoon in Bredenbury drinking and smoking pot.

On the way home, we decided it would be shorter to take the highway back. Boo seemed well enough to drive. No worries, right? We were driving along, talking and laughing about something or other, when suddenly Boo said, "Let's play chicken with a semi!"

Then he pulled over into oncoming traffic and we were facing down a semi moving at top speed. We screamed at Boo to stop playing around and get back on the right side of the road, but all he did was laugh like a crazed fool.

Almost at the last minute Boo pulled his car back into his own lane; we felt the wind push our little car as the semi blasted past us.

There's no describing the fear one faces at a moment like that. We were so angry with him, yet all the idiot could do was laugh.

When he dropped us off at our place, I couldn't get the boys out of the car fast enough.

Unfortunately, Boo had the opportunity to do that to us another time, even though he had promised not to. I always figured he would die that way.

Drug Bust

Greg and I didn't get around unless someone drove us. His license had been revoked for several years, but when we were offered a car, such as to go to Winnipeg, Greg took it. Once there, I called my friend Ivy who lived in Ste. Anne and asked if she and her family could join us at another friend's house that day. She agreed to meet us at Sheila's place.

Shortly after arriving, Sheila informed us that she had been visited the day before by the police and they had confiscated a vast number of marijuana plants from her basement. That was surprising to hear, but it didn't stop us from pulling out the drugs we had brought along.

Our kids, six or seven in all, were used to these kinds of gatherings, so they went off to play in another part of the house.

As the afternoon wore on, the stereo played 70s rock. The warmth from the sun eventually faded, the lengthening shadows lulling us into a lazy state of mind. Ah, it was good to be in Winnipeg again.

While we sat lounging around, a big bald-headed dude suddenly appeared through the living room and kitchen door with another burly guy just behind him. His sudden appearance made me uncomfortable, but I figured he was one of Sheila's friends because she had been leaning over the coffee table rolling a joint—and when she saw him, she picked up the bag of pot she had been rolling from and handed it to him. The big guy smiled.

And then all hell broke loose. He wasted no time in telling us they were cops and we were busted. We were read our rights and told not to move. As the front door of the living room was forced open, several other officers came in. I'm not sure how many police were actually there, but at this point I was pretty shaken. I'd never been busted before. Not a good feeling.

Some of the officers searched the house to see if there were people in the house other than the kids who were playing in the basement. I remember hearing a comment about all the beer in the fridge; why wasn't there any food? With all the kids we had, what were they to eat?

The first cop ordered me and Ivy to empty our purses on the table. I was rather surprised to find a gram of hash hidden in mine.

If I'd known that was there, I could have sold it, I remembered thinking.

But then I got scared. What happened to someone who got caught with a gram of hash? I'd heard plenty of stories. In those days, it didn't take much to land you in jail.

Ivy found an old dried-out joint she hadn't known about in the bottom of her purse and said aloud much the same as what I had thought. I felt really bad for having invited her along, because this was going to cause her trouble. Some friend I was.

The drama only got more intense, though, and soon I was glad to have her along. The cops wanted each of us strip-searched. Ivy had some experience with this sort of situation, and she told them that if they wanted to search us girls, they'd better get a female cop to do the job. Wow! She really knew her stuff. As naïve as I was, I would have allowed them to do it.

So they called in a female cop and the three of us girls were taken into the bathroom one at a time and were searched. That was humiliating. I felt violated during this whole procedure.

At the police station, we were fingerprinted and got mugshots taken. Now I had a record.

There were no drugs found on the men, so they took care of the kids while we girls went in and got our pictures taken.

Before leaving the station, I was told I would have to appear before a judge in Winnipeg. Up to this point, my only court experience had been getting a divorce. My court date was set for several months in the future. My main thought was, *How am I going to afford to come back to Manitoba?*

The whole experience shook my world. What if they threw me in jail? I was told that sometimes happened on the first offence. And since I was only living common-law with Greg, he had no rights to take over the care of the boys. What would happen to them?

I'd always said that my dealing days would be over if I ever got busted. Well, that day had arrived.

The next day, we packed up the car and stopped by Sheila's to say good-bye. As it so happened, Michael came over right around the time that Sheila was producing another bag of pot. We smoked a few joints and drank a few beers while the kids once again played in the basement.

All was going well until Sheila's ex-boyfriend showed up uninvited. They had a fight and he stormed out the kitchen door. He had to walk by the next-door neighbours, who were Indigenous and happened to be outside having a party of their own.

Michael had also gone out, but he returned almost immediately with blood spilling down the side of his face from a gash on his forehead.

"They're throwing tomahawks out there," he said.

I quickly grabbed a towel and held it to his head to stop the bleeding. Then the door burst open again and Sheila's ex came barrelling through the door and slammed it shut. He'd been cut, too, and was bleeding on the back of his shoulder. I heard that he had said something nasty to Sheila's neighbours to start the fight.

Before things got worse, I gave Michael the cloth and then ran down to the basement to protect our kids. They were really scared and I quickly ushered them to the furthest and darkest corner, away from the windows in case any got smashed and they were hit by flying glass. I even shut the lights off so the people outside wouldn't see us.

I did my best to reassure the kids that everything would be okay even though the pandemonium outside and upstairs told otherwise.

It was like a flashback to my childhood.

In the distance, I could just barely make out the sound of police sirens making their way in our direction. I was surprisingly relieved to have them back here.

Two officers came down the basement stairs and found us huddled together in the dark. They asked if we were okay and I shakily told them that we were now. They didn't stay long, because I heard over their radios that there was a break and enter someplace nearby and they had to leave right away.

It didn't take Greg and I long to say goodbye to everyone, then pile into the car and head back to Saskatchewan. By this time it was late in the afternoon, but we'd had enough excitement and just wanted to go home.

Thirty-Six
Three Proposals

For the most part, life with Greg was good. We enjoyed each other's company, and so did the other locals who spent time with us. We couldn't even go to a restaurant for a romantic dinner without some uninvited person joining us.

Although we were popular and knew how to have a good time, life wasn't always simple. We had our off times and after arguments I would throw in the towel and kick Greg out. That usually happened when he decided that going to the bar with his buds after work was more important than coming home to a waiting family and a cooked meal. Sometimes he wouldn't even call first to let me know he wasn't coming home.

After a few of those, I got a little irate with him. I didn't like being put last, so on one of those occasions I told him to pack his stuff and get out. I even helped him by having it packed for him. Less frustration and drama that way.

Around that time, I had enough money to take the boys for a two-week vacation to Thompson to visit my parents and friends. We hadn't been back home for a couple of years, so we hopped on the bus and off we went for an adventure.

I visited with some old friends and surprisingly enough ran into Don, the dancing instructor I hadn't had the change to say goodbye to. It was such a pleasure to see him again. He had gotten engaged and asked if I would come over to his place to meet his fiancée, which I did the next evening. She was all smiles and friendly and I liked her immediately.

After dinner, Don asked me to follow him into their spare bedroom to show me something he thought I'd be interested in seeing. He brought out a tall plastic glass, the kind one could put a favourite picture in, and in this one he had a picture of me. I was truly touched, but where had he gotten the picture?

In earnest, he turned to me and quietly pleaded with me to return to Thompson, and if I did he would cancel his engagement. He told me he had always loved me and wanted to marry me.

I was stunned. If I hadn't been with Brent back in the day, I'd probably have ended up marrying Don. I had really liked him and he'd always been there for me. I also felt sorry for his fiancée, though. This wasn't fair to her. He shouldn't have been saying these things. Gently I told him I was returning to Saskatchewan. I felt guilty as I said goodbye to the couple and wished them the very best. I never saw them again.

The next old friend I was to meet was Shane, who I'd met along with his wife at the Thompson Inn where she and Henry had used to work. We had become good friends, but I hadn't seen them since Henry's death.

Anyway, I met him at a bar and he asked me to join him for a drink, which I was more than happy to do. He and I always talked easily. I was surprised yet saddened to find that he and his wife had divorced.

After a couple more drinks, Shane offered me a ride home. First he stopped by the vendors to pick up a twelve-pack of beer. He then led me to his car, a brand-new cherry red Corvette. Nice ride! On the way, he stopped by a classy-looking house, which turned out to be his, and asked if I'd join him for a drink. Sure, why not?

The house was every bit as classy inside as it was outside. The guy had money.

Shane proceeded to tell me that when I was with Henry, he'd had a thing for me. Since that time, he had improved his situation and was making good money working for the mine. He went on to tell me that he would be more than able to support my family.

I was dumbfounded. I had always liked him, but only as Henry's friend. I didn't quite know what to say except that I was heading back to Saskatchewan. Disappointed, he drove me to my parents' house and I never saw him again. Wow, two marriage proposals in a week!

I had met other friends who'd gotten married or remarried, causing me to feel left out. The desire to marry flooded back over me. I even felt jealous of Don's upcoming marriage. I was wishing he was marrying me instead of her. I wondered what would have happened if I had taken him up on his offer.

We only stayed with Mom, Dad, and Loretta for one week instead of the two I'd planned. One night, while putting the boys to bed in one of the basement bedrooms, my dad came home drunk. I could hear him grumbling about something upstairs and immediately my old fears returned. As quickly as possible, I quieted my boys. It must have been a reaction from my earlier days, so as not to let dad know we were awake—or there, for that matter.

He was upset about something and he and Mom had bitter words. Then he came to the top of the stairs and hollered down for me.

"Barbra!"

That authority in his voice made my skin crawl. I was afraid for my children and myself.

I went submissively up the stairs so he wouldn't come down and scare my boys any more than they already were. We had words, but I can't remember what they were. The main thing is that I told him we would get out the next day.

When I went back downstairs and locked our bedroom door, my son's eyes were big with fear. They had heard what was going on.

Dad followed me downstairs and told me to let him in, but I said no. He shouted at me, then kicked a hole in the door. I was surprised that his booted foot didn't come right through.

When he saw I wasn't going to open the door, he gave up and stomped his way back upstairs and continued to rave until he eventually settled down or passed out.

I didn't sleep much that night as I relived all the terror of my childhood in that house.

First thing in the morning, I phoned for the bus schedule and packed up. In tears, Mom begged me not to go, but my fear of dad overrode her pleas. I felt awful leaving her, but it wasn't an option for me to face Dad when he got home from work. What a relief it was to be riding away from him and his evil temper.

Shortly after our return home, two friends of Greg's came by and asked if the boys and I would like to go swimming at a nearby lake. It was just what we needed. On our way, I asked if it would be okay to stop by the farm and ask Greg to join us. I longed to see him.

When we drove onto the farmyard, Aunt Jenna came out to greet us wearing her usual big, welcoming smile. The boys and I were excited to see her and the feelings were mutual. Apparently Greg had been moping around, so she went into the house and told him we were outside.

It didn't take him long to appear. He looked into the car to see who was in it and was surprised to see me and the boys. We were still supposed to be in Manitoba. He acknowledged the boys but gave me a distant look and asked his friends what was up. They told him that we were going to the lake and asked if he wanted to join us. It didn't take much to persuade him. He rushed into the house, grabbed what he needed, and soon climbed into the backseat with us.

He and I didn't talk during the drive, but he and the boys did. I was nervous and unsure of myself and could feel the distance between us, but I pretended all was well in my little world.

I'd never been to this lake before. The beach was fairly crowded, but we managed to grab a piece of it for ourselves. The boys went off to do their thing and I found myself a quieter area where I could sit in solitude.

A short time later, Greg came by and asked how it had gone in Thompson and why we were home early. I explained what had happened with my parents, and in no time we were back on familiar ground, as if we hadn't been apart. After a time, we got up and joined the others. They were relieved to see that we were back to normal, so we could all relax.

As the afternoon wore on and the beach began to empty, and a beer or two later, I felt the urge to try out the diving board out in the middle of the water. The swim across the lake took me back to the many times my brother Michael and I had done this at Paint Lake, Manitoba. We'd spent hours hanging out on the diving board. Those were treasured memories.

Scrambling up the ladder, I could hardly wait for that exhilarating moment between leaving the board and entering the water below. Taking a deep breath, I jumped and spearheaded straight into the lake. It felt every bit as thrilling as I'd anticipated.

Now, it hadn't crossed my mind to ask why nobody had used the board the whole time we'd been there, and I quickly discovered the reason. No sooner had I cut through the water than my outstretched hands met the hard bottom. The walloping impact bolted up through my hands and arms, snapping me back so hard that I thought I had broken something. The water wasn't deep enough for diving.

Dazed from the impact and thinking I might drown, somehow I managed to pull myself together. I twisted my body around to face upward, all the while holding onto what little air I hadn't yet exhaled. It felt as though my lungs were about to burst and I knew I had to surface—and fast—or else I'd black out.

With great effort, I managed to kick my legs hard enough to shoot myself to the surface and gulp in fresh oxygen. I then held myself on the surface until I could gather my bearings and see which way it was to shore. The pain in my back seemed manageable, so I didn't bother to call out for help.

I swam for a bit, then rested on my back, kicking just enough to keep myself afloat. I pushed on, turning onto my stomach, and dogpaddled for a while so as not to give in to pain. I was progressing toward the shore, and if anyone saw me out there they'd just think I was just enjoying a leisurely swim.

I began to feel confident that I would make it when suddenly I hit a patch of long underwater weeds. They grabbed around my legs and ankles and I started to panic. Surely I hadn't come this far only to drown! I kicked harder to get loose, but the weeds held on tight, and the churning kicked up even more weeds.

What do I do? I wondered.

Out of nowhere came a still, small voice: *Don't panic. Relax. Just breathe.*

So I did just that and the weeds loosened their hold. Gently I flapped my feet, trying not to churn up the weeds again, and slowly made my way out of their territory. It felt like it took forever, but I soon got close enough to shore to touch the welcoming sand under my feet.

Assessing the damage to my back, I found the pain wasn't as severe as I had feared. I was able to stand up without too much trouble. What a relief!

Leaving the water behind, I headed back to my people and pretended that all was well. I felt stupid and embarrassed. All I knew was that I had once again cheated death. I grabbed a beer, sat down next to Greg, and watched my kids enjoy themselves, grateful to be alive.

I never swam in a lake again, or even jumped off a diving board, after that day. I also believe it was the voice of the Holy Spirit telling me what to do to get out of the weeds.

Within a week of being home, Greg had moved back in. He admitted that he had been a bit scared that we wouldn't come back from Thompson.

One night after we left the bar and walked home, I fell into a state of deep thought. Greg wanted to know what I was thinking so hard about, so rather reluctantly I told him I'd been thinking that it was time I considered marrying again. That took him by surprise, because when we'd started living together I had told him that I had no intention of ever remarrying. Who needed a piece of paper? If it didn't work out, we could just go our own ways without the expense of a divorce. In other wards, no commitment.

I expected him now to say goodbye to me and move on. Instead he asked if I had anyone in mind.

"I don't know yet," I said. "I'm just pondering the idea."

While I was saying this, he walked a little ahead of me, then turned to face me and asked if I would marry him.

I looked him in the eyes and laughed. "Don't be silly."

Later in bed, Greg turned to me and asked me to marry him again. I laughed at him and told him to quit fooling around and go to sleep.

He didn't think that was funny.

"I'm only going to ask you one more time," he said, really frustrated. "If you laugh, I'll never ask you again. Now, will you marry me?"

That got my attention. I really wanted to believe him, but I figured he was just clowning around—until I saw the desperation in his face and realized he was serious.

"Do you really mean it? This isn't a game, is it?"

Pulling me closer, he reassured me that this was the real thing.

Still with my guard up, I cautiously said yes… waiting for the inevitable "Just kidding." But it never came.

"I love you," he said with a huge smile and great big kiss to seal the deal.

I sure hadn't expected that, nor had I ever dreamed of being proposed to three times by three different men in a matter of two weeks.

The next day, as soon as the bar was open, we went down to celebrate our engagement after having lived common-law for two years.

And so we planned our wedding.

Greg was my first cousin, but since I couldn't have any more children, I felt like we were given the okay. He loved my sons as his own and accepted the fact that we wouldn't have children together. We went to his family's doctor, a friend of the family, who gave us blood tests as a wedding gift.

We were to be married a couple of weeks later, on September 10, 1983 in a courtroom in Melville, Saskatchewan. It was the very same courtroom in which he and his brother Ron had many times stood before a judge growing up. We wanted a small wedding with only our mothers, Ron and Marla, my sisters Darlene and Loretta, and Greg's friend Bruce.

On the day of the wedding, Ron drove all the guests to the courtroom while the wedding party followed behind in Bruce's car. We took the back road to Melville and stopped several times to retrieve the bottle of whisky, mix, and glasses that were stashed in the trunk of the car in order to celebrate this most audacious day. As a result, it took us a little longer to get there.

By the time we had covered the forty or so miles to Melville, we were fairly lit. Actually, Greg and I had been drunk almost every day since his proposal.

When we finally made it to the courtroom, upon entering we found it packed with a lot of our friends. They claimed they had wanted to see Greg go down. He'd never been married before.

The judge who was to marry us was late, so Greg and Bruce took it upon themselves to go in search of him. Half an hour later, they came back with the news that the judge was out golfing and should arrive soon. They had gotten their information from the police station. Imagine that… two drunks looking for a judge at the police station!

During this time, everyone was having a blast visiting. My head was pretty fuzzy from all the booze. It all seemed like a joke.

When the judge finally made his appearance, he came in with a barrel of fried chicken under his arm. He called Greg and I into his chambers, along with our mothers. He found it a little puzzling that our mothers both had the same maiden names. We all grinned when they explained that they were sisters, Jenna being the eldest of the two. Eventually all the paperwork was completed and the judge sent our moms back out into the courtroom. He had some questions for me and Greg.

While we were with the judge, Aunt Jenna sat in the judge's chair and called the court to order using the gavel. Someone took a picture of her while she was up to her mischief. I heard later that everyone in the room had cracked up. She claimed that she had been in the courtroom so many times that she'd just wanted to see how it felt being on the other side of the bench.

Anyway, she was down by the time we came out. Greg and I said our vows and then left for home, where everyone was invited for a reception. On the way back, we made plenty of stops to toast the new mister and missus. I think it was hard for both of us to believe we had actually done it!

Our little two-bedroom home was full of guests by the time we got there. My mom was so disappointed with us, because she knew how drunk we were already… and knew we were going to get worse. She'd seen enough through her years to recognize our behaviour.

At one point, her displeasure got the better of her and she threw several whisky bottles into the garbage cans outside. She got caught and brought them back in. We were quite mad at her. One of those bottles was particularly expensive and it had been another wedding gift from our family doctor. He had good taste in whisky, and the money to pay for it.

If he'd only known he had bought it for a couple of alcoholics, he might have made a different choice of wedding gift.

When it came time to open the rest of our wedding gifts, Greg and I kneeled on the floor in front of the coffee table so everyone could watch. We took turns opening presents, but when it came time for one particular gift from Darlene she told me that I should be the one to open it. We were all curious to see what the little parcel held.

Cautiously, I opened the top and dug around the paper. When my hand circled it, I pulled it up… then quickly shoved it back down, with a smirk on my face. I secretly shoved the box behind me.

"Sorry," I said. "But I can't show you that one."

Everyone laughed. It was a set of salt and peppershakers stolen from a restaurant in Winnipeg, and they were full of marijuana. I wasn't about to share that with anyone.

I'm ashamed to admit it, but to me that was the best gift of them all.

After our beautiful homemade wedding cake was cut and the toasts made, I wandered outside for a cigarette and a breath of fresh air to clear my head. Ron and Marla joined me, along with several others. They were thinking of heading off to the bar for a few drinks and wanted to know if I wanted to come. I didn't think Greg would miss me, so I headed out.

Here it was, my wedding day, and I left my new husband of a few short hours behind to man the house while I took off to the bar. I actually thought it was funny.

When we walked into the bar, some of the regulars asked where the groom was and Ron told them they had kidnapped the bride. We all laughed and ordered a round.

Not half an hour later, Greg and his crew came in. We called them over to join us, but he was upset and got his own table. Fine. I ordered us another round.

Some time later, Greg and his friends joined us and we got totally wasted.

The rest of the day, and the next three weeks, are a blank for me. We didn't stay sober enough or care enough to even consummate the marriage.

When I sobered up years later, I came to understand why Mom had tried to throw out our alcohol. I'm so ashamed of the way we got married and how I treated her. It was a horrible time for her and she'd had no place to escape since she was staying with her sister, who didn't have a ride to go home either. She was rightfully ashamed of me and I had given her every reason to be. She'd come down for a wedding and ended up cleaning up after us and taking care of the kids while we partied hard. I don't remember thanking her once for all she and Aunt Jenna did for us. We just got mad at her for throwing out our booze. The whole affair was a drunken whirlwind.

Two weeks after getting married, I returned to Winnipeg to attend my trial for possession of hashish. I was very fortunate it was my first offence. I was released with a year's probation, but unfortunately I had a record now.

Thirty-Seven
Rehab

After the honeymoon period wore off and life returned to usual, there was a period of time during which we physically abused each other. I was free with my hands and punched Greg in the arms whenever I got really angry with him. One day he closed-fisted me in the ribs, which took the wind right out of my sails. I couldn't stay mad, because I knew I'd deserved it.

Another time, Greg came home at lunchtime totally drunk. He began picking at us while the boys and I tried to eat our lunch. They knew enough not to say anything, but I could tell they'd had enough. I pleaded for him to stop and leave us alone, but he just kept on and on until, without realizing what I was doing, I lifted my coffee cup to splash its contents into his face—but instead I smashed the cup into his face, breaking his nose.

Oh my god, what had I done? I was just as shocked as he was, but it at least shut him up since he had to go and take care of it.

Two days later, while I was walking alone down the street, one of his drinking buddies came up to me and threatened that if I ever laid a hand on my old man again he would come after me himself. I couldn't believe what he was saying to me. He didn't have a clue what had taken place and now he was threatening to beat me up! I wanted to drop the sucker right there in the street. What a joke. Was he for real?

Without showing him a trace of fear, I glared into his eyes and in no uncertain terms told him where he could go. Then I kept on walking. He never troubled me again.

I had a mouth on me that could make a soldier blush and I didn't back down, even when I knew I was wrong. To admit being wrong was to admit defeat, and that would be a sign of weakness. Weakness would mean I was vulnerable. If I had even a small crack in my armor, I feared letting out all my suppressed emotions. They would explode out of my soul in a fit of screaming rage.

At times it took everything in me to hold myself together.

Sadly, the abuse didn't stop there. I broke his nose a second time, probably for the same thing.

My drinking and parenting skills progressively worsened. My kids were left to themselves a lot. When they wanted me, especially for their lunch or supper, they would have to come find me. I would get frustrated and tell them I'd be home soon, but then not show up for hours. I really didn't deserve my children. I should have had them taken away from me.

Around this time, Joey had a serious accident and I wasn't there for him. He fell headfirst off some scaffolding and landed on his head. He'd been unconscious for a time and someone had taken him to the hospital.

Where was I? In the bar, no doubt.

Blayne would clean the house after many of our late night parties, which the boys always struggled to sleep through so they could go to school the next morning. They woke up to beer and whisky bottles and overflowing ashtrays. Eugene told me years later that he would drink what was left in some of the beer bottles and glasses.

I'd wake up nursing a gigantic hangover and find the house spotless after the pigsty I'd left the night before.

I'm ashamed to admit that my kids took better care of me than I did of them. Too many times, I would snivel to them about how hard life was for me with Greg. He'd either left us or I'd kicked him out. I had become the child, and they the adults.

They grew up tough, because when I played with them I played rough. When I disciplined, I was strict. They were taught good manners, and they got punished when they needed it—if I was around. I yelled and swore a lot. I had a foul mouth, yet I wouldn't let my kids swear.

Sadly, I don't remember a lot about my children's childhoods. I fed them and off they'd go. I wouldn't see them for the whole day. Sure, we took them with us when we went out and about, but they didn't have the care and support of real parents.

Even though I didn't know what they were up to, I always considered them to be good boys who stayed out of trouble—that is, except for the one time I came home from shopping and found a large box on the kitchen table. No one was in the house, so I didn't know who had brought it in.

Curious, I opened the lid and then slammed it shut, shocked. Inside were snakes, wriggling and twisting, trying to get out of the box. I went to the kitchen door and yelled all three of the boys' names and telling them to get inside *right now*. I didn't even know where they were, but I wanted those snakes out of the house, pronto.

One of the boys responded and took the box out onto the front step. When I came out, I could see snakes slithering in every direction. Then I noticed that the basement window was open and thought for sure one had crawled back into the house. I ordered my son to go downstairs and shut that window. When I got up enough nerve, I went down into the basement to see if there were any snakes crawling on the floor. Thankfully, I found none.

When I got back upstairs, I took my broom outside and tried to push all the snakes away from the house. That's when I saw Greg coming up the street on his bike. He had a phobia of snakes, and I knew if he'd see them he would probably faint.

By the time he rode up to the house, most of the snakes had cleared out to other yards. For quite a while later, every time I went down the basement I nervously looked for snakes. Whichever of my boys had brought those snakes into the house had definitely gotten his revenge on me. I'd had it coming!

Dad Has Cancer

After Dad retired at the age of sixty, he moved Mom and Loretta to a small town in northern Saskatchewan where my brother Paul lived. It was soon to be discovered that he had cancer in his throat. He battled for several years, but it was beating him.

I was soon told he was in the Saskatoon hospital and very ill. Since I owed him money, I thought I'd better get it to him before anything happened. I didn't want to be another of those people who borrowed from him and never paid him back.

Greg borrowed a car and we drove up to the hospital to see him. It was a hard experience for me. He had a private room and at first I was alone in his room with him.

"Hi, how are you?" I said.

He looked thin after having once weighed nearly three hundred pounds. He said he was in a lot of pain everywhere. I quickly told him that I had the money I owed him. He couldn't understand why I was paying him back now, but I told him that I liked to pay my debts. He told me to take it down to the front desk and they would lock it away for him.

Shortly after returning to his room, my brother Andrew and sister Ann came in. In relief, I moved away and let them sit by his bedside. I stood by a window across the room and watched as they talked and joked around so easily. I felt completely out of place. I didn't feel like I belonged, or like Dad even knew me.

I envied my siblings for their easy way with him because I couldn't interact that way. Even with him in this condition, so close to death, I still feared him. It seemed like the visit took forever to come to an end, and when it did I was glad to go, but I felt awful. I hurt inside and knew this would probably be the last time I saw him alive.

But I had accomplished what I set out to do.

Alcoholics Anonymous

Somewhere during the five years that we lived in Langenburg, Greg and I decided to try the Alcoholics Anonymous twelve-step program. The drinking had started to interfere with Greg's many jobs, and between these jobs we had to go on welfare.

When the program didn't work for him, Greg discovered that he could go to a rehabilitation centre in Regina. The centre allowed me to come along, as his spouse, so I went in order to support him as he worked out his problem.

After the fourth day in the centre, we were allowed outside for a walk, which was a big mistake. We discussed the fact that we weren't able to share a room together and decided that this wasn't for us. We casually went back inside, quietly packed our clothes, and cowardly snuck away. Of course we found a dingy bar on the way to the bus depot and hesitated only a moment before ducking inside to have a few for the road.

Back in Langenburg, I pondered the films, lectures, and counselling sessions we had attended during our four short days in rehab. I also remembered how caring the staff had been. There had been safety and a hope in that centre I'd never found anywhere else.

Everywhere I looked, I could see people living normal lives—and I wanted mine to be the same. I knew we were wrong in leaving rehab, but in my deep insecurity I had allowed Greg to sway me into believing it wasn't the place for us.

When dwelling on all this, the truth hit me: not only was I an alcoholic, I was a drug addict as well.

After more drinking and more fighting, I came to the realization that I needed to do something about my addiction, so this time I tried the rehab centre for myself. I don't remember how I was able to get there—for instance, I don't know who looked after my children—but I knew I was miserable beyond description. I needed help in the worst way.

Who would have thought I'd be walking back through the same doors Greg and I had so confidently walked out only a short time ago? This took great courage on my part.

I went through the process of being signed in and given the rules, as well as my own room upstairs. Standing in the middle of my tiny room, I took in my new home for the next three weeks. I had only a bed, a small bedside table with a lamp, a dresser, and a narrow dormer window to look out of. As I stood still and acknowledged the unbelievable fact that I actually was doing something to help myself, I found that I was void of all feelings. I felt empty, depleted... dead inside. How could rehab help me? There wasn't anything left to work with.

I was given a schedule for each day. All I needed to do was follow its instructions and show up. Somehow I managed to take in the tools I gleaned from the lectures, talks, and films and stored them away in my very mushy brain.

I knew without a doubt that this was where I was supposed to be. I met others who were struggling just like myself. Real, caring people took the time for me, which I so desperately needed.

Yet my guard was still up. I had to act like I was always in control. I could be anything you wanted me to be. I had so many different masks to wear.

This was my first real "holiday" from Greg and the kids, yet I was locked in a building and could only go out for an hour. I didn't have anywhere to go until I made a new friend or two, yet even then I didn't let them close to me.

When I was alone, I missed my kids and worried about them. There was no outside contact. I couldn't even phone and find out how they were doing. The whole plan was to focus completely on myself without any outside influences. This way, no one could sneak anything in.

At rehab I learned how addiction works and the damage it does to one's body and life. I was feeling good and doing something good for myself. I even made it to the "marbling out" ceremony, which I was so proud of myself for. We were called up one at a time to pick a marble out of a special container as our reward; it was a reminder for the days to come of what we had accomplished so far and what we hoped to establish for our future, which was to stay clean and dry.

This was my first time taking part in the ceremony, and I was excited that Greg came. I believe he was proud of me, because I could honestly say I felt new and changed, really happy, and filled with a special kind of joy. I had accomplished something purposeful.

Churchbridge was having an AA convention. Addicts from all over came with their friends and families to have a lovely supper and hear special speakers share their recovery stories. Greg and I were invited to attend by some friends we had made while attending AA. There were maybe forty to fifty people in attendance. We all enjoyed a hearty meal and great conversation.

After all the dishes were cleared away, we settled down to hear the people's many testimonies. Earlier I had been asked if I would share mine, and with great trepidation I had agreed. When my turn came, I stepped onto the platform looked around the room at the many expectant faces. As I rested my hands on the podium, I said, "Can you people see me? Because I can hardly see over this thing!" Well, everyone cracked up laughing, a great icebreaker for me to begin sharing bits and pieces of my past with these like-minded people who had come together to support one another.

The talk went smoothly, and afterward I received a loud applause. Only once I'd returned to my seat did I really shake from nerves. I shook so bad that I couldn't drink my coffee. That was the third time I had stood before an audience. I was amazed at how confidently I was able to share, but I was so very ashamed of my past.

After a few months at home, I began thinking I was cured, but in no time, with the help of Greg and some well-meaning friends, I once again succumbed to the tantalizing taste of great beer. I fell headlong into the pit once more. I failed. I failed myself, I failed my children, and I failed the people at AA. What a great big loser I was. My emotional state was in complete disrepair. I simply couldn't do anything right.

At this point in my life, I was attending an upgrading class, which involved me going back to school to learn a year's worth of lessons in just three months. It took place at Langenburg's city hall, right across the road from where we lived. I started at Grade Nine and finished that season with marks in the 90s. I had no idea I was so smart!

But I was struggling with my home life, and about three-quarters of the way into the tenth grade, my teacher saw my struggle and talked to a counsellor in Yorkton to see if she could help me. When I was told about the opportunity to once again go to rehab, I jumped at the chance. At this point I was once again separated from Greg, and Darlene and her son were staying with me. I asked Darlene if she could watch my kids while I was away for three weeks and she agreed. I was desperate to change my lifestyle.

I was sent to an Indigenous lodge just outside Fort Qu'Appelle. I did rather well the first week and a half, and during this time I shared a room with another young woman. We became friends. I felt like I belonged here, which helped me to settle in and get serious. I truly wanted to clean up my life. I needed to look at what I was doing to my family and myself.

I wanted a better life for us all, so I worked hard at it. I listened to the teachings and watched the videos with newfound interest. I did chores like everyone else, and I especially liked working in the kitchen. There were a lot of hungry mouths to feed at the lodge. I made friends easily, which encouraged me because they were serious as well.

We were preparing for some kind of event and I had been given the job of creating a poster for it. I discovered I could still draw when I put my mind to it. It took a long time and a good eraser, but the effort proved to be worth it.

I was about halfway finished my poster when an emergency call came through the office for me. We typically weren't allowed outside contact of any kind, but this call came from Greg, who was now taking care of the kids. It turned out that Darlene's ex-boyfriend, Reynold, had come back to town looking for her and found her at my place.

Just before going into rehab, I had suggested to Darlene that she drive Greg around so she could see firsthand how people hunted deer in the area. She'd never gone deer hunting before. Somehow Reynold had gotten wind of it and came looking for her. He found her at my place and accused her of screwing around with my husband. He was insanely jealous and planned to draw Greg into the conflict and do him in. It had been mentioned to us that he had possibly killed before, so we had reason to believe he might do it again.

On this day, Greg's call was to inform me that I needed to come home because he had the .303 loaded and had been sleeping with it under the bed for the last three days while he waited for this lunatic to show up. He wasn't getting much sleep because his nerves were on edge. He was scared he might shoot someone accidentally.

With great trepidation, I told him to come and get me, which he did the next evening. He had a friend drive him and on the way they picked up a case of beer, which was open in the car when I got in. I was grievously disappointed that he couldn't come and get me sober. I so wanted to stay clean. Even with my nerves being in such turmoil, I resisted drinking.

We arrived home late and the boys were glad to see me. They didn't know what was going on, as far as I knew.

It was nerve-wracking to know someone was coming after you, intending to use you for target practice. I remember the feeling of being shot at while duck- and deer-hunting, and I also remember getting shot in the ankle from a BB gun as a kid.

Somehow we managed to fall asleep that night, but there seemed to be more unusual sounds in the house than normal, which made us jumpy.

The boys went to school as usual the next day. They would be safer there.

The day remained quiet, but in the evening a call came through from Marla. She whispered, "He's here and he wants to know where Greg is hiding."

"Who's there?" I asked.

"Reynold, and he's tearing our place up."

I could hear him banging around in the background. And then he noticed that Marla was on the phone.

"Who are you talking to?" Reynold yelled.

"Just a friend—"

"Hang that f—ing phone up now."

The line went dead.

What was he going to do to them? Greg and I sat on pins and needles, worried out of our minds.

Thankfully, the boys were upstairs sleeping and didn't know what was going on.

Half an hour went by before the next call came in. It was Marla again.

"Reynold is on his way to your place," she said in hysterics. "He's got a gun!"

With Churchbridge being so close, we knew it wouldn't take him long to get here. We didn't have a vehicle to move everyone to a safer place, so Greg told me to shut off all the lights, close the curtains, and stay away from the windows. He loaded the .303 and phoned the police in Yorkton, forty-five miles away; the Langenburg police rolled up the sidewalks about 6:00 p.m., so unfortunately Reynold had a head start.

Greg told me we weren't going to be sitting ducks, so he took the rifle and an extra clip and went out the back door to hide in the shadows beside the shed at the far end of the backyard. Being we lived on a corner lot, from there Greg had a clear view of all the roads leading past our house. He also knew which truck Reynold was driving. Greg was an accomplished hunter, so if Reynold's truck came close to our house, the streetlights would announce his arrival and he'd be a goner.

Time dragged by agonizingly slow and the darkness made it all the more eerie. This was like something you'd watch on TV.

I cautiously looked out the back window to see if I could see Greg, but he was well hidden in the shadows.

As I stepped away from the window, an awful feeling came over me. I envisioned a bullet smashing through the back of my head and my brains exploding out the front of my face. It was so hard to sit still and not worry about Greg outside and my boys upstairs and what might happen to us. The anxiety of waiting made my heart pound.

About half an hour went by before I saw the lights of a police car against the curtains. Cautiously I peeked around the curtain and watched the car drive slowly past our house with its spotlight searching the ground. It drove up and down the street and around a few blocks.

Greg came in once they passed and put the gun away. The arrival of the police relieved a lot of stress, and I was glad he was beside me and alive. But what were we to do now, just wait?

Again the police drove by, but they came up with nothing. We figure Reynold must have heard that the police were on their way. We remembered him saying something about having a police scanner in his truck.

The police came to our door and assured us that they were going to watch for him.

Sleep didn't come easy that night—or the next two nights, for that matter. We were waiting for Reynold to backtrack once the police were out of the way. He was a ticking timebomb.

Our world was crumbling and we needed to do something.

Then Greg came up with the only solution he could think of. We needed to move out of town, and fast. He had an inheritance coming and asked for it, then secured a moving van, which we packed in a few hours. I had a chance to say goodbye to a few people, and then we hit the road, heading toward Medicine Hat, where I knew a childhood friend who would help us.

We were on the run. I truly believe that if Reynold had managed to take Greg out, he wouldn't have stopped there. He would have gotten rid of the evidence: me and the boys.

We had no place to stay and not much money, but there we were, two adults and three teenage boys packed in a moving van motoring down the highway.

Thirty-Eight
Medicine Hat

Before nightfall, we arrived in Swift Current, Saskatchewan and could hardly believe there were only small patches of snow on the ground here. We even saw a gopher running about! We'd just left heaps of snow behind us.

Being too tired and emotionally drained to go any farther, all five of us crammed into a hotel room before continuing on the next morning to Medicine Hat.

We had arranged to meet my childhood friend Elaine at a local restaurant. We figured Reynold wouldn't think to look for us here, and Elaine's mom, Marion, agreed that we could stay at her place until we were able to secure a home of our own.

I managed to stay sober about a week before caving in and having my first beer and toke with the others in the house. From there on, the old me was back, the so-called party girl. I was too weak to fight it.

When I drank, confusion caused me to doubt everything about myself. I was lost and severely broken. It didn't take much for tears to spill. I was a walking, talking wreck of an empty shell.

It also didn't take much for Greg and I to tear into each other. It was close to a month before Greg got us on Welfare, found us a house, and landed a job. I was truly grateful to Marion for putting up with us.

The size of the city terrified me. I was afraid to walk around the block in case I got lost, and just crossing the streets set my nerves on edge. Our new home was close to downtown, which was a relief. At least I was capable of shopping on my own here and not getting lost at the turn of a corner. We rented the top half of a house which had two other suites. We drank with one of the other men who lived there. I liked this place very much.

We were also within walking distance of several bars, so once Greg found them it didn't take long before they became his home away from home. He found work there, too, even though he was primarily a roofer along with his many other trades. We stayed on welfare until we were settled and didn't need their help any longer, and before long the boys were into their school routines and had begun to explore the town. I didn't see much of them.

Almost a year into our lives in Medicine Hat, Greg and I proved that the geographical move hadn't changed us. I was once again a full-blown mess, and Greg was the same. One night, we'd been drinking excessively and the inevitable fight broke loose. He left late in the night and said he would be back to pick up his belongings in a day or two. He was good to his word, except I hadn't expected him to take most of the furniture as well.

It felt like he'd brought us to a scary city only to dump us. We were to fend for ourselves. I had been totally dependant upon him, and he knew it. At least we had our beds.

After the boys went to school, I'd pace around the empty kitchen and living room in despair. I sat on an empty shelf and smoked my last joint. My thoughts racing, I lifted my head and looked out of the window at big fluffy clouds hanging in the sky. I searched for some sign of the God I had heard of, but where was He?

In soul-wrenching desperation, I cried out, "God, if You're real, help me." Then I bowed my head and cried. I was alone, afraid, and had no answers. I also didn't have any money. I just didn't know which way to turn, and honestly I didn't expect God to answer.

When Greg didn't return in the following days, it became evident that I had to go back on welfare. I had no knowledge of how to apply, though, because Greg had always taken care of that. To make matters worse, when I got to the office where I met the social worker, my mind was in so much confusion that I couldn't comprehend what she was saying. I sat across from her like a child, her words entering one ear and coming back out the other.

The social worker directed me to another person who enrolled me in the second semester of New Worlds for Women at the Medicine Hat College. This was a course intended to prepare women to enter the workforce. I had never really worked, as I was always a stay-at-home mom. I felt bewildered about the prospect of going to this college, but at least I would be getting paid to go, enough for me to support my family.

My first day walking into the college was overwhelming. College? Who would have thought that possible? The place seemed huge. I did, however, manage to find the admittance office and hesitantly walk through the door.

I can't remember how many other women were there on my first day in class, but it sure did help to know there were so many my own age. I found the desk furthest from the instructor, as old habits die hard. I was resentful, moody, and kept people as far away from me as possible.

As the days passed, I eventually began to open up to a couple of the students. And wouldn't you know it, they liked their drugs as much as I did mine. They became my suppliers and we hung out together.

Dad's Death

Dad passed away on November 27, 1987. The funeral brought up many conflicting emotions, because somehow I'd never thought he would actually die. While growing up, he always said, very convincingly, "I'm the most miserable son of a b— who ever lived and I will never die." And I honestly believed him.

So to see him in the coffin with one eye partly open, as though he was going to get up out of the coffin,[19] was shocking and eerie. I just couldn't wrap my mind around it. He was really gone! He couldn't harm anyone anymore.

Although he had mellowed out in his last years, my memories of him at his worst were just as alive as ever.

Even though I went to the cemetery to witness his departure, I still couldn't believe he had actually died. I couldn't cry, not then and not later.

Becoming a Christian

After I finished New Worlds for Women, I decided to go back to school instead of finding a job. When I'd left Langenburg, I had been almost three quarters of the way through Grade Ten, but when I was evaluated the teachers placed me back into grade nine. I was extremely disappointed at first, but I sucked it up and went to class.

Many evenings after supper I sat at the kitchen table and did my homework along with my sons. It was the most special time I can remember with them. If I needed help, one would help me and vice versa.

By now Greg had returned, but he didn't like that I had homework every night as well as on the weekends. I had to cram, too, because they packed a year's worth schooling into just three months.

I still smoked weed and drank beer, but hanging out at the bar wasn't an option. It was for Greg, though. With all my schoolwork, I guess maybe he felt left out. I did my best to spread myself out between my husband, children, and school. I felt like butter spread thin over hot toast.

In the middle of the semester, I met an ex-drug dealer outside the Social Studies classroom. His name was Antonio, and as it turned out he was in every class I attended. He and his male friend took me under their wing and helped me when I was struggling with my schoolwork.

They also talked a lot about Jesus. They evangelized every chance they got. I eventually met their wives, and they too talked about Jesus. They could see my hunger for God, so Antonio and his wife Cindy invited me to a local church and I accepted their invitation.

On July 17, 1988, two days after my thirty-fourth birthday, we attended an evening church service. There were a lot of people entering into the building and they looked genuinely happy to be there. They were hugging, shaking hands, and laughing. This was truly different from another church Greg and I had tried a year before. At that one, everyone looked so serious, and by the time we left I felt like I'd been beat up with a baseball bat. Pain had coursed through my whole body and I couldn't understand why. Needless to say, I never went back.

But this one was really different. I could feel the joy and peace. I don't remember a word the preacher spoke, but at the end of the service there was an altar call for anyone who wanted to come up and accept Jesus as their Lord and Savoir. Without hesitation, I walked up to the front, broken and defeated, and

---

[19] I wasn't the only one to comment on how strange this was.

recited what is known as the sinner's prayer. I humbly asked forgiveness for all my sins and asked Jesus to come into my heart and be Lord of my life. I didn't quite know what "Lord of my life" meant, but I wanted it. I hadn't done such a great job orchestrating my own life, so I was quite sure Jesus couldn't do any worse. I was amazed at how peaceful I felt when I left the church that night.

> Jesus is "'the stone you builders rejected, which has become the cornerstone.' Salvation is found in no one else, for there is no other name under heaven given to mankind by which we must be saved." (Acts 4:11–12)

After asking Jesus into my heart, it didn't take long for everyone around me to notice the dramatic change in my personality. I was definitely different. I didn't want to drink, didn't want to get stoned, didn't want to swear, and really didn't want to listen to any of my good old party tunes. I destroyed all my albums while my sons looked on in disbelief. As I smashed every record to pieces, they probably thought I had finally lost it. I'm talking well over a hundred albums here.

Then I went to work on my reading material, which was full of illicit sex, betrayal, and filth. I also destroyed all the Jehovah's Witness books and pamphlets, along with other religious materials that didn't line up to my new understanding.

The next to go was all my drug paraphernalia—the pipes, roach clips, rolling papers, hot knives, and pen cases. I acquainted them with the garbage can. I was determined that they would never make their way into my life again. Anything with skulls or snakes, anything that brought glory to Satan, had to go. I had served him long enough.

Another thing I noticed was that I didn't want to take my Lord's name in vain anymore, and it troubled me deeply when I heard anyone else doing it. Using His name in vain is a verbal assault towards God and Jesus.

> You shall not misuse the name of the Lord your God, for the Lord will not hold anyone guiltless who misuses his name. (Exodus 20:7)

I even gave up riding motorcycles, because riding them gave me a false sense of power and a very bad attitude. I told God I was giving it up until He said I could have it back for the pure enjoyment of the ride. I received many invitations to ride, but I turned them all down. That wasn't easy.

A little more than ten years later, God sent an old friend who loved biking to give me a ride. He was the guy whose bike I had threatened to kick over because it wasn't a Harley Davidson. As it turned out, he and his wife bought a Harley Davidson, which to me was the Rolls Royce of motorcycles.

"Some little girl told me to buy a real bike," he said. "So I listened to her and got one. You want a ride?"

Well, I couldn't very well turn down an invite like that, now could I? I told him if he was taking me for a ride it had better be more than just around the block. I mean, I wanted a *ride*. So he took me out to the Trans-Canada Highway and cracked it open. We had the sun, the clouds, the wind, and the rain. It was the greatest ride ever!

Anyway, back to purging my house. I was finished with my old life once and for all. No one had told me to get rid of all this stuff; I just didn't want it anymore. It felt unclean.

I even stopped using my favourite F-word. That's when I realized God had performed a supernatural miracle on me. I had tried to quit drinking, drugs, and swearing on my own, but never was able to accomplish it, even with the help of AA and rehab centres.[20] What I had needed all along was Jesus.

God had answered my prayer. He didn't care that I was stoned. He only cared about my heart, and my heart was crying out to Him that day. He had a plan!

Thank You, God! Just whispering the name of Jesus is a powerful prayer. It goes straight to heaven and every word is heard and recorded.

> *Until now you have not asked for anything in my name. Ask and you will receive, and your joy will be complete.* (John 16:24)

What did Greg think of all this? He lost his drinking buddy the night I went to the altar and accepted Jesus as my Lord. He didn't know what to think of me—first the AA meetings, then rehab, and now religion. What was next? What had become of his wife? She was praising God and going to church. The dirty books had gone out and the Bible had come in.

His mannerisms seemed to say, *I hope she doesn't expect me to change, because that's not going to happen.*

So he drank more, was gone longer, and fought harder. He'd seen the change in me and probably couldn't wait for this new phase to run its course. He wanted me to go back to normal—to drinking, smoking up, swearing, screaming, crying, and punching out walls and mirrors. Who in their right mind would want that back?

I'd hit rock bottom, felt so defeated and broken that I knew I couldn't put my life back together on my own. I had no peace, no joy, and no hope for the future. All I was doing was existing, surviving to get through another day.

The regrets of my failure at motherhood can still come back when I least expect it. Such regrets are hard to let go of, but they also keep me from ever wanting to go back to the old ways.

Old Life, New Desires

Before I even knew You, Lord
I was but a clump of hard dry clay
The kind that lay around with no purpose
Usually drunk or stoned most days
But when Your Spirit began to move
Beckoning and calling me by name
The desires for the old way of living
Brought no satisfaction, just bearable pain

---

[20] I'm not saying these things don't work. It's just that they didn't work for me.

Prayers of the saints were answered
Your Word and Spirit got through to me
Altering my very existence
The influences I had and the words that I'd speak
And now a great crowd of witnesses watch me
To see what I'm going to do
And my greatest heart's desire, Lord
Is they'll see me standing firm for You

Yes, You are the Great Potter, Lord
I'm a miracle, what else can I say
In Your hands I'm soft pliable putty
To shape and mould with each new day
My life is surely a testimony
To bring glory and honour to Your name
Help me, Lord, never to forget
The old life from which I came.

Thirty-Nine
A New Life

One lazy afternoon while everyone had left the house, I decided to lie down on my bed and talk to God. After a short interval of being in His presence, I heard a knock at my front door and reluctantly got up to answer it.

It was just over a week since I'd accepted Jesus as Lord and now here were the Jehovah's Witnesses standing at my door. This time I wouldn't allow them in. They tried to minister to me, but I told them politely that I was no longer interested in their teachings or their books. They wanted to know why, so I told them that I had asked Jesus into my heart, and now He'd set me free from my addictions, something that had never happened in all the years I'd listened to their doctrine.

They tried to argue with me, but I stood my ground as best I could with the little understanding of Christianity I possessed. I then asked them to leave and never come back. With that, I politely closed the door.

Relieved at their departure, I went back into my bedroom and lay down again to talk to God. While praising and worshipping Him, I suddenly felt something touch my foot. But when I looked down, I saw nothing there.

As I lay still, I once again felt this something walk slowly up my leg. I couldn't see anything, but I felt it. When it reached my shoulders, it began to shake me—violently. I felt hostility emanate from this unseen thing. It was truly creepy.

Then, from out of nowhere, I remembered that someone had told me to use the name of Jesus against the working of Satan and his demons. In a choked voice, I managed to squeak out the name of Jesus and tell that thing to get off me and get out of my home, which it did immediately.

I was shaken to the core of my being. So Satan and his demons were real! The only thing I can figure out from this encounter is that a demon attacked me through the false teachings of the Jehovah's Witnesses and that it was really angry with me for turning the Witnesses away. It had wanted to scare me, and it had, but then it got cast off of me and out of my house for good. I was set free of it and got a great firsthand lesson in demon warfare and wrestling against the powers of darkness.

> *For our struggle is not against flesh and blood, but against the rulers, against the authorities, against the powers of this dark world and against the spiritual forces of evil in the heavenly realms.* (Ephesians 6:12)

This is proof that what I received when I went up to receive God was truth… and the truth set me free.

Another day, while leaving a friend's house after an afternoon of visiting, I had to walk through a park. By the time I reached the first bench, my right foot swelled up for no reason at all. It got so big that I couldn't fit my foot into the sandal I was wearing.

I sat on the bench and wondered what I was going to do now. I couldn't just walk barefoot home. Then I heard a voice in my head: *Use the name of Jesus.*

I did what it said. "In the name of Jesus, I command the swelling to go down."

Instantly, the swelling was completely gone. I was amazed! The power of prayer was real. Wow! I slid my foot back into the sandal and continued home.

As a new baby Christian, I was hungry to learn. When I received my first Bible, I was told to start reading from the New Testament. While reading, I also discovered that I needed to be baptized, so I asked my new friends if they knew of any church that would baptize me. The one I was attending didn't have a baptismal pool.

As it turned out, just up the hill from where I was living was a church that was having a baptismal service that evening. When I got there, I was directed to the pastor's office. As I drew up to his door, it opened and several people filed out. It turned out they had just been instructed on what baptism is about and what to expect. Well, I was too late for that, but the pastor didn't mind. He took my name and told me he would see me that evening and baptize me.

I told Greg and my sons that I was getting baptized and asked if they would come and watch. Greg and Joey came along. When I came out of the water that evening, Joey said my matted hair made me look like a drowned rat. A young man who speaks his mind! But even so, I felt renewed. I also knew I was doing what God wanted me to do.

Full water immersion symbolizes the death of our old lives, with all that was ugly and ungodly being buried and being resurrected into a new life in Christ Jesus. In other words, the old man is gone and the new man is raised to newness of life.

> *We were therefore buried with him through baptism into death in order that, just as Christ was raised from the dead through the glory of the Father, we too may live a new life.* (Romans 6:4)

Not long after being baptized, I discovered that a Christian was to pay tithes. Since I didn't have a job or any money of my own, I had nothing to give. So I asked God for a job, so I could tithe.

My first job was cleaning the house of an elderly couple. It took three hours to clean their home once a week at $7 per hour. I made $21 and was so proud of myself when I tithed $2.10 that week.

Then I discovered that a Christian was to pay offerings as well. At first I could only give fifty cents, and even then that was a lot of money since I had so little to spend on groceries and pay my bills. Greg was still drinking and we both smoked, so grocery shopping was skimpy.

But I saw God bless my tithes and offerings many times. I seemed to get more groceries even though I spent the same amount. I found great sales and as a result felt extremely happy.

"Will a mere mortal rob God? Yet you rob me. But you ask, 'How are we robbing you?' In tithes and offerings. You are under a curse—your whole nation—because you are robbing me. Bring the whole tithe into the storehouse, that there may be food in my house. Test me in this," says the Lord Almighty, "and see if I will not throw open the floodgates of heaven and pour out so much blessing that there will not be room enough to store it. I will prevent pests from devouring your crops, and the vines in your fields will not drop their fruit before it is ripe… Then all the nations will call you blessed, for yours will be a delightful land." (Malachi 3:8–12)

Then Jesus said to them, "Give back to Caesar what is Caesar's and to God what is God's." (Mark 12:17)

Shortly after becoming a Christian, God spoke to me about putting a book together—and I freaked out. *No way,* I thought. *I can't do that. Besides, who's going to read anything I put together? If this is really coming from You, God, then You have to send someone to help me.*

Not long after my talk with God, I was talking to the secretary of our church, Marina, who volunteered to type the book out for me! I also told my friend Joyce, who lived next door, about writing the book and she offered to help as well! God went beyond what I'd asked Him and gave me two people to help.

While I was attending rehab, I had collected poems on drugs and alcohol because they spoke so deeply to me. I also found other people who wanted to submit poems. By May 15, 1991 my first book was printed and I named it *Something Beautiful*. God used that little book to touch people's hearts.

Later, in December 1998, I updated the book and changed the title to *From the Prison to the Palace*.

Mom came from Saskatoon to visit around this time, and as she sat at my kitchen table she noticed a For Sale sign in front of a three-story apartment building across the street. I guess her wheels got to turning because she ended up buying the building. She and Greg discussed renovations, and in no time we moved into the bottom floor, taking up two of the suites.

At first all appeared to go well. Greg, the boys, Mom, Loretta, and I began ripping down plaster and slates in the walls between the living room, dining room, and kitchen in order to transform it into one big open area. Other members of the family helped when they came to Medicine Hat to visit.

Work on the apartment progressed slowly, and the more Greg drank the poorer was his workmanship.

Greg wasn't pleased with my newfound Christianity, and so he leaned more and more to the bars. One could say we had become unevenly yoked. We were living in the same house, but our lives were separate. He was still stuck in the rut he was in before. It's funny that it was his idea to go to rehab the first time, yet I was the one who found out that I had the problem as well and did something about it. I wanted to become a better wife, a better mom, and just an all-round better and happier person.

The change had a big cost.

One evening while the boys and I were watching TV, Greg came home drunk and in a very lousy mood. He ignored the dinner I had kept warm for him and without a word went straight to our bedroom. We watched him slam the door, then went back to our show.

Unexpectedly, the bedroom door flung open and Greg glared at me. "I don't want this book in here."

He threw the Bible at me, and it landed on the floor near my feet. With that, he slammed the door shut again.

I had learned by then just to let him be. I picked up the Bible and we continued watching TV. Yes, we were disturbed by his unhappiness, but there was nothing we could do about it.

While we were living in that big old apartment, my children began attending church with me. Each one gave his life to Jesus and joined the youth group and found enjoyment and new positive friends. I was so proud of them.

The only one who wasn't happy about this was my lost and lonely husband. He continued to drink and pick fights with me, but we kept praying for him.

During a drunken episode in the middle of winter, he came home and I told him it was terribly cold in the boys' bedrooms. Greg went about fixing the problem. He grabbed what he thought to be the caulking gun and proceeded to caulk around the inside of each tall window in their rooms. He said we could clean them off in the spring.

It was later discovered that the caulk he'd used was actually glue. He had glued all the windows shut. Did we ever get a laugh out of that! One thing was certain, however: there was no more cold coming through those windows.

Another time, Greg was going to fix the dryer. I wasn't in the room when he started, but when I walked in he was leaning over the front of the dryer and placed two knives on something in the back. We heard a sudden loud pop and the knives went flying in different directions. As did he!

He managed to recover from the shock, but I was coming to the conclusion that it wasn't a good idea to ask him to fix anything unless he was sober.

We had a florescent light attached beneath the cupboard over the kitchen sink, but the cord was too long and kept getting in the way, so Greg decided he would solve the problem. And of course he had been drinking.

Taking out my best butcher knife, he cut into the cord to splice it. Well, he had left the light on so he could see what he was doing. Cutting into that cord resulted in the biggest shock of all shocks.

Once again, he did recover, but my knife didn't fare so well. The heat surging through the wires melted part of the blade. I kept the knife as a reminder of how funny the incident was. I swear he had a death wish. His drinking was literally killing him.

Not long after Greg threw the Bible out of our room, his behaviour worsened. One day he called and told me he would be staying at Pastor Wyll's place in order to sober up. Pastor Wyll was once an alcoholic himself, so he knew what Greg needed. Greg told me he'd heard the voice of God speaking to him loud and clear while he was out drinking that afternoon. Afterward he had urgently taken a taxi to the church I attended and submitted his life to Jesus.

He spent three days violently detoxing on the bed Pastor Wyll gave him. He then spent a few more days to make sure he was ready to come home.

When Greg finally got back to the house, he was a new man. He had his own Bible, which he read constantly. He didn't go back to the bars and he worked diligently on Mom's apartment. To say I was ecstatic would be putting it mildly. We became a real family.

A little more than a year after I turned my life over to Jesus, I began crying out to Him to help me quit smoking. I smoked two packs a day and had smoked a lot of drugs, which inflicted a great deal of damage on my lungs. By evening I'd be sitting in a chair with my arms crossed, rocking back and forth with tears in my eyes as pain ripped through my chest. It felt like someone was jabbing a sword through me. I had the smoker's cough to go with it, but I couldn't find the will to quit. I'd tried many times but failed.

One Sunday at church, as I was trying to sing, I kept getting interrupted by coughing. Phlegm was choking off my vocal cords. Finally, out of pure frustration, I cried out to God, "I can't even praise You. Help me."

A week or so later, while preparing to make dinner for the family, a deacon from the church named Lee stopped by. I served him coffee and he joined Greg at the table. As they spoke, I was at the counter preparing to cut an onion to make hamburgers. As I reached for the onion, I felt my hand being moved and placed on my package of cigarettes instead, which was further down the counter. That was weird.[21]

Because our little kitchen was thick with cigarette smoke, I turned to Lee and asked if God had sent him to pray for me about my cigarette habit. He sighed and a look of utter relief crossed his face. He told us that God wanted him to pray for me.

I put the hamburger in the fridge and sat at the end of the table next to him. He got up and, with Greg's permission, placed one hand under my neck and the other on my upper back. As he began to pray, the Holy Spirit came over me. I felt the blood in my whole body begin to tingle.

When he finished praying, I was so stoned in the Holy Spirit that I couldn't move even if I had wanted to. I stayed like that for some time while Lee and Greg continued to talk.

Then Lee turned to me and, pointing at his own chest just below his shoulder, he asked, "You have a pain right here, don't you?" I confirmed that I did. He got up, pulled my chair sideways and said, "You had better be right, Holy Spirit." He drew his right hand back and slapped me across my right cheek, sending my head flying to the side.

Who comes into your house and slaps you across the face? Well, I didn't feel the slap at all, and the pain in my chest immediately disappeared. Imagine Lee's relief that it went just as the Holy Spirit had designed it to. There wasn't even a mark, and afterward the Spirit came on me even heavier.

---

[21] I truly believe an angel took my hand and placed it there.

Unable to move, I sat there in the anointing for about twenty minutes, all the while experiencing the sensation of every blood vessel tingling throughout my body. I believe my blood was being washed clean.

When I could finally move, Lee finished his conversation with Greg and stood in front of me once again. He said that the Holy Spirit wanted him to tell me that I had brand-new baby lungs and that I would never smoke again. He added that if I tried to smoke, I would become fatally ill. Then Lee left.

After that, all my cravings for cigarettes was gone. I mean, really gone!

That night, my brother Lawrence drove into town. He was still trucking, so we went to the coffee shop to meet him. We had to push tables together once others from the family joined us. As we sat and had coffee, everyone started passing around cigarettes like they were candy.

Even though I hadn't desired a cigarette after Lee had prayed for me several hours before, I suddenly wanted one—and Greg's cigarette was sitting in the ashtray beside me.

With great caution, because of what Lee had said, I picked up Greg's cigarette and took a drag, but I only inhaled half and blew out the other half. If I was going to get sick, then hopefully I would only get half-sick. Now, wasn't that logical reasoning on my part?

Since nothing happened, I took another drag off the cigarette, blowing half the smoke out before inhaling. Only this time, right before my eyes, I envisioned two great talons ripping my lungs apart. I doubled over with pain and tears slid down my cheeks. In great shame, I asked God to forgive me. He had known I would test Him.

The pain didn't last long, but long enough to prove that God had indeed set me free from cigarettes.

Shortly after Greg's conversion, Mom had decided to sell the apartment block and move back to Saskatoon, although we would be able to continue living there until it sold. We expanded our living quarters to take over two full floors of the building.

It was then that we began to take people into our home who needed a place to stay while they tried to get their lives back on track. Some were married women with children who couldn't handle living with their addicted husbands, others were men and women with addiction problems, and we also took in teens with nowhere to go. We opened our home to anyone who was in trouble and needed a hand up.

One young man, William, was around the same age as our sons. His parents lived in Lethbridge, but he was attending school in Medicine Hat. He stayed with us for quite some time and became like one of my own sons. He still is, to this day.

Since we had such a large dining room and kitchen, we started a weekly Bible study in our home, with Pastor Wyll leading it. We started with a few people, but in no time our numbers climbed as high as thirty people. It was crowded, interesting, and extremely enjoyable. The study and discussions would last for several hours. We had a large coffee urn and many brought food to share. No one was ever in a hurry to go home.

Then came the day Greg and I decided we needed to renew our marriage vows. We'd come to realize that our first marriage had been a complete mockery of what God held sacred. So we held a simple wedding in the living room. I asked my friend Joyce to be my bridesmaid and Greg asked her husband Allan to be his best man.

Since I didn't have a dress and couldn't afford to buy one for this special occasion, Joyce lent me one of her beautiful dresses. She also did my hair and makeup. I felt like a million dollars! Others helped with the arrangements: wedding cake, food, and flowers. With our sons in attendance this time, along with many of our friends, we both stood in front of Pastor Wyll, this time perfectly sober and in our right minds, and repledged our vows.

During this period, I was also learning about forgiveness and why one needs to forgive. One evening, while everyone was out, I began seeing tormenting images of what my father had done to me and the rest of my family. I was so overwhelmed by the suddenness of these visions.

There were many thorns in my past, but these were the longest and deadliest, the ones that had been stored away for far too many years because I hadn't known how to deal with them. Standing by the kitchen counter one day, uncontrollable screams of despair burst out of me. In aguish, I slammed my fists over and over again, crying out at the top of my lungs.

The memories kept coming and I felt that I was on the verge of going insane. When I finally became too exhausted to go on, I heard God speak softly to me. It took a while to understand what He was saying, and then it came to me that if I wanted to be free of the control he had over me, even from the grave, I needed to forgive him and allow God to heal me.

So, with great determination and a lot of hesitation, I finally came to a place of surrender. I forgave Dad and turned him over to God. I then asked God to forgive me for hating him so much. God forgave me for holding onto all that fear, neglect, abuse, and violence. He brought to my life a peace that surpassed human understanding. I felt like I had been washed clean.

I also found that when those memories of my father later trickled through my mind, they didn't hurt me any more. I was free!

Forty
Our Own House

Allan and Greg partnered together to run a used car lot. They did quiet well from my understanding, though I wasn't part of the business. But there came a time when our friendship with Allan and Joyce suddenly changed. Joyce stopped calling and visiting. She simply disappeared from my life, and then they moved to another part of the city.

Just before this took place, Greg had gone back to drinking and stopped going to church. He also didn't want to have anything more to do with the car business. Because I'm not a businessperson, I simply accepted his decision and asked no questions.

It wasn't until many years later that I learned the truth. Joyce told me that Greg had approached Allan and demanded an insane amount of money for his half of the business. Naturally they'd thought I knew about this, as I was Greg's wife. They took Greg to our pastor, to try to get some counsel on the situation, but I knew nothing about this meeting. Out of the goodness of Allan's heart, at that meeting he offered Greg a smaller amount of money just to settle the matter, and with the pastor's encouragement Greg took the deal. He shouldn't have, because when they'd started the business it had all come from Allan's start-up money.

I was so embarrassed and humiliated when I found out about this. With much shame, I told Joyce that Greg had screwed others out of their money as well.

Greg was a deceiver, but what really bothered me was the fact that no one ever asked me if they should lend to him. I would have been the first to tell them not to do it. And when I found out he cheated these people, I always felt responsible to right the wrong by paying them back, simply because Greg was my husband. Not that I had the money, but I would have made payments.

Eventually the apartment building sold and we were fortunate enough to find a house right across the street. In fact, it was the same house Joyce and Allan had lived in. There was room enough for our boys and William.

After we moved, William's younger bother came to join us for a couple of months until he had to return to Lethbridge. Then there was a guy who just couldn't get his life on track; he stayed with us until he found his own place.

We had a somewhat crowded home, but it worked and everybody got along.

Still, the house was hot and stuffy. One day, I decided to join Joey out on the screened-in porch. It was a warm summer night and as we sat Joey asked if God was real—and if He was, did He ever think about him? We talked about it for a bit, and then I bowed my head and asked God to show Himself to Joey, so he would know that He was real.

When I lifted my head and opened my eyes, I gasped.

"Look Joey, look across the valley!"

All along the tops of the houses danced the northern lights. It looked like they were suspended from one end of the cliff to the other. In sacred awe, we got up, left the porch, and marvelled at the sky. Suddenly, the lights began approaching toward us from across the valley. They seemed to stop over our house and turn into the shape of a dove.

"Is this God?" Joey asked.

"It has to be!"

The image of the dove remained for a time and then disappeared. I could feel the presence of God all over me that night, and Joey and I both knew it had been an answer to my prayer and his question.

Yes, God is real and He hears the voices of His children. It was a holy moment.

Around this time, Greg decided that he wanted to adopt the boys. I was okay with this, but I wanted him to ask them first. Joey and Blayne were happy to keep their own names, but Eugene, not having a father, said that he wanted to be Greg's son.

So we went on a search for his Aunt Terri, Henry's sister. I would need Henry's death certificate in order for Greg to adopt Eugene. Terri and I had kept in close contact for many years, but somewhere along the way I'd lost touch with her due to us both moving around so much.

I said a prayer and then I called the operator to see if I could get Terri's phone number just by using her name. The operator said that they normally didn't give out numbers unless someone also knew the address. I explained my situation and she did me the favour of initiating a name search across all of Ontario. She found three numbers from three different areas of the province for me to try. I thanked her profusely.

I asked the Lord to show me which number to call. One number stuck out, so I dialled it and immediately Terri answered. Awesome! I told her about the other numbers and she explained that she had been in those places, but then moved on.

Anyway, I told her why I was calling and she said she would get the certificate as soon as possible. From there, we caught up.

The certificate didn't take long to come and the adoption was in the bag. My son had his own dad, and I was able to give Greg a son!

For whatever reason, tears began running down my cheeks one day while kneeling beside my bed in prayer. Then the phone rang. Because no one else was home, I got up to answer it. It was a friend from church who I hadn't talked to in some time.

The woman hesitated and then revealed that she had something she needed to share with me. It was something the Lord had told her to tell me, only she had waited three weeks before coming up with the nerve to do so.

She went on to say that the Lord was going to do something for me that I had thought absolutely impossible. This was to show me that there is nothing too big for Him. After we talked a bit, I thanked her and hung up. I didn't share this conversation with anyone.

About a week or so later, Greg came home and told me that we had a chance to buy a house. Now, if there were anything in the whole world I would have thought completely impossible, this was it. Me, owning my own house? Greg had been talking to a realtor, and the realtor was coming by the next day to speak to us.

The next day, a young man came over after supper and explained how we could purchase a house without any money. It had something to do with him lending us the money, and then us giving it back to him. As I said, I'm not business-minded, so I didn't know if this was legal or not.

Greg and I went to see the house they'd been talking about and it suited our purpose. We really liked it. So Greg called the realtor back and told him we would accept the deal. I didn't understand all the jargon, but I trusted Greg and went along with it.

Because I had a perfect credit rating and was working full-time at a pizza place, the realtor said it was a go. He took out a large bundle of bills held together with an elastic band, and then he handed it to Greg. They did some paperwork, after which Greg handed it back to the realtor. After the paperwork was completed, the place was ours.

My friend had truly heard from God. God had made the impossible possible!

Shortly after moving in, I had one of those rare moments when I had the house completely to myself. I took the opportunity to sit in the living room and pray. It was wonderful and I felt very close to God.

Suddenly, a thought popped into my mind and I repeated it out loud: "What would it be like without Holy Spirit living inside me?" No sooner had I spoken those words than I felt Holy Spirit step out of my body. Instantly everything around me turned blacker than night. Never in all my life had I ever felt so alone and afraid. It was dark and sinister. I sat on the edge of my couch, rocking back and forth, face in my hands, sobbing uncontrollably. Within seconds, my face was soaking wet in tears. While still crying, I pleaded for God to forgive me and asked the Holy Spirit to come back—and believe me, I meant every word of it.

Instantly, I felt the Holy Spirit step back inside me, and immediately my tears dried up. The light was back and the peace that surpasses all understanding returned. I knew I wasn't alone anymore. I swore I had gone down into hell for those few terrifying seconds, though it had felt like an eternity.

I will never forget that experience as long as I live. I believe God allowed me to experience this so I would know that the Holy Spirit is real and never wander away from God. I am so grateful.

We weren't long in the house before Joey moved out at the age of nineteen and got his own place. He still blames me to this day. He had told me he wasn't ready to leave, and I know now that he was right. But when I was growing up, when you turned eighteen you moved out—that is, if you hadn't gotten kicked out first. And if you weren't in school, you moved out and got a job.

Soon after, Blayne joined Joey, and not long after Eugene went to stay with my mom in Saskatoon.

I missed having the boys at home, but we were still taking in people who needed a place to live until they could get their lives back on track. We hosted Greg's brother's family for a while when they needed help.

We only had the house for a year, and halfway through that period Greg returned to drinking, stopped going to church, and no longer paid the bills. I couldn't afford to keep up the house payments and other bills, at least not with my meagre wages. Greg made great wages as a roofer, but he had begun supporting the local watering hole again. I didn't see much of the money, so the house had to go. Just like that, we were back to living in an apartment. And if there was any money leftover from the sale of the house, I didn't see it. He stole my gift.

Our next stop was Upland Drive. I have no idea how long we were there, maybe a year, but before long our marriage fell apart again.

Forty-One
Train Wrecks

I've been through so many relationship train wrecks that I lost count. Always the train pulls gradually out of the station and everything appears auspicious. The miles slide by, clickity-clack. Security and anticipation drape their affectionate arms about my shoulders while I contently lean into my seat to enjoy the ride.

Greg and I had made the promising commitment to start fresh once. What I hadn't suspected was that I was being swallowed up by the cunning words of a well-practiced narcissistic personality.

There, far ahead of the engine, are broken and missing pieces of track. There are no warning signs, thus making it too late to slam on the breaks. Suddenly the car veers from its designated path, wrenching violently as it's flung onto its side, skidding precariously over rocks.

Once again the train has been derailed, leaving in its wake carnage scattered in every direction. The ride is over and the only thing left to do is pick up the mangled pieces and rebuild.

Between 1992 and 2003, I moved eleven times, all of which turned out to be temporary homes. I lost count of how many times Greg moved. I had no roots to speak of and Greg didn't have what it takes to permanently stop drinking, although he tries. He just couldn't decide which side of the fence he wanted to be on.

Well, while I lived alone at the Dunmore apartment, I stood in the middle of the living room with my eyes closed, talking to God. I asked Him to help me take my eyes off myself and guide me to do His will.

I was given a moment's glimpse of Jesus hanging upon the cross. At first I was looking at Him from above, the top of His head. I was in awe! I mean, it really blew me away.

"Lord, how do I pray for my family?" I asked.

"Take your eyes off My head and look at My feet."

Suddenly, I could see His feet clearly. I saw the nail sticking out of his feet and the blood flowing from their wounds. I was instantly repelled and had to turn away.

"Why are you repelled?" He asked.

I began to cry. "I hate pain and hurt. I hate seeing people suffer."

"But I did it for you," he said. Tears gripped me as I grasped what He was saying to me. "My child, you are worth it. I was looking at you when this happened. I did it for you. You see, you belong to My kingdom and I will bring you back. Doesn't a potter take special care of his creation, protecting it from harm? So it is with you. So it is with all My children. My love is greater and deeper than the human mind can comprehend. My love will keep and protect My children. My love is greater than all eternity."

But God demonstrates his own love for us in this: while we were still sinners, Christ died for us. (Romans 5:8)

As I looked around my living room, I saw ornaments made by unknown potters, and I realized that when I packed them up to move, I would take care not to break them. I realized, too, that that is how we are as God's people. The potter sells his creations in the hope that they will be cherished and protected, just as God places His people before us so that we will cherish and care for them as He does each of us.

"I have given this family to you, Barbra," God spoke to me. "If you cherish your ornaments, how much more your family?"

Since that conversation, I've tried hard to treat my family and others the way God wants us to treat one another. But I have to be honest: I'm human and I've failed a million zillion times at this. Still, I haven't given up. I'm gradually making progress. When I meet someone I don't like, guilt kicks around inside me and I have to turn to God and ask His forgiveness for my attitude. I have to ask Him to help me to see them through His eyes and love them through His love. When I've done that, the most remarkable thing happens; I start to like them. *Start* is the key word here. It doesn't happen all at once, but a little at a time, until I can feel His care for him living and breathing inside me. To get to that point, I've often had to plead for God's help.

Once again Greg stopped drinking and came back to church, so I let him move back in with me. By this time I was again working as a pizza cook. My hours fluctuated, but I worked most evenings and would return home around two or three in the morning.

Since I was making this extra money, I asked Greg what was the one thing in his life he had always wanted to do but never had the courage to try. He told me that he wanted to learn how to play a guitar.

So for Christmas, I found an affordable guitar and gave it to him. He immediately began to learn chords and practiced, practiced, practiced. He put beautiful cords together, but the songs had no lyrics. It was a joy to listen.

I came home one night at three o'clock and found that Greg was in bed. Before going to sleep, I sat at the table to unwind from the hectic night's work.

Suddenly, a few interesting sentences began forming in my head. I reached for pen and paper and wrote them down.

My dear darling husband
Your struggles I can see
I long to take you in my arms
And hold you close to me
When we share our thoughts together
Though we don't always agree
But sharing my thoughts with you, dear
Means so very much to me

I see you as someone special
A proud buck you do stand
Holding your antlers high
Almost daring any man
I see you when I awake
I see you throughout the day
I see you in everything I do
Because you're my man and that's okay

Yes, I did marry you
But have only one regret
We've been through many rough times
And they're not over yet
So here I sit writing
This love letter to you
Haven't done it in a long while
But it's my way of saying "I love you"

Within a few minutes, I had finished a full-length poem. It described the depth of our love in only few words. I named it "Love Letter."

Leaving it on the table for Greg to read in the morning, I went tiredly to bed.

A couple of days later, he asked me to listen to a song he had composed. I was astonished to discover that he had put chords to the poem—and it was beautiful! It was our first song.

Years later, we went into a studio and recorded it along with three other songs.

Sadly, this period of our marriage didn't last. We soon separated again and I once again found myself on my own.

Since the apartment had two bedrooms, I asked God for a Christian roommate to share the expenses. At church that Sunday, I was introduced to a woman named Marlene, who had been praying for a place to rent. As it turned out, her husband Delbert didn't have enough work to support them back in Saskatchewan and so she'd managed to secure a job for three months here in Medicine Hat. I liked her immediately. She had spark! I just knew she was an answer to prayer and she moved in as soon as she could collect her belongings.

We didn't see a lot of each other, as we often worked different shifts, but when we did get together our friendship bloomed. Marlene had an awesome sense of humour and we could really talk and laugh! She encouraged me on my darkest days. She understood what it was like to miss a husband. In a way, she was like a mother, sharing with me the great wisdom and comfort I so desperately needed.

I had a lot of growing up to do and God was putting the right people in my life to help me catch up on the years I had lost to drinking and doing drugs.

Marlene took me to her hometown of Shaunavon and introduced me to her family. I fell in love with them, too, and felt like I belonged. They taught me many valuable lessons about how a real family lived. I wanted to be part of a family like that.

I discovered that Marlene and Delbert had started a couple of churches up north outside of Edmonton. They also owned a large ministry that distributed free second-hand clothing and furniture, in addition to being involved in ministry on the local Indigenous reservations.

When Marlene discovered my book of poetry, *Something Beautiful,* she felt it would suit their ministry perfectly. It contained poems about alcohol, drugs, and other behaviours that could cause a person's live to derail. So she wrote cheques through the ministry to buy books from me—and when she ran out, she bought more. The books were touching people's lives!

All the money I gained from selling these books went back into making other books. Their purpose was strictly to minister to people, not to earn a profit. In fact, I usually gave the books away.

I printed my books at a small printing shop where a friend of mine worked. Since each book was costly to produce, I couldn't pay to print very many at a time.

Well, one afternoon while I was assembling new books and had their pages spread out across the counter, two nuns walked in. While they waited their turn, they watched what I was doing and asked about my books. I told them that the books were used to minister to hurting people who were caught up in addictions. Even before the book was assembled, the nuns wanted to buy it.

The nuns then told me a story of a young woman they knew who was involved in heavy drugs and was talking about suicide. They wanted to give her one of my books in the hopes that it would help her. I quickly finished assembling the book and gave it to them. They insisted on paying for it. Who argues with nuns?

I never thought I'd hear from those nuns again, but not long after our meeting my phone rang and a quiet voice on the other end asked if my name was Barbra. I told her that it was. She explained that she had received my book from some nuns, and the book had moved her so deeply that she'd given her life to Jesus. Now she wanted to meet me personally!

I hopped on a bus to go meet her. We talked for about an hour, after which I had the opportunity to pray with her. In tears, she hugged me goodbye and thanked me for bringing hope to her screwed-up life.

If she thought she was privileged to have met me, she had no idea how much she had inspired me. I couldn't believe what God was doing with this little power-packed booklet. The book has been distributed across Canada, and one of the stories in it even went overseas to China after someone requested that I read it aloud at my friend's funeral.

Anyway, Marlene stayed three months and then returned home, but we never lost touch. I became close friends with her daughter Mae, who had a five-year-old son, Alexander. We spent many adventurous hours together, including spontaneous road trips. I also got to know her sister Florence and we would get together in powerful prayer, then watch God answer the prayers.

Whenever the stress of life gets to be too much for me, I catch a ride to Shaunavon, where this family welcomes me with open arms. They're like the family I never had. Whenever I visit, it's a great excuse for a big family dinner, which makes me feel so very special and wanted.

Shortly after Marlene left, Greg returned—again. This time, I took him to Shaunavon to meet my new family, and when we came back our van was loaded from front to back with used clothing from Marlene and Delbert's ministry. It was enough to stack high in our living room with only a narrow pathway to get from one end of the room to the other. We called in all the families and friends we knew, and encouraged them to bring people they knew, and take away the clothes by the bagful. After everyone had taken what they needed, we packed up the remains and took it to the Salvation Army.

One day, I just happened to turn on the TV and caught the end of a Christian television show produced in Winnipeg called *It's a New Day*. The guest speaker on the program was talking about addiction, and then came the book offer: *The 12 Step Serenity Bible*. I didn't have much money, but the book was free, so I dialled the ministry's phone number and ordered the books. And while I was at it, I accepted prayer.

A month or more went by and I forgot about the book—that is, until it showed up in my mailbox. At first I was excited and flipped through the pages. I found it to be very different from other books I'd read on addictions and AA. So I placed it on a bookshelf to be read later and then forgot about it.

By this time, life with Greg was on a downward spiral. His drinking and spending was out of control, not to mention he was still going to the bar after work and staying until closing time. I often felt that it was again time to move on, so I prayed about the situation and watched the newspapers for rental opportunities.

It wasn't long before I came upon a cheap but clean basement suite that was in my price range. It was the middle of the month, so I told the landlord I would take it at the end of the month and put down a deposit. The suite was within walking distance of work and there was a bus stop only half a block away. It was perfect!

I didn't say anything to Greg, because our marriage was already intolerable and I didn't want to make things worse. Besides, we had lousy communication skills. He'd bully me and I would react in anger.

A week later, after getting off work at four in the afternoon, I came home to our empty apartment and suddenly felt an overwhelming urge to move out immediately. I asked God that if this was His prompting— if it was, He needed to provide a mover and some boxes. He would also have to give me favour with my new landlord, who would have to allow me to move in early.

Putting the move in God's hands, I phoned the landlord and he agreed to meet with me at a restaurant across the street from where I lived. I was honest about my situation and without hesitation he passed over the keys to my new suite and said I could move in immediately. Taken aback, I thanked him and hurried home to gather my belongings.

Next, I phoned my workplace and asked the delivery driver if he knew of anyone who could help me move. Since he was getting off work in an hour, he said he would see what he could do.

In the meantime, I again prayed and asked what I should take with me. As I walked through the apartment, I gathered dishes, silverware, pots and pans, sheets, blankets, pillows, towels, and other personal belongings. I would leave Greg lacking for nothing, but my TV, stereo, and VCR were coming with me. He'd already pawned them off once before and I'd had to borrow money from my brother-in-law to buy them back.

Being an avid reader, I then went to the bookshelves and asked God which books I should take. I then ran my hand lightly over the books, and when I sensed a book I needed I pulled it out and placed it on the pile. Quickly I came upon the long forgotten *12 Step Serenity Bible*. Really? Well, I just shrugged my shoulders and put it with the others.

Not long after gathering everything I wanted to take with me, I heard banging on the apartment door. I opened it to find a crew of guys who hung out at my workplace, along with the driver I had spoken to earlier. I was absolutely flabbergasted! They'd even brought boxes, so I started filling them while I instructed the guys what to take out to the truck and car which God had so graciously provided for me.

The only other furniture I took was the single bed and a matching dresser that had been given to me two weeks prior by my landlady and her boyfriend. At the time, they had been breaking up, too.

I had moved into my new home within an hour. Before the guys left, my bed was set up and the TV stand was placed where I wanted it. All the electronics were hooked up and working, and the housewares were set in a corner to be dealt with the next day.

It had been a very long and emotional day and I was mentally and physically spent. With my last bit of energy, I made up the bed and gratefully crawled into it. It took a while for my mind to quieten before falling into a deep sleep, one which I knew would not be interrupted by arguments, anger and tears.

Two days after moving, I awoke to a dreary, overcast morning that matched my mood perfectly. I felt the need to take the lengthy walk to work. The walk wasn't so bad, as it was downhill, but going home afterward would present a steep incline.

Upon reaching the bottom, I heard a voice whisper in my ear: "Look up."

There was no one in front or behind me, so I ignored the voice and continued on my way.

Again the voice said, "Look up."

When I did so, at first all I could see was a dark cloud spanning the whole sky. What was this about? As I continued to stare, I saw it—a tiny ray of sunshine peeking through the cloud. The cloud then separated and began to form into the shape of a flying eagle and the sun's rays burst fort. I was absolutely mesmerized! Drinking in the awesomeness of this event, I felt the sadness and misery drain out of me, replaced by joy beyond understanding. I knew God had done this for me! My spirit soared as I watched the beams of light slowly fade as the clouds joined back together.

Bursting with happiness, I quickened my steps so I wouldn't be late for work. Then I heard it: a song. Over and over again, four lines raced through my head.

Wait, Lord, I need to get a pen and paper, I thought.

Reaching the door of my workplace, with trembling hands I fumbled about in my purse trying to find the keys. As soon as I was inside, I grabbed a pen and piece of paper and waited for the song to start over again:

I will soar on the wings of an eagle
I will soar higher than before
I will go where I've never been before
And I will soar with Jesus my Lord

I knew the song was a promise from God. Even though my world had fallen down around me, I knew God was with me and I would rise above this storm, just as eagles do during a storm. They soar high above the clouds and wait it out, then return to earth when it's over.

As I would discover in later years, there was so much more to the promise. This song also relates to a Bible verse in Isaiah, which I still cling to when the storms in my life break lose:

He gives strength to the weary and increases the power of the weak. Even youths grow tired and weary, and young men stumble and fall; but those who hope in the Lord will renew their strength. They will soar on wings like eagles; they will run and not grow weary, they will walk and not be faint. (Isaiah 40:29–31)

The next day, while I was looking for something to read, I was strongly drawn to the *12 Step Serenity Bible* again.

"Okay, Lord, what do You want to show me?" I asked aloud.

"Write the precepts."

What the heck was a precept? I didn't have a dictionary, so I didn't know what this meant, but I was intrigued and knew that He wanted me to read this book.

"Okay, but You'll have to show me what You want me to do."

I later learned that the word precept refers to a commandment or direction that's meant as a rule of moral conduct. It occurs in a few different verses of the Bible:

I meditate on your precepts and consider your ways. (Psalms 119:15)

…that they might keep his precepts and observe his laws. Praise the Lord. (Psalms 105:45)

So I opened the book and began to read.

That book was the beginning of a long and many times painful journey out of the world of insanity in which I had lived. Its contents drew me to the light, and once I started reading it I just couldn't put it down. I even went so far as to stuff it into my purse so I could read it on the bus on the way to and from work.

But when I came to step four, which instructed me to make a searching and fearless moral inventory of myself, I didn't understand what I was supposed to do, even after reading the chapter twice. I felt hopelessly perplexed and couldn't move on until I understood this part of the book.

God, if there's anyone else in this city who has this book, please show me that person, in Jesus's name, I prayed.

That same evening, one of the delivery drivers, a Christian Biker named Bear, came into the kitchen and noticed the book.

When he commented on it, I asked excitedly, "Do you know anything about it?"

"Yeah, I go to a twelve-step group and we're studying the book," he said.

"When do they meet and can anyone go?"

"They meet tomorrow night at seven."

Then he gave me the address. This was awesome! Talk about an instant answer to prayer.

The next day was my day off, so with trepidation I took the bus and made my way downtown. I didn't like going to new places by myself and I wasn't good at finding my way around, but I wanted this bad enough that I needed to take the chance.

When I walked through the door, I found a woman sitting alone at one of the tables. By the looks of it, I had arrived early. She immediately welcomed me and introduced herself as Fay. She was the one teaching the twelve-step program.

I told her why I was there and she said I could join them, but they were already on step nine or ten. Well, I figured since I was already there I might as well stay.

I didn't participate in the class as others did. Instead I just sat and nervously listened.

At the end of the class, Fay offered me a lift home as she was going in the same direction. We sat outside my place and talked for more than an hour. She listened and understood my situation. By the time she left, I knew this was the direction God wanted me to go.

Forty-Two
Making Amends

A couple of weeks after I had moved out, I still had the keys to Greg's apartment. So I decided to go over to return them.

I knocked on the door, but he didn't answer. Inside I heard music playing, though, and I'd seen the lights on through the window. I knew he was home.

Using the key, I walked in and called his name. As I passed through the kitchen, I saw them—Greg on the living room couch holding hands with a woman I'd never seen before.

If I was surprised, the look on his face was priceless. We were still married and he was still a professing Christian. How could he?

In an uncontrollable rage, I picked up the closest thing to me, which just happened to be a half-filled glass pot of cold coffee, and flung it against the wall, just missing a large window. The pot shattered, sending coffee and shards of glass flying everywhere. Then I grabbed a pizza pan on the counter and frisbeed it in the same direction, sticking it deep into the wall. He was very lucky it wasn't his head.

After a few choice words, I threw down the keys and angrily, slamming the door behind me. It was a stormy walk back to my place and I shed many bitter tears on the way. I wanted to kill him. I wanted to hurt him every bit as much as he had hurt me, if not more.

In all our years together, I had never once thought he would screw around on me. Even when we were separated, we never saw anyone else. So far as I knew.

Then a new question arose: was this the reason he hadn't come home?

By the time I reached the haven of my apartment, I was ready for a meltdown. Shock and trauma engulfed me. In burning tears, I hammered on the kitchen counter with my fists. The realization struck my mind like a bolt of lightening that I had lost him this time, really lost him.

Suddenly, I was startled by a knock at the door. What now? In frustration, I opened the door and saw my son Joey standing before me. He could see I wasn't okay. When he came in and closed the door behind him, I had no alternative but to tell him what had happened.

Then my strength gave way and I broke out in unwelcome tears. He gathered me up in his strong arms and held me protectively while the tears fell and the war raged in my heart. My mind was saying, *Please don't let me go*, yet I felt I couldn't stay in Joey's arms long; I didn't know how to allow such love and tenderness in.

His words were gentle and reassuring, sticking me back together like bonding glue, but all I wanted to do was destroy everything, to scream and slam my fists. I also didn't know how to deal with Joey's unhappiness and anger towards Greg.

Everything was getting worse, and my mind kept telling me that I had to be strong. *Don't bring Joey into another one of your messes, Barb. Come on, Barb, stop crying. Pull yourself together. This isn't helping.*

My maternal instincts were kicking in.

I seldom cried in front of my sons. I showed anger, yes. Tantrums, yes. Crying? Not so much. I tried to be secretive about that.

I pulled away from Joey and told him I'd be okay now. Once he was assured that I would get through it, he left. But he salvaged what was left of my heart that day. The tenderness and love he showed was so precious to me, even though at the time I felt undeserving of it.

I continued to attend the weekly Bible studies. Fay became a very good friend and supported me in prayer, even letting me phone her when the situation got to be too difficult to handle. When she didn't hear from me, she phoned. I depended heavily upon her.

Fay was the one God chose to help me through this transition. Lucky her.

When she introduced me to her family, I had an extremely hard time understanding the fact that they accepted me without conditions. I spent a great deal of time at her place. Line upon line, precept upon precept, she was able to get through to me about how wrong my lifestyle had been and what I needed to do to change and become the person I hadn't known I wanted to be. She picked me up for meetings to make sure I attended. I was hungry for truth and lapping it up like ice cream.

At last I found out what AA's fourth step was all about: make a searching and fearless moral inventory of yourself. This was when I really found out how screwed up my life had been from the very beginning. I found out that I had assets and defects, even though I'd thought I had only defects. I was truly surprised to find I actually had some assets.

One of the hardest things I had to do was make a list of all the people I had harmed. Then I searched them out and asked for their forgiveness, at least the ones I could still find. I had to take a sheet of lined paper and write their names. Before I knew it, I was at the bottom of the page, and these were only the names that came to me in the moment.

I had my work cut out for me. I prayed and asked God to show me where these people were and to give me wisdom, courage, and the right words to speak.

What a humbling experience that was. I didn't do confrontation well. As a matter of fact, I ran away from it. I had been so beaten down by my past, and confrontation made me panic. But one by one, the Lord brought into my life the people from whom I needed to ask forgiveness. With each one, God's grace was on me. They all forgave me and some said that they hadn't even known there was a problem. But I knew and had to rectify it.

This process took months to accomplish.

Soon I came to the last person on the list, but she had moved out of town. What was I supposed to do now? I asked God to put her in my path.

A few months later, I spotted her while riding the bus. She was seated upfront while I was seated at the back. The bus was so full at the time that I figured I would wait until she got off downtown and then catch her there. After all, I didn't want anyone else listening to our conversation.

Well, she got off before we got downtown. I kicked myself.

Again I went to God, only this time in tears and shame. I pleaded with Him to give me another chance to get it right.

A week later, there she was on the bus again and she did get off downtown. So I rushed off the bus to catch up to her before she transferred onto another bus.

She was truly surprised and happy to see me. I didn't waste any time and got straight to the point. With great sincerity, I apologized and waited for the rebuke, which never came. She smiled and said, with so much love, "Barb, you have never done me a wrong. There is nothing to apologize for." With that, she gave me a big hug then caught her bus.

I was so relieved and thankful. I praised God for giving me another chance and walked away in awe.

After that encounter, I never saw her again.

There were of course many more people to whom I had to make amends to, but I did it as they came to mind. With each person, I felt freer and happier. I wasn't carrying all that anger and resentment around anymore. When I forgave them and asked for their forgiveness, I was set free from all the junk in my life.

Fay was such a valuable instrument of God, but He also introduced me to another valuable woman, Gail. Together, Fay and Gail stood by me when I was at my lowest points. They prayed for and encouraged me, fighting for me to succeed. I'm so grateful they never gave up on me. I felt the need to call upon them almost every day.

That's how broken and messed up I was. Greg had left me feeling so unwanted and betrayed, as though I was a failure as a wife. I couldn't even call myself a woman, yet alone a girl. There was too much shame in the word *woman*. Growing up in my dad's house, to be a girl or woman had been a defect of character, and I had seen myself as defective—flawed, a nothing, a no one.

I was high maintenance for Fay and Gail, so codependant, love-hungry, and empty. The tears I'd held back for so many pained-filled years began to spill at the littlest thing. For one who had prided herself on being so tough and strong, I became a baby, a snivelling mess.

Just to make it clear, these women were sensitive to my needs, but they never babied me. They told the truth and never minced words. They were honest and straightforward. When I was with Fay and Gail, I knew I was on my way to learning how to soar like an eagle!

As it turned out, Fay played guitar and piano and sang for the homeless at a local seniors centre. Once a month, the centre would serve the homeless a full-course meal, and she encouraged me to help. After the meal, she'd entertain and share the word of God with the people who had come to eat.

I loved being part of this ministry, and when Fay discovered my love for singing I began singing with her. What a nerve-wracking experience that was. I was so nervous, in fact, that I insisted that she had to pray for me every time we had to sing.

Our songs were very well received, but when we were finished I would shake like a leaf on a blustery day. It just wouldn't do to have anyone see how nervous I was, though; I had to look natural!

I also went with Fay to help cook meals at the church when it was her turn to volunteer. She was introducing me to a whole new world which I very much wanted to be part of.

About six months after leaving Greg, I felt the Lord telling me to return to my husband. He swore he hadn't had an affair, that he had only been helping this woman out when she was having trouble with her spouse. He was very convincing and I had no proof that he was lying, so I accepted his explanation. And when God says to go back, you go back.

But from that day forward, I was constantly suspicious when he didn't show up when he supposed to.[22]

I introduced Greg to Fay and her husband. They became friends.

I understand now why God had wanted me to move away from Greg. It had been the right time to start the twelve-step program and meet Fay and Gail. God had begun cleaning up my heart, healing my emotions and training me for the work He was calling me to do.

After several years of hard work and healing, I teamed up with Fay to help share this remarkable program with those who are really serious about changing their lifestyles. I learned the importance of forgiving those who had hurt me, and how to ask for forgiveness from those whom I had hurt. However, I found it harder to forgive myself. I just can't say it enough times; forgiveness is the key to freedom.

Instead of going back to the same apartment, Greg found a house for us on Twelfth Street. I brought all the furniture I had acquired, while Greg left his behind for those who had been sharing his apartment. This place was a much better location, as it was two blocks from my work. Also, it was wonderful to live in a house with a backyard and a deck! Best of all, it had a huge lilac bush, which is one of my favourite spring flowers!

Between 1993 and 1994, we became grandparents four times. Blayne and Lillian had a son on April 29. Joey and Adele had a daughter on July 28. During this same period, Eugene and Lane miscarried their first baby, a boy, they called their "angel baby." But on January 25, 1994, they gave birth to a healthy baby girl.

When all the families came together for visits and special occasions, it was truly an amazing sight to see the three babies lying side by side, kicking and laughing on the floor. We were very proud parents and grandparents!

---

[22] I found out years later that I had been right. Greg did have an affair with that woman.

Unfortunately, the bliss I felt living in this house only lasted about a year. I had to pack up and leave again because Greg returned to drinking.

So I went back to the confinement of apartment living. Not long after moving to a place on Southview Drive, I was laid off from my pizza job. Fortunately, I then found a full-time position at the Viener Centre, a place for seniors that provided dining, recreation, and learning. I worked in the kitchen doing food prep, washing dishes, and helping with Meals on Wheels.

In the spring of 1995, the South Saskatchewan River flooded its banks. Because the centre was right next to the river, the main floor saw three feet of flooding. After that, our doors closed indefinitely. The local hospital graciously opened up their kitchen for us to continue with the Meals on Wheels, but my hours were cut to part-time.

I found another part-time job, this time working at the Hudson Bay Restaurant. I worked seven days a week, most days working from 8:00 a.m. until 10:00 p.m. between my two jobs. I would go home between shifts just long enough to change uniforms, rest for an hour, then head off again.

Eventually, the Viener Centre reopened and I quit my job at The Bay. And while this was going on, Greg and I went through another cycle in our relationship, with him moving back in.

While in this apartment, I received a call from Eugene's Aunt Terri. Strangely enough, only a week or two before she called I had asked God if I'd ever meet this woman in person. As it turned out, she was calling from Edmonton and wanted to come to Medicine Hat to visit. She arrived the next day!

For several days she, Eugene, and his family had the chance to get to know one another. And later, when Terri went back to Ontario, she told her mother Marj about us, and the next year they both came for a visit. They were both such lovely people. And to top it off, Greg and I shared the love of Christ with Marj and she asked Jesus into her heart.

When Marj returned home, she packed up all of the belongings Henry had had with him the day he died and sent them to Eugene. She had kept them in her attic for twenty-one years.

Mom and Paul

By this time, Mom had been diagnosed with brain tumours and underwent radiation and chemotherapy. She was given only six months to live.

I managed to scrape together enough money to visit her while she and Loretta were still living in their apartment in Saskatoon. During that trip, I was shocked to see that Mom had lost all her hair and a great deal of strength. She told me about radiation procedure and how much it frightened her every time she had go through it.

I could only stay a few days to help, as they were preparing to move in with my sister Ann. I volunteered to wash Mom's walls, and in return she blessed me with the very last quilt she'd ever made.

The first time I saw that quilt, I fell immediately in love with it. The checkerboard pattern had sixteen large red and white squares with tiny pink roses against a minty-green background. Each red square had a large white dove in the middle, and the white squares had a red heart. The red squares reminded me of the blood of Jesus and the doves represented the Holy Spirit. The white squares symbolized purity and the hearts represented the love of God. The back of the quilt was made from a soft fabric of tiny rosebuds with green stems. The rosebuds reminded me of Mom and Dad's nicknames, Rose and Bud.

Shortly after I reluctantly returned from that trip, quilt in hand, I received some extremely bad news. On May 25, 1996, my brother Paul's body was found in his garage. His death was declared a suicide, but to this day the cause remains questionable.

There are no words to describe the grief I felt for Paul's wife and their two little girls. The night of his death, they were out of town visiting her parents only to return home the next day to discover the tragedy. My heart ached for them and the death of my brother, but I had no way of knowing how I could comfort them. Many times there's just nothing anyone can do.

It was equally hard to watch two of my older brothers literally hold up our mother as she walked into the church for Paul's funeral. She was utterly devastated. Being so deathly sick, bearing the loss of her son was simply too much for her.

Not long after the funeral, I heard that Mom was doing poorly, so I went to see her in the hospital. I entered her room to find her hands and feet tied to the posts of her bed with the siderails up. The nurse explained that Mom had been given the strongest medications, but they barely touched the pain, which caused her to thrash about. Oh how she had suffered.[23]

I didn't know if she recognized me, but I sat next to her and softly sang one of her favourite hymns, "Amazing Grace." It appeared to bring her a little comfort and she settled down somewhat.

I didn't have much time with her before two of her sisters joined us. At that time, I moved away from Mom's bedside so they could sit nearer to her. They encouraged me to stay, but I felt they had more rights to her than I. My heart was so heavy.

The one thing that truly comforted me was the fact that I had visited Mom a couple of months before. In her small, dimly lit room, I had sat on her bed and talked about Jesus and where she would go after she died. She had been open to what the Bible said on the matter, so she'd prayed and asked Jesus into her heart.

The Bible says the only way to the Father is through His Son. I had gotten the impression that she'd said the prayer more to reassure me than for herself.

The next time we'd talked about where she was going, I was riding with her in the back of an ambulance as the paramedics drove her to the hospital. This time she prayed the prayer with sincerity because we both thought she wasn't coming out alive.

I was so relieved to know that one day I would see her in heaven.

Just four months after Paul's death, on September 1, 1996, Mom passed away. It was Darlene's birthday, a devastating blow to her.

The very same day as Mom's funeral, Mom's older sister was lying in a hospital not far away. As Greg and I prepared to drive home to Medicine Hat, we discussed whether we had enough time to run up and visit her, but because it was so late and we had a long drive home we decided to stay on the road. The next day, we heard our aunt had passed away, and that it had happened right about the same time we had been driving out of town that day.

---

[23] This reminds me of the way in which she had needed to tie me down as a baby when I, too, had been in unbearable discomfort.

Just before Mom died, she told me that she had constant nightmares of the day she had thrown the fork and injured my eye. She'd wake up crying, and sometimes screaming, in the night. She just couldn't forgive herself... and that really saddened me—not for what she had done to me, but for what she had been going through all those years. I didn't know, because we never talked about it. I guess every time she looked at me and saw my prosthetic eye, it was a reminder of what she'd done.

As we held each other close, we cried and I told her that I never once blamed her. I knew she hadn't intended to harm me. She was the one person in this whole wide world who I had truly trusted. I always knew she loved me.

It's so hard to forgive ourselves for the awful mistakes we make. But I've found that the more often I give my mistakes over to God, the less power they have to torment me.

Forty - Three

1996 to 2002

During the next seven years, I moved at least seven more times when either I left Greg or Greg left me. But there were good times, too. When Greg was sober and back in church, he joined the music ministry, playing guitar and singing. I began singing in a barbershop quartet, because a friend of mine was in it. I gave it a try and truly enjoyed myself. By the end of the season, we and other groups performed on stage at the Medicine Hat College. People actually paid to hear us sing! That was an amazing experience and a dream come true. As a little girl, I had always pictured myself on stage singing. Well, it happened.

We also started a little group called the Rumpus Room Jammers. Fay and Greg would bring their guitars and we would sing, then others began to bring their instruments and join in with us. It caught on so well that before long we were going to people's houses to hold praise and worship gatherings. Our numbers grew to forty or more people per gathering. We would jam for two or three hours, then have coffee and feast on whatever food had been brought.

From those gatherings, Fay, her husband Joseph, their friends Ralph and Joan, and Greg and I decided to form our own band. Joseph didn't play, but he was an important member who helped carry the guitars, amplifiers, and other equipment. We called ourselves The Doorkeepers and played country gospel. Our objective was to minister Jesus Christ through song to those who would otherwise not want to hear about Him. We knew music has the power to get inside a person and plant seeds of truth.

We played at many functions and in several towns. We weren't great by any means, but we loved to share the gospel.

One of the functions we played for was the Full Gospel Business Men's Fellowship. They offered a delicious buffet dinner and brought in speakers to share their testimonies. If anyone needed prayer at the end of the evening, they were welcomed to come up and someone would pray for them. They've been holding these meetings once a month for as long as I can remember.

We were asked to provide the music on several occasions, which was fun and nerve-wracking all at the same time.

Of course, we only went to these meetings when Greg was off the bottle. One time, he was asked to share his testimony, and he agreed. His words were recorded, and this is what he said:

I was born in Yorkton, Saskatchewan, born and raised on a small farm about forty miles east of there, in a little place called Churchbridge. There was really nothing there until about 1960–61, and then they found potash and it boomed. And as it did, I grew older and I boomed with it.

I went to school there. I took up ball and hockey. I was very avid in those two avenues. Rather small for the hockey season, and in order to survive out there you did your best, you fought the hard game, and afterwards to fit in with the crowd you usually started drinking with them. I got into that pattern and it went on for years and years and years.

When I was seventeen, I got a job on the CPR as an assistant station agent and it lasted about two months. And then I found out that from two in the afternoon till 11:00 o'clock, the night shift was cutting into my drinking with my buddies, so I quit and it progressed like that for another twenty-five or thirty years.

From there I went up to Thompson, Manitoba and I worked up there for a month, then quit. Then I went out to Ontario and worked out there for about five years, but the booze was always a part of it. It was a consistent thing. And from there I came back to Saskatchewan and I was there for a while. And then I went out to B.C. for a bit.

I kept following the seasons, playing ball and hockey wherever, and I was good enough where I could always fit in with a team. Everybody on the team was always a good drinker, so I was in my glory with it throughout.

In 1981, I was at home nursing a tremendous hangover and my cousin stopped in—he drives for a trucking company out of Winnipeg—and he picked me up. I had nothing to do and he wanted me to go back to Winnipeg with him, so I did. I then met Barbra, she's my wife now, but I hadn't seen her for many, many years, and about two years later we got married. Our marriage was not made in heaven. It has since been redeemed there, I hope.

The drugs and the booze was still a going thing. A very close member in our family was having troubles up in Winnipeg and she came down to where we were and needed a place to stay. Her boyfriend followed her and he wasn't a very nice fellow. When he came there, we didn't know a whole pile about the situation or anything else; it was just that she was in trouble and she needed a place to stay. We always opened our doors, even when we were in the world.

The situation turned very violent. He had probably knifed a few people up in Winnipeg and there was a roomer that he might have even killed one or two. And this was the kind of guy we were dealing with. My wife was in an alcohol centre in Fort Qu'Appelle, Saskatchewan and I was still drinking. For three nights, I slept with my .303 loaded. It was scary, really scary. So I phoned her and I said, "You got to get home here." Because I was losing it. This guy seemed to come and go by night and the cops couldn't stop him or anything else. I was actually to the point where if one of my good friends would have popped up at the door at 1 o'clock in the morning and would have knocked on it to have a drink with me, which they did a lot of, the chances are then I would have just pulled the trigger. So it was a bad situation.

I had an inheritance coming, and so I told my wife that we were moving to either Saskatoon or Medicine Hat. So we chose Medicine Hat. We moved here the spring of '87.

About one year later she found the Lord and I moved out. I couldn't understand it. I never been involved with anything like that. I knew about God. I heard the name spoken, but Jesus was an unfamiliar name. And I didn't realize that He'd gone to the cross for me. My wife tried to tell me about Him and it went in one ear and out the other.

So I rebelled for about two years. Then I was sitting in the motel one afternoon and I don't know what happened. I was drunk, but I got up and I walked out and around into the alley to the taxi stand and I told the driver to take me to the church and I didn't even know where it was, but I knew the general direction.

So he got me there and I can remember Pastor Gordon was the pastor at the time and I went into the church and I just started crying and said, "You got to save me. You got to save me." That's all I knew; I had to be saved. I didn't know anything about it except the bits and pieces I held on to that my wife had talked about.

So I gave my life to the Lord in that drunken state and I lay in a bed at another pastor's house for four days suffering from alcohol withdrawals, and shaking and I got back into it. Then I wasn't sure if after that if I had been saved because I was drunk when it happened, so I went back again when I was sober and did it over again and since then I've had a few slips. It's nothing you can really pinpoint. I've always gotten up. The fear is one day I wouldn't be able to.

But I haven't been able to comprehend the love of Christ and I've been thinking about that the last couple of days. I know that when I come home from work and my grandchildren are there, they run out of the house and they yell, "Hi Grampa, Gramp, Gramp." And I suppose that's what the Lord wants me to do, to run to him and say, "Father, Father." Or when I do something and one of them imitates me, I know the feeling that I get and I start smiling. I feel pretty warm inside that this little person is copying me and I suppose that is what the Lord wants me to do, to copy him.

So it was a new revelation and it's worth going for. He has brought me out of the muck. He has brought me out of the mire after every slip, fall, walk away from the

Lord, whatever it's called. He's always picked me up and He's always blessed me. He has never left nor forsaken me, even in the worse moments. He brought me through suicidal thoughts. He brought me through so much. I thank Him for what He's done in my life, in my family's life. He's given us some very close brothers and sisters in Christ. People have prayed for me and people I could always talk to, even though I didn't, were there and I thank the Lord for them.

You can tell that Greg was very nervous, but he was a hundred percent sincere. Except he kept returning to his old habit. He just couldn't get free.

We all had a desires to record a CD, so we saved enough money and made an appointment to do the recording in Wetaskiwin, Alberta. After the recording, we drove to Camrose and played at a seniors lodge, then stayed the night in a hotel.

Another time, Fay booked us into doing a full service at a church at Burstall, Saskatchewan. After the praise and worship, Fay preached a powerful message. I was asked to share a bit of my own testimony, too. We were well received. We also had the privilege to play at a conference in Sylvan Lake, Alberta. That was wonderful!

When our CDs arrived, we lost count of how many we sold and had to order more many times. I still give them away from time to time.

Our band played once at the Riverside Memorial Park bandstand in downtown Medicine Hat, and several times at the Kin Coulee Park bandstand during a Christian jamboree. That was a lot of fun, like a miniature Woodstock.

Fay and I were asked several times to lead the praise and worship for Women's Aglow meetings. I was nervous when this happened, but Fay wouldn't let me back out. I was forced to meet my fears straight on and the Holy Spirit always made His presence known.

One day, I asked Greg to write down all the outstanding debts he had accumulated over the years. I needed to know how much we owed, and to whom. It was time for him to be honest with me, and he needed to do this if he was going to walk the straight line.

Well, he started writing, and by the time he had finished I was shocked and disheartened. It was a staggering amount of money, more than $20,000. How had it gotten to be so much? At that time, a hundred dollars was like a thousand dollars to me. And there was absolutely nothing to show for these debts except bill collectors and angry friends and family. Also, we were broke. How were we ever going to pay this off?

I was so naïve. I didn't recognize the wheeling and dealing Greg did with the people he associated with. I trusted him right from the start of our relationship; after all he had been my knight in shining armor.

And yet I could remember, right from the beginning, that Greg would talk his mother out of her pension cheques. He would spin a great story to make her give him the money. After leaving her place, we'd go straight to the bar, buy beer, pay a friend for gas, and end up at a party somewhere later one. He did this on several occasions.

I once asked him if he'd ever paid his mom back, and he had said she wouldn't take it. I should have been smarter and realized then what I was getting into.

The first time he stole from me was while I was back in school. After classes one day, I went to the hardware store for something and was approached by the owner about something Greg had bought from him. I didn't know what he was talking about, but I asked how Greg had paid for it.

"With your family allowance cheque," the owner told me.

I had never given Greg my family allowance! So the man showed me the cheque—and sure enough, Greg had forged my signature.

I left the store very embarrassed and angry.

When I found Greg and confronted him, he concocted a very lame story which led to a fight. I told him if he ever did that again I would report him to the police, and I meant it. He never touched another one of my cheques. But he still got away with it, because I didn't get my money back.

He had a whole bag of tricks and was never without money for very long, whether he worked for it or not. He once talked a car dealer into allowing him to purchase a '52 Chevy by making payments—without my knowledge, of course. He made maybe two payments, but the guy never saw the rest of his $750. It was amazing how easy Greg could find ways to rip people off, and by the time we left Saskatchewan he owed a lot of people a lot of money.

Shortly after moving to Medicine Hat, we joined the local co-op, which had a furniture store. Greg ran up a large debt and in no time the bill collectors came calling. And whether I lived with him or not at the time, they also called me. I thought he had been paying it off, or so he said. Not so.

I'd even given him money to pay this debt, but somehow that money never made it to the co-op. I dreaded answering the phone, because I wouldn't know if it was a creditor or friend who wanted their money.

Greg's drinking really cost us. We worked hard, made good money, and never took holidays. I shopped at second-hand stores—which is nothing to be ashamed of if you really need to—and learned to do without new clothes. I also skimped on good healthy food and visits to the dentist because there was never enough money.

Greg would get himself set up in business, buy the best tools, and then when business went bad he'd pawn his tools and binge. I lost count of how many times this was. In desperation, to pay off one personal debt, Greg sold all his work tools as well as his truck to pay someone. Then he went drinking with the leftover money. And out of the blue he'd come up with enough money to buy new tools when he finally sobered up. Wasn't it amazing that he could come up with enough money to buy these things while I had to bus or walk to work? He never rode the bus; if he didn't have a vehicle, he took cabs.

The worst creditors were our friends. Greg borrowed a thousand dollars from a very close and dear friend of mine, who then approached me on the matter and asked when Greg would return the money. I just looked at him, dumbfounded, unaware of what he was talking about. He was angry, which put me right in the middle of a bad situation. I was always the last to know and yet I took the brunt of people's disappointment and anger.

Yet not one of these people asked me first if they should lend Greg money.

All the while I tried to keep my head on straight and keep my marriage intact, because the Bible said that you shouldn't get divorced. I had made vows, for better or worse.

He went to my girlfriend's store and bought me a gift and told her he would pay her later. I ended up paying for it. The same with the guitar he bought me. Then there was the $1,100 vacuum he figured I was so deserving of; it took me a couple of years to pay that one off. Good vacuum, but not for that price and all the interest.

Greg taught Eugene how to shingle a roof, and he became so good at it that Greg would put him on a job and walk away to "look for other jobs," which he'd find at the local watering hole. He'd sit there all day getting wasted only to return to the job site at the end of the day. He'd pay Eugene a lower wage than they'd discussed, then pocket the rest.

Of course, I wouldn't find this out until the kid exploded over the fact that his father had ripped him off yet again. I was so angry that he would use his own son this way. I also found out, after the fact, that he borrowed from our other two sons and never paid them back either. Was there anyone he didn't screw over?

With Greg as a husband, I never knew what to expect. In fact, I never knew if I was married or single from one week to the next—or if I'd have furniture, be able to pay rent, or be moving onto the streets. I worked hard, but it was never enough to meet the bills.

Even during all my years of drinking and going drugs, I always paid my debts. But Greg seemed to have no conscience. Nothing really seemed to trouble him. He spun lies as though they were truths and believed them all.

I was still stupid enough to believe that if only he would surrender to God, he would change and become an honest man. For as long as there was breath in his body, I hoped he would turn his life around and get right with everyone, especially God. At times it felt like a losing battle, but I just kept on praying for him.

Forty-Four

Miracles

I always walked with my right foot pointing inward instead of straight ahead. This bothered me because my right shoes would wear out quickly. So I asked God to straighten out my foot.

One night at church there was a healing call for people to have their legs and feet prayed over. I went up, sat in a chair, and the evangelist asked me to place a foot into each open palm of his hands. He held my legs and feet straight before me, supporting them loosely, and then placed them side by side and we could see that one leg was longer than the other.

With authority, he spoke healing over my legs and feet in Jesus's name. In amazement, I felt my right foot turn all the way to the right on its own, until it was completely flattened in the evangelist's open hand. I couldn't have turned my foot that far on my own if my life depended on it. As the foot slowly moved into position, I felt the most unique sensation. Then I watched the leg grew outward to match the length as the other leg.

I'd experienced this once before when someone prayed for my back, and my hips twisted completely on their own, coming into perfect alignment with my back. I even grew a quarter of an inch that day!

God loves to amaze us.

Around this time, Greg was drinking and not paying the bills again, and this time I was determined not to pay them for him. My brother Andrew was staying with us on the day we received an eviction notice. We only had a few weeks to either pay up or move out. This was my first eviction, as I had always paid the bills when Greg didn't. But with the help of the twelve-step program I realized that I was enabling Greg by taking care of his financial responsibilities. I wasn't going to do that anymore.

I also wasn't going to run off and get my own apartment and let him persuade a friend to bail him out.

I had prayed about this and felt strongly that this was what I needed to do. I completely trusted God to work this out. Was I scared? Absolutely! Like my mother, I had always run away when life got too rough. This time, I was determined to break that cycle, no matter the cost.

The first services to be turned off were the cable and telephone. Greg asked me why they were off, so I nervously told him the reason. I also told him that the utilities would be next to go, and then I reminded him that if the rent wasn't paid in a week we would be evicted. Telling him this was no easy task after so many years of being manipulated and controlled by him.

This angered him so much that he left. I didn't see him until the next day when he was hungover and miserable.

The day before our eviction, while driving around in my friend Mae's truck, I looked in the newspaper for apartments to rent. An ad for a one-bedroom apartment jumped off the page at me. Since we were already driving around town, we thought we might as well go by and have a look.

We stopped in front of a three-story brick building. The area was well-kept and pleasant to the eyes. Not only that, but it was close to a bus stop, and my church was only halfway down the block. How perfect was that?

We met with the landlord and he showed us the suite he had just finished painting. He had also installed new carpets. The place looked so fresh and inviting.

I asked about the damage deposit, the rent, and the utilities and was amazed to discover it was affordable for me. He told me that the building was only for single women and then asked if I was interested in taking it. I was really tempted to say yes on the spot, but instead I told him we were only looking. But I really liked it.

Before Mae dropped me off at home, she told me to call her after she was done her next shift because she wanted to help me pack and move to wherever I was going. I was truly blessed to have a friendship like that.

Next morning, Andrew and I were sitting at the table when Greg dragged himself out of bed. He said good morning and we returned his greeting. I got him a coffee and he asked what I was going to do that day. I asked him if he had the money for rent. He didn't, so as casually as I could I told him we were moving today. He looked shocked and asked why. I told him this was eviction day and we had to be out by midnight. He said that he'd thought he had another two weeks before the end of the month. I assured him we did not.

He then asked me if I had a place to move to and I told him that I didn't. With a stunned look on his face, he asked, "Where are you going to go?"

"With you."

"What? But I have no place."

"Then I guess we're both going to live in the streets."

"That's not fair to you. You don't deserve this."

"I have no other choice, Greg. You're my husband and I go where you go."

Those were the bravest words I ever spoke. My insides were shaking like an earthquake.

God, please don't make me go with him, I silently pleaded. But I had to completely trust God in this.

"Can't you find a place?" he pleaded.

He knew he had gone too far this time. He didn't want to drag me around with him. I knew he loved me in his own way.

"I can find a place if you give me permission to go without you," I said. "But you have to tell God that you're releasing me."

He understood what I was saying, so out loud he spoke to God and gave me permission to find my own place, with the knowledge that he wouldn't be moving in with me. He then got up from the table and went to the bedroom, changed, and headed for the door. I asked where he was going and he said he was going to look for a truck and boxes to move us.

Poor Andrew. He sat through this whole ordeal without saying a word and didn't know what to do. He just looked at me with concern written all over his face. I simply told him that Greg wouldn't be back, that he had gone to the bar and would find a place to stay with one of his drinking buddies.

However, the good news was that I had looked at an apartment the day before and could now go over to Fay's place right away to use her phone and see if the apartment was still available. Andrew said he would start getting things ready to be packed. He had already found a place to stay since I'd warned him beforehand that we would no doubt be moving.

I was so grateful for Andrew's help, since he was an experienced mover.

As I got ready to go out, I asked God if there would be enough money to give something to Andrew so he wouldn't be leaving empty-handed.

I got ready to walk out the door, but before I did, I heard the Lord say, "Barbra, you didn't curl your hair."

"What?" I thought I was hearing things.

He said it again. "You didn't curl your hair."

"Okay, I'll curl it."

With that, I turned back to go into the bathroom. Just when I finished styling my hair, I heard a loud knock on the apartment door. I hadn't expected to see Mae standing in front of me with a great big smile on her face, but there she was, cheerfully asking if I was ready to go.

"Why aren't you at work?" I asked.

It turned out there had been some mistake on the schedule and she didn't have to work after all. I told her that I was just on my way to phone the guy at the apartment building to see if that unit was still available.

"Let's just go there and ask him," she said.

Excitedly, I let Andrew know where I was going and he assured me that he had plenty to keep himself busy.

When we got to the building, the landlord was just stepping out of the vacant apartment with a screwdriver in his hand. I asked if the apartment was still available and he told me it was.

We went into his place, and with his wife in attendance we discussed my situation. They said I could move in right away. So I paid the rent, did the necessary paperwork, then told them that I needed to go to the bank to get the damage deposit, change over the utilities, and get my phone hooked up while I still had a ride because Mae could only help for a short time.

Mae and I picked up boxes and papers, then went to see about getting a change of address. Surprisingly enough, the utilities, cable, and phone were able to be hooked up that very same day! We finished just in time for Mae to drop me off at home before heading off to work. She said she'd come back afterward to help again.

Andrew had gotten everything ready. He had done a lot of work in the time we were gone, including taking pieces of furniture apart. We went through the fridge to see what food I would take and what food I could spare for Andrew to take with him.

Shortly after, I heard another unexpected knock at my door. It was Fay, telling me that she had time to take over a few small loads. Everything was falling perfectly into place!

I left Andrew to pack while Fay and I loaded up her little car, which took time seeing as I lived on the top floor of a three-story building with no elevator.

After paying the damage deposit, I waited excitedly for my new keys. To my amazement, the landlord not only handed me the keys, but also gave me $20 back from the damage deposit, just in case I needed it for something. That brought on a flood of unexpected emotion and tears stung the back of my eyes. Immediately I knew this was the money I had asked God for, something to give Andrew. I profusely thanked him! The day just kept getting better and better.

After Fay left, I happily went up to Andrew and handed him the $20 the Lord kept aside for him. At first he didn't want to take it, but I explained that I had prayed about this and this money was from God. He had no choice but to accept it!

Later that evening, my sons and daughters-in-law came over to help for a short time. Their help was most welcome and moved thing along. We were like a beehive of activity.

When it was getting late, Mae came back with her truck so we could start moving the bigger stuff out. As it turned out, her brother had come into town from somewhere around Edmonton and offered to help. Everyone's kindness and generosity was amazing.

By 11:30 that night, the last load was out. I checked to see that everything was clean and nothing left behind, as I had promised my landlady.

Was I happy about all this? No, not one bit. I had tried hard to keep our relationship together. I'd been in a battle to see if I would trust God to take care of me, and once again I saw the mighty hand of God move on my behalf!

This was a miracle in the making.

Another supernatural event happened some time later, during a period when I was back with Greg. At the time, we were renting the upstairs floor of a house and a young woman rented the basement. I got to know this woman, and during one of our many conversations I casually mentioned how much I would like to own my own home again, but I felt there wasn't a chance of that ever happening.

What were the odds of her being a loans officer at the same bank I used? Whatever the odds, that's exactly what she was. She took it upon herself to check my credit rating and informed me I could purchase a place if I wanted, with her help. I was ecstatic, having not even known I *had* a credit rating!

Not many months after her telling me this, Greg and I found and moved into our very own trailer with a brand-new living room and kitchen suite.

We had moved into the trailer around the middle of summer during a time when I wasn't working. Instead I took a much-needed break to enjoy our new home and rest.

What I enjoyed most was going into the private backyard. We lived on the outskirts of the neighbourhood, overlooking the bald prairie. Our cat loved it, too. She was able to roam freely and catch all the mice her heart desired.

One night I woke up around two in the morning and sensed that something was horribly wrong. Finding it impossible to go back to sleep, I slipped quietly out of bed and went into the living room so as not to disturb Greg. I felt an urgency to pray, so I went to my knees and began to pray in tongues. I had no idea what I was praying for, but God knew.

During the prayer, I began praying a hedge of protection around my sons and their families. About an hour later, I felt the urgency lift then I went back to bed and fell into a deep sleep.

After seeing Greg off to work the next morning, I sat at the kitchen table typing out new songs for our band. Unexpectantly, the front door opened and in came Blayne, who was once again staying with us. He was working on an oilrig north of Edmonton and we weren't due to see him for another week.

As I studied his face, I noticed that he had a pained expression—and he was limping. I immediately asked him what had happened and he told me that he'd been in an accident at work at around two o'clock that morning. While a new drill pipe was being hoisted up into place, it had slipped loose and fallen to the ground, hitting Blayne across his thigh. Since he could barely walk, he'd gotten into his car and drove all night to come home.

Horror-struck, I asked him if he'd gone to the hospital to get it checked. He hadn't, but he would go after he'd had a bath to soak his leg. All he really wanted to do was go to bed. Well, he was a grown man, so I didn't push the point—although I very much wanted to. I went to prepare the tub for him, and when I walked into the bathroom I heard in a very clear and precise voice, "It could have been his head."

Suddenly I remembered that the Lord had woken me up around the same time that night to pray. I was praying for my son's life to be spared! In God's mercy, he not only spared Blayne's life, but his leg as well.

This isn't the only time God had me fall to my knees and pray for my sons. Blayne told me that he and one of his crewmembers were standing on the floor of the rig one day when the top let go and fell to the ground around them. They found themselves standing in the middle of steel girders. God spared their lives.

Joey had a similar experience. While at work one day, processing cattle, his job was to cut open a cow's gut and let the entrails fall out onto the table. When he was making the cut, the knife slipped and nearly hit him right in the chest. The only thing that stopped it from stabbing him in the heart had been a tiny button on the front of his shirt.

"You must have been praying for me, Mom," he said to me later.

While working as a roofer, Eugene several times fell off roofs, even while he was harnessed. He should have died, but he and I believe God's angels worked overtime for him.[24]

After Blayne moved out, we had another young man move in. Dalton was my friend Gail's son and he was just at the age when it was time for the chick to leave the nest. He wasn't quite ready to have his

---

[24] It's my opinion that harnesses are more dangerous than not wearing them. They just provide one more thing for a roofer to trip over. I know because I occasionally roofed alongside Greg.

own place, so what better option was there but for him to stay with someone he knew? Dalton lived with us in the trailer for several months, and it was a joy having him there and getting to know him. I was sad to see him go.

Come spring, as soon as I could, I got on my hands and knees digging up the grass in the backyard. I wanted to plant new flowerbeds to make the yard come alive with colour. I could hardly wait to see what the plants would look like full-grown and blooming.

I never got to see them. Greg went back to the bar and we had to sell the trailer. Because of this, I also needed to return to work.

However, God did grant me my heart's desire—to have a place of my own, even if it was for only a short time.

Talk to God

Has your life become like a never-ending whirlwind
Just like a ball in a pinball game
Bouncing wildly from one crisis to another
And you had no choice and no one to blame
You need to talk to God

There are days when the world just keeps closing in
And you feel like you can't go on
It's like banging your head on that ol' brick wall
And all you've got to show are the bruises
You need to talk to God

Cast your cares on the Lord and He'll sustain you
He'll never let the righteous fall
Faith is letting go and trusting in God
Trusting in God to catch you
You need to talk to God

Forty-Five
Moving Again

At one point, Greg found us a nice duplex to rent on Elm Street. It had two rooms upstairs with a partly finished basement. I loved the balcony, sitting outside and watching the world go by.

After selling the trailer, I made sure all the debts I knew about were paid. But wouldn't you know it? A couple of months later, we got a bill in the mail telling me that I owed the bank $800. Greg of course forgot to tell me about this one. It turned out that while moving our furniture to the new place on Elm Street, he got into a small car accident. Instead of reporting the accident, the other driver settled for a payout of $800 so his insurance wouldn't go up.

Anyway, the bill was there and it had to be settled. I was stuck paying it only because the bank account was in both our names. I went to the bank and had Greg's name removed before he could do any more damage.

Strangely enough, Greg confessed to me that as long as he went to church and followed God's word, we were happy and blessed—and whenever he went back to the bars, we lost everything including each other. How very true. That's exactly how it played out.

There was no such thing as a social drink for Greg. It was stay sober or drink to oblivion, and that's what he did night after night. I became like my mom when Greg didn't come home after work. I'd have his dinner warming while trying to watch something on TV, to keep my mind from worrying about what kind of mood he'd be in when he got home. Every nerve stood at attention, waiting for the inevitable no-win confrontation.

When it got to be too late, I'd go to bed and hopefully fall asleep and not be woken up. One thing I noticed was that Greg would get out of his vehicle and walk to the door in a good mood, but then when he entered his whole demeanour would change. He knew he was doing wrong, so he would start a fight just to get the attention off himself and onto me. He knew exactly how to rattle my cage.

Before he'd come home, I would put away the sharp knives, should I have the urge to shut him up permanently, ending the torment his words caused me. Whether I remained quiet or tried to answer him, he would spew words at me until I wanted to scream. It was like a physical beating, only there were no marks on the body. His words destroyed every beautiful feeling of love I'd once had for him.

"Just leave me alone," I'd scream as I went from room to room, trying to escape him. "Please, leave me alone."

But he would follow and keep yapping.

There were times when I locked myself in the bathroom, sitting on the edge of the tub, rocking back and forth, shaking like a leaf while he banged and yelled on the other side of the door. When I replied to him, he would twist my words, distorting everything I said. Then he would leave me shaken, confused, and crying.

The only difference between him and my dad is that Greg wouldn't lay a hand on me. He knew I wouldn't take that from any man. What I really wanted him to do was hold me and tell me everything was going to be okay, but he didn't; he'd just get into his truck and drive to the bar.

Sometimes he didn't come home at all, and that would make things even worse. Was he with another woman? Had he gotten into an accident? Had he killed someone while driving around so drunk? I felt so trapped in this ugly relationship.

The many nights he'd come home way after the bars were closed. I would lie in bed, pretending to sleep so he wouldn't start in on me. I'd hear him banging around, every nerve in my body jumping. Tears would silently slide down onto my pillow.

Even after he finally passed out, I would lie awake long into the night and be utterly exhausted the next day. There were days when he would straighten up for a time and life would get back on kilter, but it never lasted long.

I came to the conclusion that I needed to get a job before I killed him. He wasn't worth going to jail for and I was no murderer. But he was driving me insane. Mentally and physically, I was getting sick.

I talked to one of my girlfriends, who knew a woman who worked as a cook in the oilrig camps. This woman phoned me and it turned out she was looking for another cook to work there. So she hired me and I was able to head up as soon as the camps opened for the season.

This sounded like the perfect job. I would be gone weeks at a time making good money, and I wouldn't be running from my marriage. I could just work. I was told the work was hard, but that didn't matter to me. It couldn't be any worse than the hellhole I was already living in.

In the meantime, I kept myself busy with family, friends, and church. One day while sitting with friends next to a large window at church, a Salvation Army pickup truck drove by. We commented on it as a possible job opportunity, but then we thought no more about it.

A few days later, the same truck drove by me. It kept crossing my path, which led me to wonder what was up. Before this, I've never noticed them.

A couple of weeks later, I received a phone call from the manager at the Salvation Army homeless shelter. He had heard about me from a friend of mine who worked there and wanted me to bring in a resume.

What? I hadn't applied for a job there. I told him I already had a job, then I thanked him for calling and hung up. I sat there looking at the phone and remembered the various jobs I'd gotten when God had arranged for companies to reach out to me. That's often how I knew that an opportunity was from Him.

After accepting the camp job, I had kept praying and asking God if that really was where He wanted me to go. Something about it didn't feel right. The strange thing is that I had disturbing dreams after I accepted that job. So I petitioned the Lord, saying that if He didn't want me to go up north, the sign would be that the shelter manager would call me back. There didn't seem much chance of that happening. Usually if you turn a company down, they file your name under G. for garbage.

The next morning, the same manager phoned me back and said the same thing. I was dumbfounded; so I told him I would bring my resume in shortly, since I lived nearby to the shelter.

As I walked there, I again asked God, *Is this really from You? If so, would You show me one more time, so that I'll know that I know this is where You want me to work? I don't want to be where You don't want me, or else it won't work out. If You want me at the shelter, I will quit the other job. So please just show me.*

Then I heard God tell me to look down. By this time, I was crossing a bridge… and as I looked down off the side, I saw the Salvation Army truck drive under the bridge—the very same one I'd been seeing for days.

"Okay, Lord, I'm all for it!" I said, laughing. "Give me the right words to speak. Thanks, Lord!"

I was immediately ushered into the manager's office, and before I knew it I was hired and starting the next night. I couldn't believe it.

When I got home, I called the cook from the oilrig camp and declined her offer.

I did my best to cope with home life and worked the midnight shifts at my new full-time job. During the night, I cleaned the downstairs area where the men slept, washed the bedding and towels, scrubbed the floors and bathrooms, and rearranged and stocked the pantry. If I had time to clean rooms and sanitize used beds before I went home, I did. There was always something to do. I also conducted head counts, which meant taking a flashlight and quietly opening the men's bedroom doors to make sure everyone was accounted for. I didn't like that part of the job, because it felt like I was invading their privacy.

Many nights, the women and men would go outside into the backyard when they couldn't sleep, either to smoke or just to clear their heads. Many would stop and talk with me while I folded laundry.

I had many opportunities to pray for those who wanted prayer. Since I had been through so much myself, I could well understand where they were coming from. There wasn't much they could share that would shock me. If anything, I would shock them, which helped me gain their trust. I wasn't afraid of working around them, knowing that many had come from undesirable backgrounds like my own.

One night while cleaning near one of the bathrooms on the women's floor, I heard a woman crying inside. I went up to the closed door and asked through the door if she was okay. When she slowly opened the door and allowed me to come in, I asked if I could be of any help. Soon we were sitting on the floor of the bathroom, with her pouring out her heart.

Not long after, the door opened again and in walked another young woman who also shared her story. After a while, their tears dried up and I prayed for them. By the time they were ready to head back to their rooms, we hugged and they had smiles on their faces.

I was also called in to work day or evening shifts when needed. On these shifts, I could interact with everyone who used the facility. When the clients came in from outside, I had the job of checking their bags and conducting body searches for drugs, alcohol, needles, and dangerous weapons. Some of the weapons we took from them were enough to make one shutter. Their weapons and meds were given back when they left the shelter.

I learned how to do intakes, which entailed entering the clients' personal information into the computer to see if they were suitable to stay. If someone had been drinking or doing drugs, they weren't allowed to stay, as the centre was a dry facility for men, women, and children. If they had been banned due to an altercation, they weren't allowed back until a certain amount of penalty time had elapsed. If any altercations took place, I had to write up an incident report.

I learned to file their meds and passed them out when needed. I also had to deal with the police officers who came in looking for people to make arrests. I cooked meals, prepped vegetables, and prepared soup for the soup kitchen. Eventually I was also asked to read a daily devotional with the morning crowd and pray with them before they headed off for the day.

I truly loved what I was doing and gained the trust of many who used the facility.

Greg Moves Out

The trouble at home only escalated until one of us had to go again, and this time it was Greg. I was interfering with his life. He needed the feel of excitement and freedom which came through the kind of stimulation that only a bar or party brings. Because I was trying so hard to live a normal life, I wasn't very stimulating.

Sometimes the loneliest people in the world aren't the ones who live alone, but the ones who live with someone who claims to love them but doesn't.

One very late night, at 2:50 a.m., God spoke these encouraging and uplifting words, which I was desperate to receive:

Wipe away the tears of the past.
For today I am doing a new thing.
The old fades as colour in the sun.
The fresh is as a new garment before it is washed.
Fear robs one of peace of mind.
Liberty restores and heals the mind.
Cast off the old and replace it with new.
There are new things every morning.
Fresh manna from heaven.
Reach out to grasp it.

Ask for it and it will be given.

Walk in faith.

When you need more, Jesus will give you the exact amount needed at the right time.

Stretch forth your hand and receive without reserve.

For I am a generous God and have more than enough in my storehouse

for each one of my children.

I shall never run out of mercy, grace, liberty, generosity, and faith abundantly.

I will not hold back for those in need.

I am not the kind of God who would play on your heart and emotions.

I am a serious God.

When I act, who can stop it?

I come through at the right time.

Rent your heart before Me.

Be honest in *all* you do.

Trust Me to keep you and restore you back to health and clarity of mind.

See and taste that the Lord is good.

Desire more seeing and more tasting.

This is pleasing to Me, for I will meet you where you are at.

I will touch you in your heart; that is where the change takes place.

When the heart changes, your character changes.

And when your character changes, the people, as well as yourself, will see the changes.

The changes will always be for your good and My glory,

because only Jesus can heal a broken and contrite heart.

My health was failing as I gave in to all the stress I had endured. My shoulders and arms had become extremely painful. During the night, they would fall asleep and go so numb that I struggled to roll out of bed. During the day, I could barely lift an empty plastic glass off the counter. In order to put my arms on the table, I would have to lift one arm, then reach down with that hand to lift up the other arm. I'd have to do the same to take my arms off the table.

I couldn't even hold my newborn granddaughter for more than a couple of minutes before pleading with someone to take her away before I dropped her. Not being able to hold my grandbaby hurt more than the pain in my arms. It made me want to cry, but that wouldn't have helped everyone around me.

Going to work was the hardest. I had to completely rely on the Lord for help. I'd pray His word back to Him: *"but those who hope in the Lord will renew their strength"* (Isaiah 40:31). I said, "Lord, the pain is so great tonight, but You said You would meet me in my weakness, so I'm going to start cleaning and I need Your help." As I started washing down the bathroom, the joint pain in my shoulders would scream at me, but I'd have no choice but to press on.

Within fifteen to twenty minutes, the pain would stop and I could do the rest of the night's work with just twinges of pain to remind me that it was still there. I'd just praise and thank the Lord for His help in getting me through another shift.

At home, it would start over again.

This condition went on for a few months, but I would tell the Lord that no matter how much I hurt, I would praise Him anyway! And I did.

> *Trust in the Lord with all your heart and lean not on your own understanding; in all your ways submit to him, and he will make your paths straight.* (Proverbs 3:5–6)

Every move Greg or I made was painful, and not long after Greg would move out I would experience the relief of much-needed freedom. But the loneliness always seeped back in and soon Greg or myself would wonder what the other was doing. It was a cruel mind game.

I wasn't alone for very long this time, since my brother Andrew unexpectedly breezed into town again and needed a place to stay. I gave him the partly finished basement, and he set up a home there.

I loved having Andrew with me; it was the other nine he brought with him I wasn't so fond of. He set up nine fish tanks with a piranha in each. Ugh. I'd watched too many movies with piranhas and couldn't think of them as house fish.

But at least the house didn't seem so empty. He stayed until he found his own place.

Forty-Six
Cancer and Divorce

I don't remember how long Greg was gone this time, but when he returned it was to inform me that his doctor had told him he had cancer in his right lung. It was so severe, in fact, that he had to go to Calgary and have it removed immediately.

Suddenly, all the troubles of the past seemed insignificant. His father had passed away from cancer and we had watched him go downhill quickly and painfully. Greg had taken his death very hard.

He would need someone to care for him once he was released from hospital. Since there wasn't anyone to take care of him properly, I told him he could come home. I'm far from a nurse, but I was the best he had on such short notice.

I didn't know what to expect, but I was willing to give him my all. I remembered only too well what it felt like to go into a hospital alone and wake up from a surgery alone. It deeply saddened me that I couldn't be there for him because I had to work. Besides, I had no way of going to Calgary.

I don't know how Greg got to Calgary, but the day of his surgery was immensely hard for me as no one was able to contact me to let me know how it had gone. But God, in His infinite wisdom, made a way. While talking with my friend Mae from Shaunavon, she came up with a solution. I got the night off work and she drove into Medicine Hat, picked me up, and took me to Calgary the evening of his surgery. He wouldn't be expecting us.

It was a huge hospital and something of a challenge to find our way around. Mae was a great help and support to me as we searched for his room. When we asked about the surgery, we were told that the doctors had removed his lung and he was in a great deal of pain but responding well to treatment. This was good news.

Upon locating his room, we were asked to wait outside the door a few minutes while a couple of nurses worked with him. As we stood waiting, I heard the most heart-breaking cries of agony coming out of Greg. I cringed inside. I could see the male nurses adjusting his body into a more comfortable position on his pillow. He also had an IV line sticking in his back.

He had always been such a strong man when it came to pain, gritting his teeth and smiling and pretending all was well. This time there was no pretending; it was more than he could bear, and I felt helpless. His cries forced me to turn away and hold back my tears.

Mae did her best to console me. What a wonderful friend! Her presence alone was comforting. I just needed to know for myself that he was going to be okay.

After what seemed to be an eternity, but lasted only about five minutes, we were allowed to go in and see him. He looked so fragile and small and spent of all strength. His face was distorted in pain and his breathing laboured. He was also hooked up to an IV and a monitor. The incision on his back where they had cut him started almost in the middle of his shoulder blades, ran straight down to the bottom of his ribs, and cut across to his side. It had been stapled shut and looked much like a zipper. I couldn't for the life of me understand why there weren't any bandages to protect the wound from infection. Later I was told it would heal better if it was exposed to the air.

As I walked over to his bed, he did manage a genuine smile amidst the pain and I knew he was happy to see me. He tried putting on a front, but he didn't fool me. I'd known him too long for him to get away with that.

He shared a room with three others, so he had plenty of company. He said the nurses were great, which was comforting to know.

We couldn't stay long, as Mae had a long drive to return home and he needed his rest, but it was worth the trip just to let him know that I was there for him. We may not have been living together, but that didn't do anything to change how I felt after all the years we'd spent together, through good and bad. I was still there for him.

For the next couple of months, he slept on the couch, where he was most comfortable and could watch the TV. I tried to meet all his needs while I was home, but I worked the midnight shift; during those times, if he needed anything I was only a phone call away.

After a lot of practice, he began to walk from the doorway to the sidewalk, progressing a little further each day. We lived only three houses away from a neighbourhood school, and he would make his way around it. As there were still patches of snow on the ground, he had to be extra careful not to slip.

On several occasions, I asked him if he wanted company. At first he was all for it, but after a time he hesitated at me being with him. He'd also started taking a cup of coffee with him.

I wondered about the hesitations. He walked more often and for longer periods of time, and I figured he was just following the doctor's orders and strengthening himself. This was strange, as he hadn't liked to walk that much; he had preferred to drive.

As it turned out, I soon discovered that someone was smuggling in cigarettes and liquor for him, probably when I was at work or sleeping during the day. The strangest thing is that I couldn't smell either one on him, yet I could on other people. This also explained why he had suddenly taken up chewing gum!

Well, once the secret was out it didn't take him long to get back to his old way of life.

One evening while I was working on something at my computer, he came into my office and start yapping off again. I asked him to leave and let me finish what I was doing. But no, he was in a belligerent mood and needed to blow off some steam. The old game was back on. I went from one room to another to get away from him. I didn't want to fight.

When I finally went back into the office, he followed me in and said the wrong words to me. I lost it, grabbing him by the front of his shirt and slamming his back into the wall with all my might. Then I drew back my arm, my fist ready to paste him in the face. The only things that stopped me was the look of pain on his face and his body sliding to the floor. Instead I dragged him out of my room by the ankles, pulling him down the hall.

I had had enough. I swore the next time he did that I would kill him, and I meant it. I then marched back into my room and slammed the door. I didn't hear from him the rest of the night.

For a while, Blayne lived with us again. The rig he was working on was here in the Medicine Hat area, and this time he was living up north. He was a joy to have around—that is, when he wasn't working or sleeping.

As our situation got worse, I felt that I needed to do a twenty-one-day fast and pray. That meant no food for three weeks. Up until this time, I had been able to fast three days. But twenty-one? Mae decided that she would do one as well, so we supported each other by phone.

I asked God to close my stomach for three weeks if this was of Him, which He did. I drank water and clear juices. For nourishment, I drank only the strained broth of boiled vegetables. Some people were concerned about me fasting for so long and also working, but I found that I had more energy and God sustained me.

It was amazing how quickly those three weeks went by. At the end of it, I went to Shaunavon so I could be together with Mae when we ended the fast. At midnight, we got Chinese food… and it never tasted so good! You're not supposed to come off a fast with solid foods, but soup just wasn't going to cut it.

During the fast, my prayer times were powerful and God became more real to me. There was a lot of change in my persona. I felt stronger than ever before.

One morning, before getting off the midnight shift at work, I looked out the front window and noticed a big red sign in the window of the fourplex apartment right across the road from the shelter. The "For Rent" sign jumped out at me. With high hopes, I talked to God about it and then left the decision in His hands. I didn't have enough money yet to afford a place, but I would have it by the end of the month.

Two weeks later, it was taken. I guess I was meant to stay put for now.

But a couple of months later, the sign was back and I had the money this time. I felt a stirring in my spirit that it was time to move, so I phoned the owner and immediately got an appointment to see the place.

The next day, I met with the owner after my shift was done. As I walked inside and took the stairs down to the basement suite, I instantly fell in love with the place. It was airy with big windows and had two large bedrooms, and the fact that it was right across the road from work was a major selling point.

By this time, Greg was back to working. There were some good days, but the bad ones destroyed the good ones. I told Blayne I was getting my own place and if he wanted to stay, that was up to him, but I had room for him if he needed it.

This time, I let Greg know that I was moving out. He was indifferent but said I couldn't have the furniture. I told him I would take what I had bought and what I needed.

On moving day, I got help from Gail, her son Dalton, and my daughter-in-law Lane. When they came, Greg was just waking up from an all-nighter after having been passed out on the living room couch. The first thing he did was reach for the glass of whisky that had been left on the coffee table from the night before. That was to stop the shakes he got every time he came off the alcohol.

He wasn't disrespectful to Gail or Dalton, but he kept glaring at Lane. Finally she asked him why he was glaring at her, and he said something like, "I thought you were my girl." In other words, why was she helping me? Lane just told him that he knew what he had done wrong—and left it at that.

Knowing that I'm deathly allergic to cigarette smoke, Greg deliberately lit a cigarette and filled the living room with smoke. He knew full well I would have to keep walking through that cloud as I carried things outside.

When his drink ran out, he walked up to the wall and took off a large picture I had bought him. He then left the house and returned a half-hour later with a fresh bottle of whisky, having pawned the picture. He then sat on the couch, scowling.

I was so relieved when the last load went out. I'd left a small freezer in the basement with the intention of Blayne bringing it over for me when he had the time. I then left the keys and closed the door behind me.

Much later, I talked to Gail about how embarrassing it had been for her and Dalton to have to face Greg like that. She just assured me that they'd been more concerned about my safety. Dalton had been prepared to defend me if Greg tried harming me. That touched me in ways not many people can understand unless they've been through it themselves. I had taken his bullying for so long that I had gotten used to having to deal with it by myself. So having these people by my side meant the world to me.

Soon all my boxes were piled up in the new apartment. The only furniture I had was my bed and the TV cabinet with my electronics. I would have to buy kitchen and living room furniture as I could afford them. But I was used to starting over.

I set up the TV unit and sat on the floor to relax. While I was down there, I asked God what I could use to make the floor a little more comfortable. Suddenly, He reminded me that I had a blow-up mattress. I pumped it up, threw a blanket over it, and added cushions. What more could one ask for?

I thanked God for the instant answer. I had the most important thing: peace!

Three months later, I got a call from my old landlord. He came to see me and told me that Greg was three months in arrears on the rent, and my name was still on the lease. I don't know why that surprised me, but it did. I told him I would pay as I could and find someone to take over the lease. But he could see the situation in my new apartment; I was using an outdoor plastic patio set and an air mattress in the living room. He told me not to bother with Greg's bill. He would take care of it.

I was extremely relieved. I had enough bills and I was living paycheque to paycheque.

One might ask why I felt responsible for Greg's debts. The Bible told me that when he and I had come together in marriage, we had become one in the spirit. I understood this to mean that I no longer had my own identity; he and I were joined together as one. And this principle doesn't just apply to marriage; if you have sex outside of marriage, you also become one in the spirit with that person.

So his debts were my debts. In sickness and in health, for better or worse, and so on. I had said these vows and I was going to keep them to the best of my ability.

Anyway, I did find a friend of mine to take over the place. That was when I discovered that Greg had sold my small freezer as well as Blayne's very expensive and valuable car speakers. The freezer I didn't mind so much, but stealing from Blayne was a whole different story.

I also received quite a shock when I walked by a used furniture store one day and saw my living room and kitchen suite for sale. Just another inconsequential blow.

For years, my marriage was full of deep-seated disappointment. Each one was like a wrecking ball slamming into my heart, sending chunks of flesh flying in all directions. I just didn't have it in me to put myself back together again. There wasn't another try left in me.

So I cried out to God, *Do I really have to stay in this marriage? Please show me if it's okay to leave for good this time.*

Greg hadn't changed. If anything, he had gotten worse. He had a mistress, and her name was Miss Alcohol. I had seen her many times in my dreams. She'd be sitting on his lap or walking past me with her arms in his. She was a bottle with no legs, arms, or even a head, yet she had enough seductive influence to take my man away from me and keep him in her iron grasp.

After twenty-three years of this train wreck, I sought the counsel of my pastor to see if I could end this once and for all. He gave me all the information he had about our denomination's stance on divorce. In terms of whether I should do it, he didn't say yes, nor did he say no. Instead he gave me the information and left it to me.

When I left the pastor's office that day, I felt like I was walking on air. I saw a vision of a tiny bird sitting on the rung of its open cage door, not yet knowing if it should fly out of captivity or stay in its familiar cage.

With much prayer, I found a paralegal who within a matter of four months drew up divorce papers and had them served to Greg.

I had a few reasons to divorce Greg. One was that I felt the need to remove myself from between him and God, so they could fight it out between themselves. Another was that I couldn't stand to watch him literally kill himself one drink at a time.

His binges lasted anywhere from one week to six or seven months. During these period he couldn't eat regular meals and he lost weight until he was skin and bones. He would get to the point that he smelled so terrible; he didn't shower, shave, or comb his hair. His addiction brought him to the place where it was necessary for him to have a drink as soon as he woke up. To sleep, he had to pass out.

I just couldn't watch it anymore. By divorcing him, he wouldn't have any more power over me.

On April 8, 2003, I received the final divorce papers that declared I was no longer one with him.

Divorce has an ugly stigma attached to it. The worst is the shame of being part of a failed union. All my dreams of ever having a true family died. My greatest hope had been that some day Greg would find deliverance from alcohol, that he would allow the Lord to heal his heart and all the hurts and deep wounds he carried.

One part in me was hugely relieved that it was finally over, but the other part was filled with a deep sorrow.

Not long after our marriage ended, I picked up a newspaper and was shocked to see a picture of Greg's car turned upside-down on the front page with Grey lying on a stretcher. Apparently his car had hit an icy patch on the road and he'd lost control.

Later I heard the real story. He had been at a party, and the host had wanted him to stay the night since he was so wasted. But he was determined to go back to the bar.

He was fortunate to come out with a few bumps and bruises. It was a good thing no one else got involved in the accident. The car was a total write-off.

Shortly after that episode, he packed up and went back home to Saskatchewan.

Forty-Seven
New Beginnings

Life was peaceful and I enjoyed working at the shelter. It wasn't always easy, but then nothing ever is. I slowly built up my home, getting all the furniture I lacked. In fact, I was very thankful for and proud of my home. With God's help, it became a warm and inviting place to live.

So life was good.

That is, until one day I was working on my lawn and I heard the Lord say, "You are to go to Saskatchewan and see Greg." I hadn't heard from Greg since I had moved out for the last time about a year before.

I stopped in my tracks. What?

This time I heard His voice again, only clearer.

"When do I go, Lord?" I responded in disbelief. "If this is really from You, You'll have to arrange for a driver to take me and provide the money for the trip. You know I don't have any. I'll also need a place to stay, since there aren't any hotels in Churchbridge. And what am I supposed to do when I get there?"

I didn't hear a thing, but I felt like He was waiting for something.

"Okay, if this is of You, I'll do it."

With that, I felt His peace and went about my day.

The next day, my foster son William came to Medicine Hat to have his taxes done at the same place that I did mine.

While we were heading together to the tax office, I heard the Holy Spirit say to me, *You need to go to Churchbridge.*

When I wondered if that was really from Him, the Spirit hit my body hard. When that happens, the power of God passes through my upper body and my shoulders scrunch up. The power is so great that my body can't handle it, and sometimes the power causes my body to jerk involuntarily. That's when I know for certain that the Lord is speaking to me. It may look strange, but God has His own way of getting my attention. He did say in the Bible that His people would be peculiar!

If this is from You, Lord, then William will agree to be my driver, I prayed. *But if he can't go, I'll know I'm not hearing from You.*

So I cautiously said to William, "This is going to sound really crazy, but I'm going to put it out there because God won't give me any peace on this. Are you interested in hearing what I'm being told?"

When William said he was, I told him what the Lord had been speaking to me. He didn't flinch a bit. If anything, he seemed excited.

"When do you want to go?" William asked, his face lighting up. "Today? We could go today!"

This took me by surprise, since I didn't really want to go see Greg. "Are you serious?"

"Yeah. I can go after we get these papers to the tax office."

"Whoa, wait a minute. Don't you have to ask your wife?"

I was certain she wouldn't agree to this, but when he phoned her she just told us to have a good time. I couldn't believe what I was hearing.

Okay, Lord, I have the ride, and I can use my credit card to pay for it, but I still haven't got a place for us to stay.

Then I heard Him tell me to call Aunt Jenna. With trepidation, I pulled my phone out and called, hoping I wouldn't get through to her. But of course she answered her phone, so I asked if she would be okay with William and I coming to Churchbridge that night and staying with her.

Well, she was overjoyed at the idea.

There it was. I had all the confirmations I needed. I was to go immediately.

By the time William's taxes were taken care of, it was almost six o'clock in the evening. We stopped by my place to pick up an overnight bag, got some fast food for dinner, and picked up muffins for Jenna at the grocery store. Then we hit the highway.

I could hardly believe what we were doing, but at least it would be an adventure.

It was an eight-hour drive to Churchbridge, and on the drive William and I could talk about anything.

We reached Churchbridge in the middle of the night with music blaring in the truck's speakers. I couldn't believe how fast the trip had gone. It felt as though we had been transported and only been in the truck for a couple of hours.[25]

Jenna had beds prepared for us, and when we walked into the house I explained to her that the Lord had sent me. I needed to see Greg for some reason, but I didn't know what it was. Being a believer, she understood. She agreed to call him in the morning to make sure he was home.

The next morning, Jenna and I enjoyed a coffee and caught up on our families. I had brought my wedding band with me and chose my words carefully as I handed it back to Jenna. It was her wedding band and she was pleased to have me wear it when I married her son, but now I explained that the wedding band was hers and I felt privileged to have been given it when Greg and I married. Now I felt that it belonged in her family and should stay there. She looked at me in surprise and accepted it gracefully.

---

[25] A road trip, time with my boy, and an adventure… in my books, it just doesn't get any better than that!

When William roused himself, we left to meet Greg at a restaurant for breakfast. He looked much healthier than I'd last seen him, which made me happy. I didn't have much to say other than catching him up on how the kids and grandchildren were doing, but thankfully William did a great job filling in the empty spaces!

All too soon, breakfast was over and it was time to return home. We gave our hugs, said goodbye to Jenna, and thanked her for having us. I really loved that woman. She was a good aunt, but as a mother-in-law she was perfect! She understood me.

We took Greg back to his apartment and he invited us up. He had an antique clock that he wanted William to have.

After talking a bit more, Greg walked us down to the truck and gave William a big hug and handshake. He then turned to me, hugged me, and thanked me for coming to see him. The look on his face, just before driving away, seemed to plead, *Take me with you.*

The trip home was once again very fast. Yes, God was definitely in this, but I know it hadn't just been about returning the ring. That had only been a bonus. It was about something the Lord wanted done, but I didn't yet know what it was.

A month or so later, Greg returned to Medicine Hat. A young couple we knew had driven him down and he went to live with our son Eugene. In the early days, he made the rounds, seeing all his friends again. He came over to see me as well.

We began to date, and in no time we ended up engaged again.

Not long after, Greg started to feel sick a lot and he said that he needed to see his family doctor. As we sat in the waiting room, we were like a couple of kids, joking around and keeping the mood light; I knew that he was nervous about what the doctor might find.

Finally his name was called and he went in to see the doctor. I waited for him for quite some time and grew concerned. When he came out, he had a sombre look on his face. But since the clinic was filled with so many other waiting patients, he didn't tell me what the doctor had told him until we were outside.

First, the doctor had been surprised to see him after two years. He told Greg that usually a patient died within a year of having a lung removed. When Greg described his condition, the doctor came to believe that the cancer had returned, so he ordered tests.

His theory proved correct. Greg needed to immediately undergo chemotherapy for his other lung. This was devastating. I assured him that he didn't have to do this alone, that I would be at his side if he wanted me.

With a brave front and much determination, shortly thereafter Greg and I walked hand in hand towards the hospital's cancer clinic. Neither of us had ever walked this hall, so we didn't know what to expect. The important thing was that we were doing this together.

We were received with kindness, and once again we joked around and tried to uplift one another while waiting for the appointment.

When his name was called, with heavy feet we went forward to be welcomed by a kindly nurse who showed us into the room where the treatment was to take place. The room looked comfortable enough with six tall-backed leather chairs and a wall-mounted TV. We had the room to ourselves, which helped us to relax somewhat. I sat powerlessly by as the nurse hooked him up to an intravenous bag. All the while, we kept up a light-hearted conversation with her.

The treatment took about an hour and we passed the time by reading magazines and talking. We did our best to hide the fear we were feeling.

When Greg went home to Eugene's, he discovered that he couldn't stay there anymore; there was too much partying and other activity going on there day and night. He knew he wouldn't get the care he needed, especially with his immune system being so weak. The only alternative was for him to stay at my place while he was in treatment.

With the second treatment, I figured I should do something useful, so I brought my sowing needles and thread along with a pair of jeans that needed hemming. While I sewed, the nurse was quite interested in hearing our story, how we had divorced and yet had chosen to walk through this nightmare together.

For this appointment, Greg didn't feel well. It was getting harder for him to keep up the smiling and the chatter, and after it was over he was quite tired.

I took him home to my place as soon as possible. He lay on the couch for some time and didn't want to eat. I felt frustrated watching him waste away.

As the days went by, he needed to consume a special drink to keep up his strength because he had no appetite. From his drinking and the cancer, he had lost a great deal of weight, and now with these treatments he was losing more.

The third treatment was much harder still. Because he had to lie down, they took us to a different room where there were beds and warm blankets. There were several other patients here, so we weren't alone. Our hearts went out to these other couples. Some were so sick that my heart broke to watch them, especially knowing that we were in the same predicament.

We engaged the couple next to us in conversation, and that helped. We told them that we would pray for them, and later that day we did. Unfortunately, we never saw them again because Greg decided he couldn't go through any more treatments. He was dreadfully ill, and with his type of cancer there really wasn't a cure. He decided to live out the rest of the life without the effects of the chemo.

While Greg was recovering, he once again returned to God. He read his Bible and prayed. Peace returned to his face, even though he didn't feel well. During this time, we weren't intimate, since we weren't yet remarried. He knew we couldn't go against the Word of God, which tells us that a couple needs to be married first. We wanted God's blessing on our marriage, so we were both willing to wait this time.

It took a while before the chemo cleared out of Greg's system and he was strong enough to start rebuilding his life. In the meantime, he was granted government support to get his own place, as he couldn't return to work.

As soon as he was strong enough, he asked me to go with him to find an apartment. We discovered a basement suite he really liked and immediately paid the damage deposit on it. Our next adventures were to find furniture and household items. We enjoyed ourselves immensely, traipsing around the stores in search of the right items. We had so much fun that we became like the people we'd been when we first met. It was incredible. The Greg I knew and loved was back!

Inevitably the day arrived when Greg moved all his treasures into his new castle. I hadn't seen him this happy in many years. It did my heart good to see him truly enjoying himself.

Because he wasn't healed enough to carry anything remotely heavy, I would wait for him to tell me where he wanted each piece placed.

When it was time for me to go home, I felt sad leaving Greg behind, but he had plenty to keep himself busy. The cat that lived upstairs had invited himself into Greg's apartment and introduced himself. Greg adored cats and they always took a liking to him.

In the meantime, I spoke to my pastor about remarrying. When I mentioned Greg being my first cousin, the pastor explained that it was wrong. I had known that before but married him anyway because I couldn't have any more children.

But according to God's word, marrying your first cousin was incest. I'd never heard it put that way before, so I definitely had to end this engagement.

I saw Greg a lot at first, but as the weeks passed his visits became fewer. It wasn't hard for me to guess why. He had made some new friends and gone back to drinking. When I found out about it, I knew there was no chance of us ever being together again. This seemed to confirm the pastor's words about incest.

On one of Greg's visits, I told him that I couldn't marry him and handed him back the engagement ring. I saw even less of him after that.

Greg's brother Ron came to town to visit a short time later, which meant they would be on the party circuit. One very late evening, Ron called me in desperation to tell me that Greg wasn't breathing right. What should he do? I told him to get Greg to the hospital immediately.

For Ron to phone me, I knew Greg had to be in seriously bad condition. Ron didn't have much use for me.

Ron took him into the emergency room and the doctor diagnosed Greg with pneumonia. Oxygen and medications were administered on the spot. He was close to death.

I visited the next evening and Greg was happy to see me. I only stayed a short time, since he tired easily and had other company.

Greg was kept in the hospital for a week. The day before he was to be released, I visited him and before I left for home we hugged and stole a last kiss. I told him to take care and with great sadness I left.

Somehow I knew things were going to be very different, but I didn't know just how different.

The End

On September 6, 2006, after Greg was released from the hospital, a very nice couple Greg had introduced me to phoned me to ask if I had heard from Greg. They hadn't seen him for a few days and wondered if he was okay. I told them I hadn't seen him since his hospital stay. But I asked if they would go to his place and check on him.

Not too long after, they called back. They had knocked on his door, then tried his window, but there hadn't been any response. They asked the landlord to unlock Greg's door in order to check on him.

When they ventured inside, they found him dead with his head resting on the couch; the rest of his body sat on the floor between the couch and the coffee table, where his Bible lay open. There had been a peaceful look on his face.

According to the landlord, the cat had been scratching at Greg's window the night before. I believe the cat knew.

They all called the coroner and waited for him to come.

While I heard this news, shock surged through my body. I held the receiver in my hand in disbelief, like a replay of the day I had heard about Henry's death. Staring into space, tears trickled down my cheeks. I could envision Greg sitting upright on the floor, just like he used to do when we were together.

I can't remember what I said before putting down the receiver. Shock had me immobilized. What should I do? Where was the rulebook for these situations? How should I act? What was expected of me?

Call the kids. Yes. Yes, that's what was next.

I called Joey, who said he was heading over there and would join the couple as they waited for the coroner. He felt it would be easier on me to stay home, but I wanted to come. Oh, God, how I wanted to be there for Greg.

I don't know where Eugene was and had no way of telling him that his father had passed away. Blayne and his family were living in Fort Saskatchewan at the time, so they needed to be notified, too. Lane and Adele rushed right over as soon as they heard. Their sad, helpless looks almost destroyed me. I just didn't have anything in me to comfort them. With all my heart I wished I could, but I couldn't stay in the same room. I told them I was going to lie down.

With that, I went into my bedroom to hide.

Sitting on the edge of the bed, I screamed accusing thoughts: *You left me again. You abandoned me again, you bastard.*

Rage rose up within me and drove me insane. In a savage outrage, I slammed my foot into the bedside table and drove my fists into it as well, not caring how much it hurt me. But I just couldn't find any satisfaction in beating something that wouldn't fight back.

I wanted to destroy the whole bedroom, to smash everything that was smashable, but my bedroom door suddenly flung open and four arms wrapped themselves around me, tying my hands to my side and gently forcing me to the floor.

"Don't, Barb," they told me. "Don't do this."

My two girls managed to get me seated on the floor beside the bed. Because I could hear their own tears, I let them hold me, afraid that I would hurt them if I did what I really wanted to do. How strange that was for me to show real feelings; I had always believed I had to be the strong one, but instead I allowed real sobs of agony to gush out of me. I wanted to scream the whole building down, but I didn't act on the impulse. I didn't want to scare my girls anymore than I already had.

The rest of that day is a complete blank.

I wrestled with myself before telling Eugene that I needed to see Greg's body at the morgue. He drove me to the hospital and requested a private viewing for me. Not being Greg's wife anymore, I had no authority to arrange a viewing on my own.

Eugene and I sat in a small room while they prepared Greg's body. Our talk was a bit awkward, as I felt like I was in another world and this wasn't really happening. It hurt so much to see the pain my son was in, even though he did his best to hide it. I knew he was concerned for me, and that brought me comfort, but I didn't know how to console him. Containing my own emotions was all I could handle.

When a guard came into the room and told us they were ready, Eugene slipped his arm protectively around my shoulders. We came to the room where Greg's body lay, and Eugene and the security guard stood back, giving me some privacy as I walked up to the table holding Greg's empty shell. I allowed my thoughts to recall the past we had shared and the last days we'd shared.

My heart hurt so badly. For nearly twenty-three years, he and I had danced around our relationship. With each push to shove, our home had gotten rockier. We'd torn at each other's souls, always trying to see how far we could push the other until they broke.

The trials and tribulations had been endless, yet here we were, finally going our separate ways once and for all.

It hurt. It hurt so damned bad. We loved each other, but we'd led very separate lives. Like oil and water, we didn't mix.

How dare you leave the earth and leave me behind? I challenged him. *Do you realize there's nowhere in this whole wide upside-down world where I can reach you? Not even by phone! You abandoned me again, only this time forever. I insisted upon seeing you today, because I just had to see you one last time before the funeral arrangements begin. You know what that's like. I had to know you were really gone.*

It wasn't like when I had been told about Henry's death. Back then, I'd had no proof, not until I finally saw his death certificate twenty-some years later.

Was this some kind of joke, Greg being dead? But no, there he was, snugly wrapped up in a flannelette sheet just like a newborn baby on a hospital gurney. His skin was so cold, lifeless, and void of colour. His right eye was slightly open and I could see the beautiful blue staring right through me at something unseen behind me. It made me shudder.

As my eyes travelled the length of Greg's lifeless body, I knew this truly was the last time I would see him outside a casket.

I looked at his feet and noticed that one was left partially unwrapped. This reminded me of the many times his feet had been cold.

At least your feet will never be cold again. Heaven probably hasn't any snow or cold. And just think, you'll never hurt again either. I touched his cold and lifeless hand one last time. *Take care, my love. I'm so very sorry for all the hurt and pain we put each other through. It really was quite the adventure.*

No more would we squabble over trivial things. No more would we turn our backs on each other. And no more would we hold each other close.

Back when we'd kissed in the hospital, I wish I'd known it would be the last one. I had been able to tell he didn't want me to leave, and truthfully I hadn't wanted to go. If I'd known we were saying goodbye, I would have looked harder, hung onto him longer, and told him how much I truly loved him.

I must have really loved you, because I kept coming back, I thought. *Well, they're waiting for me to leave so your body can be put back in the freezer. Our son is waiting to take me home.*

Greg was given a funeral service in Medicine Hat. It was understood that he would be buried there, because the government was paying for the funeral. But those plans changed. Eugene wanted to honour his father's wish to take his body home to Churchbridge and lay it to rest in the family cemetery.

As there was no money to send Greg's body by hearse, Eugene's uncle paid for a rented van. Eugene took out the passenger and back seat, placed the casket inside, and drove his father home.

Greg's family held another funeral service for his friends to say their goodbyes, but because the ground was so wet they couldn't dig a proper grave. His body was therefore taken to Yorkton, where he stayed for quite a while until his family could lay him to rest.

Then, at last, all who held him dear were finally able to release him and begin the healing process.

Forty-Eight
Life Goes On

In hindsight I felt that I had in some way kept my marriage vows. I hadn't gotten involved with anyone after I'd divorced Greg, and I had only divorced him by the world's standards, not by spiritual standards. I had prayed for him and had gone to him when he had need of me. I was only ever a phone call away. I had listened and loved him. I just hadn't been able to live with him.

I had also felt that if I stepped out of the way between him and God, he wouldn't be able to lean on me and would instead call out to God, which I believe he did in his last moments of life. I think that's why God sent me to Saskatchewan. God had known that Greg would follow me home. If he had died in Churchbridge, he might not have made his peace with God.

With all my heart, I wished I could have stayed married until death parted us, but I conceded that God knew what He was doing.

For a while I continued to work for the homeless shelter, but I felt the Lord telling me it was time to move on. Six years of midnight shifts had worn me down. Work and sleep, work and sleep… there had to be more to life than that.

In October 2007, shortly after coming home from work, I received a phone call from my friend Joyce. She wanted to know if I would be interested in taking a job at the Champion's Centre, a Christian non-profit organization where she was the manager. They provided supportive living for men on low income.

The job would be as a prep cook, and I asked her about the wage. It was too low. I could have paid my bills, but there would have been no money left for food. I couldn't take the job.

She understood, but before hanging up she invited me to drop by the centre for a free coffee. I said I just might do that.

Even before now, I had often thought about going over to the centre. There was something about the place that piqued my interest.

After hanging up on Joyce, I remembered about the method by which I had found my last few jobs. I once again decided to call on the Lord.

"Lord, if this is the answer for my new job, You need to show me," I prayed. "I'll go down after I sleep and collect on that coffee."

And that's what I did. When I walked through the door of the centre, Joyce and another woman named Bernice were sitting at the staff table having lunch. Joyce was surprised yet happy to see me and immediately offered me a higher wage than we'd discussed on the phone.

As I had already worked out the amount I would need to live on, I knew that this new offer would work for me. But first I collected on the coffee. She told me what the job would entail, and then she gave me a tour of the kitchen. I started opening drawers and cupboards to see what was inside. That was very strange behaviour on my part.

When we came to the huge walk-in cooler and I stepped inside, suddenly I knew without a doubt that I was home. I walked out of the cooler, looked at Joyce, and said, "I'll take it."

That evening, I handed in my two-week notice at the shelter.

Just before leaving, though, I simply couldn't help pulling a little prank. There was one client who liked to tease me. Well, after he left early one morning for work I went downstairs to his room and stuffed one of his pillowcases with crumpled-up newspaper. It looked like a head. I then used other pillows to form a body, and dressed it with a discarded long-sleeved turtleneck top and pair of gloves. The dummy appeared to be sleeping, and it looked quite authentic. I purposely left the door to this client's room open when I left.

I later heard that the client hadn't been very happy to come back and see that someone was sleeping in his bed. In a rage, he'd marched into his room with every intention of throwing the bum out.

"Barbra!" he'd yelled when he learned the truth.

I was told that the staff upstairs heard him all the way in the office! The next time I saw him, he gave me the biggest scowl. I enjoyed keeping him on his toes.

By taking this new job, God was also answering a long-time pray for me to reconnect with Joyce. I so desired to have her friendship back. She had a big heart and I loved her as a sister.

Joyce told me after I'd been there a while that God had spoken to her and told her to call me and offer me the job. Absolutely amazing!

I helped Joyce cook lunch for the men who lived at the centre, in addition to assisting with the hot meal program, which fed forty or more homeless people six days a week. I also made soup for fifty or more homeless people at the St. Barnabas Church.

A year later, I was diagnosed with carpal tunnel in both hands and had to have surgery to correct them. As symptoms, I'd experienced a lot of shoulder pain and my arms had been falling asleep.

After two months, both hands were healed enough for me to return to work. When I returned, Joyce, in her wisdom, decided to rent part of the kitchen to another business which made sandwiches for convenience stores and gas stations. Because there was no longer enough work for me to remain working full-time, the other company hired me for four hours a day, which made up for the hours I had lost.

It was quite an adjustment. The sandwich company lasted nearly a year, and after that a decision was made to turn the dining room into a place that served hot breakfasts to the homeless and anyone else who was in need to get out of the cold or heat.

When it looked as though I knew what I was doing, Joyce turned over the whole kitchen to me, unexpectedly promoting me to cook, as well as giving me back my full hours.

"I can't do this!" I said to her.

She called back, "Yes, you can!"

Eventually she was proved right. She had faith in me and pulled abilities out of me I hadn't even known I had.

After a couple of years, Joyce stepped down from management and a woman named Bernice took her place.

Because we needed donations and fundraisers to keep our doors open, our board of directors thought we should host a Christmas fundraiser with a silent auction. They secured the large church we'd used the year before, ensuring there would be plenty of space for the many tables we needed.

For live entertainment, Bernice and I decided to put together our own band. She played drums and found a bass player while friends of ours played guitars and we sang. We only had a short time to practice, but we managed to come up with a routine. On the night of our performance, we sounded pretty good. It was a fun night!

While singing one of the songs I wrote, my granddaughter Rose recorded us on her phone and said she was going to post it on Facebook. I warned her not to, but later on, when I heard what we sounded like, I wished she had.

Unfortunately, not long after that Rose's dog chewed her phone to bits. If the song had been on Facebook, I could have gotten a copy of it, and now it's lost. It just goes to show that I was too critical of myself and afraid of what others might think. How dumb that sounds today.

During the summer of 2009, Fay asked if I would visit the Remand Centre and minister the gospel twice a month with her and a guy named Adam. We brought our guitars and I brought music sheets so the inmates could sing with us.

Each time we went, we had to sign in and leave our belongings in a locker. We were then escorted through doors that slammed and locked behind us as we proceeded to the chapel. The whole time, we were monitored. The slamming never bothered me, nor being locked in. I remembered there had been a time when I should have been behind bars myself, but in God's mercy I'd been spared.

When we arrived in the chapel, we would wait for the inmates to be lined up and brought in. Once everyone was settled, we'd sing a few songs. Then Fay would preach a powerful message and end the service by asking if anyone wanted to give their life to Jesus. Once or twice, I shared a bit about my own life and how God had rescued me.

Some of the inmates gave their hearts to Jesus, and that was so rewarding!

Before leaving, the inmates would often come forward in tears to talk about themselves, shake our hands, and thank us for coming. Going to the Remand Centre also helped me to better relate to the people who frequented the Champion's Centre after their release.

After ten months, I felt my season there was done. To this day, Fay still faithfully preaches at the Remand Centre and teaches the twelve-step program. The men are giving their hurting lives over to Jesus and changing their lives. There's an awesome move of God going on in our jail.

Forty-Nine
Back to Thompson

In May 2011, God instructed me to go back to Thompson. I needed to revisit my old stomping grounds to deal with the mess I'd left behind.

I know there are pastors who would say I had already been forgiven when I gave my life to Jesus. That is absolutely correct. But there were attitudes, unresolved hurts, anger, pain, and unforgiveness in my heart that just wouldn't leave, even after I'd asked Jesus into my heart. I would have to go back into my past and face what I had done, then turn it all over to Jesus.

In other words, I had to acknowledge my wrongs and ask Jesus to help me change. I know this works. When I can't change something in my life, I ask the Holy Spirit to show me the root of that problem—and when He shows it to me, I relive it in my mind, feel all the emotions that are still connected to it, then ask for forgiveness and give it to Jesus. And He heals me! So simple and it works!

I knew God had forgiven me of the mess I'd made of my life in Thompson, but I couldn't get past the guilt and shame I still carried. To make sure this trip was what God really wanted me to do, I asked Him to provide the time off, finances for travel, access to a hotel, and all the taxis I'd need in order to get around Thompson.

I asked Joyce, who had returned as manager, if it were possible for me to take some time off from the centre and she managed to provide me with a week.

By some miracle, I got in contact with an old girlfriend, Emma, who I hadn't seen in many years. She still lived in Thompson, although strangely enough she was moving out of the province at the end of that very month. She had a truck and said she would be absolutely delighted to share her apartment with me and take me to all the places I needed to go.

God had left no stone unturned. He'd provided everything I needed, only better. With God, all things are possible.

By this time, I'd been feeling constantly ill for more than a year with an overwhelming feeling of weakness that would drain the strength from my body. While it passed over me, my legs would feel like they were about to buckle. It would come over me at work, but I had a job to do and I sure didn't need people fussing over me or finding me lying in an undignified heap on the kitchen floor at work. So I'd pray and keep pushing forward.

I saw my doctor and she put me through a multitude of tests, from bloodwork, cardio tests, and ultrasounds, hoping to locate the problem. On several occasions I ended up in the emergency room hooked up to the heart monitor, yet we couldn't figure out what was wrong.

Because nothing was found, I began to think it was all in my head. But I couldn't convince my weak legs that it was a hoax, and for a while I ended up taking nitro-glycerine tablets.

One night I pulled an all-nighter in the emergency room, hooked up to the heart monitor, but again they found nothing. I was released at 7:30 in the morning.

Even though I hadn't slept, I asked my daughter-in-law Lane to take me to work instead of going home. I couldn't afford to miss a day's wages. She and my boss weren't too pleased, but I worked anyway.

Soon I was ready to board a plane to Winnipeg. As I took my seat, the illness made its presence known once again. My blood pressure was frightfully low. Fortunately, the seat next to me was empty, so I lay my head on the wall next to the window. The dizziness made me feel like my life was ebbing away.

Under my breath, I whispered to God that if He wanted to take me home, it was well with my soul to go—but if He did, it would freak out the other passengers.

Somehow He strengthened me and I was still very much alive as I switched planes in Winnipeg and headed north to Thompson.

Upon my arrival, Emma met me at the airport. What a pleasure it was to see her! As we joyfully hugged, it felt as though no time had passed at all and we were picking up where we'd left off.

While waiting for my luggage, though, a familiar fear griped my heart. It was this very window where Jeannette and I had picked up that package of weed so many years before. How utterly stupid I was to have taken such a risk with my children's lives, as well as my own. I silently asked God to forgive me and asked if He would help me forgive myself.

As we headed into town, I asked Emma if we could stop at the bridge that crossed the Burtwood River. When we got there, I climbed carefully down from her truck onto the ice- and snow-covered embankment. From there, I went to the huge rocks I used to climb over and the small pools of water I had swum in when the water levels were low. As I stood alone listening to the familiar sound of the running river, my heart was heavy with the knowledge that my mother's ashes lay at the bottom of the river somewhere under this bridge. It had been Mom's wish to have her ashes poured into the river as her final resting place. One of our closest friends had made that possible for her. I'd known I would have to visit and thank her before I left town.

As I entered my old stomping grounds, I found that the town had changed immensely. I discerned a metaphorical dark cloud hanging over the town like a shroud, even though it was a bright sunny day. Even the newest-looking buildings seemed old to me. I asked the Lord what it was all about and I kept hearing, "Decay, decay, decay." Yes, the place looked as though it was rotting.

Emma took me to her apartment, which was built on the cliff overlooking the town. I had always wondered what it would be like to live in one of these buildings. I'd once had the opportunity to swim in the indoor pool here, but that was all. My heart's desires were being answered! Emma lived several stories up and her view over the city captivated me.

She had been packing, so her home looked like a tornado had hit it, but there was a cot waiting for me in the midst of the many boxes.

I was tired and weak and should have rested, but as soon as I dumped my luggage we went out to explore. We found the restaurant where I had found Henry after he'd taken my butcher knives and gone looking for the guy who stole his jacket. The place had changed so much that I hardly recognize it. We lunched and talked about the good ole days.

Emma showed me the town's new flower shop, where I bought two bouquets of a rose and baby's-breath for Mom and her friend. We sought out the friend who had poured her ashes in the river and found her at home, across the street from where I grew up. At first she didn't recognize me, but when I told her who I was she was more than happy to invite us in.

I thanked her immensely for carrying out Mom's wish and gave her the rose to show my appreciation. As she was making coffee, I looked around her place, amazed at how little it had changed. It felt like old times.

Emma and I didn't stay long, as I wanted to revisit the river, so we hugged and said our goodbyes. At the river's edge, I stood a few minutes talking to Mom, telling her how much I missed her. Then I thanked her for all she had done for me, bid her goodbye, and threw the rose as far out into the water as I could, watching it float away out of sight.

As the days flew by, we began to revisit the places I needed to face. The apartment where I had lived with Henry, the mall where I'd stolen food,[26] the Fox Bay apartments, and the tavern where I'd overdosed.

I even found out that an my old family doctor was still practising medicine and got talked into seeing him again. When we entered his office, I explained to him who I was and thanked him for taking such good care of us. He remembered me and gave me a big hug.

There were so many more places too see, and each place caused different reactions and emotions to surface, along with heart-wrenching tears of regret.

Emma was so patient and understanding as she watched me bare my soul over the course of these five days. I was so grateful that God had chosen her to help me.

At last we came the hardest place of all: the train station on the outskirts of town. It looked so much smaller than I remembered. On this day, the station was locked up and there was no one around in any direction.

Since we were there by ourselves, I asked Emma if she wouldn't mind staying in the truck; I felt strongly that I needed to be alone.

---

[26] I hardly recognized it. The mall had changed in structure so drastically that I was lost as soon as I walked through the doors.

I approached the front door and the large window. With hands on either side of my face, I peered in to see what it looked like inside. It hadn't changed much. My heart felt tighter and beat faster as I made my way around to the back of the station. I stood on the all-too-familiar platform looking up and down the tracks, memories flooding back to me. Sobs broke loose from my throat and tears cascaded down my face. Fear and pain ravished me from the inside. Once again, I was that little girl full of anxiety and fear, waiting for the train to arrive before Dad caught us.

I suddenly bent over in a raging scream, releasing the fear that tore at my heart and ripped through my body. I felt myself going crazy as I descended deeper into the black hole of my past. I cried out to God for help, but deeper and deeper I fell. Anguish erupted from my soul.

I turned this way and that, struggling to get loose from the tentacles that held on so tightly. I turned on the building, and with ear-piercing screams of fury I hammered my fists against the wall, trying to alleviate my terror.

How many times had we escaped by rail? Each time I was not to make a sound… but this time there was no one to shut me up. Between sobs, I began to forgive Dad and Mom.

When I finally ran out of tears, a calm descended upon me. I felt God's presence embrace me. There was still the odd shaky sob, but I remained in place until I finished talking to God. I forgave everyone from my past and asked God to take the little girl home to heaven.

Just like that, I felt something unseen leave me. It was over! It was done! My heart didn't sting anymore.

In utter weakness, I slowly walked off the platform and made my way back around the building to where Emma patiently waited. I was drained, yet thankful to leave that place once and for all. I had been the hunted, but now my pursuer could harm me no more. I was free!

At the end of our visit, it was hard to say goodbye to Emma and the few old friends I still had in Thompson. I felt so good saying goodbye this time, and this time I wasn't running out of town; I was leaving on my own accord.

I had been ill the whole time I was there, and the plane seemed to promote the illness. As we flew again, once again I felt like I was dying—and not long after returning home, I finally discovered what was ailing me. Who would have thought it? I lacked vitamin D3.

Closing the Champion's Centre

I was happy to return to work and help as many men and women as I could, by giving them a smile or saying something silly to make them laugh. In some cases, I had to put up with bad behaviour, so I learned to defuse it. I had to remind those people that they were guests of the centre, and if they didn't want to come in and behave like a guest they were asked to leave, either with or without a police escort.

Many were out on the streets because they simply didn't like rules, but when they came in on my turf, they had to follow the rules or leave. They would be allowed back the next day if they wanted to behave.

I was told on several occasions that when someone was doing something wrong deliberately, another person would say, "Don't let Barb catch you doing that." They knew I wouldn't put up with bad behaviour, and for that I gained a lot of respect. It didn't matter to me how big or tough a person might be, I'd stare them down. If I let them get away with anything, I knew they would end up running the place. That just wasn't going to happen.

And then there were the ones who'd walk through our door with little to no reason to go on living. Somehow they would seek me out and I'd listen to their tragic stories. We would talk a bit, and then I'd ask if I could pray for them. Many welcomed the prayer and experienced the touch of the Holy Spirit. Later, I would watch them leave with a confident stride in their step and a newfound hope tucked away in their hearts. Some would come back days later to tell me of the change that had taken place because of the prayer.

While sharing their problems, some would break down in tears and I'd hold them in my arms and let them cry. Sometimes they just needed someone to listen and care. I had the privilege of sharing Jesus with them, and some would ask Jesus to come into their hearts.

The worst for me was when I was told that a regular had died. Some of these deaths were horrid.

One day, a young man who was very dear to me came to me with swollen bruises covering his face. He also had cracked ribs and was nursing his arm in a sling. He told me that three guys had tied him to a chair and beat him. A week later, I was told that this man was found dead in a basement. Many of us believed he had been murdered. A couple of people who knew who might have done it then shared with me their suspicions, but I couldn't go to the police since it was only hearsay.

With each death, I'd leave the building for privacy. I'd walk through the back door, break down, and cry. Being homeless is a very dangerous way to live, and when working with these clients we never really knew who or what we were dealing with. But most of them were simply out in the streets because they'd lost everything for one reason or another.

And then there were those who I hadn't seen for some time. I'd ask around to find out if anyone had seen them. After hearing that I was looking for them, some would stop by the centre just to let me know they were okay.

"Barb is like a mother hen with her wings covering over her chicks," someone once said to my boss. In many ways, the clients did become my kids and family.

The people who touched me most were those who came in, ate their breakfast, and sat restfully drinking their coffee. Before leaving, they'd come over to me or another worker and thank us, telling us how much they appreciated all we did for them!

This place wasn't just a job. It was my ministry, and I loved being a part of it. The rewards didn't come in paycheques or titles, but in hugs and tears when I helped people overcome their struggles.

I eventually moved up the ranks from prep cook to cook, then from supervisor to co-manager, and eventually to manager. I never saw that coming!

The Champion's Centre was closed on September 15, 2019, for lack of funds. My last day was September 13. In total, I was given thirteen amazing years there, being able to make a difference in people's lives. After I left, I heard people say that it wasn't the same without me. What a kind thing to say! Several also told me that I'd helped them and they were grateful.

Well, that's the God I serve! He changed my heart and filled it with love for the destitute. Why not? I myself had been destitute.

I'm proud to say that I was a member of the wonderful caring team of the Champion's Centre. It has now been laid to rest and another caring centre has come in to continue the job of caring for the struggling people in our community.

Epilogue

When I look back over the years and the many painful trials I faced, I shake my head in awe and am reminded of a word from God that was spoken over me many years ago. He said that I was like a small, partially opened rosebud, and as He heals me I will open more until one day I come into full bloom.

I'm also reminded of the dream which I wrote about in the book's introduction—the beautiful garden filled with a multitude of flowers, the path that led around a corner to a hidden place, and the twisted patch of thorny vines, much like balled-up barbed wire. There was a ray of sunlight revealing a small opening, and inside the opening was hidden a beautiful blue rose. The vines crept forward with the intent to destroy the rose and I felt its sadness and distress.

Suddenly, a strong hand appeared, reached into the opening, and forcefully pushed the thorns away.

I believe this dream reveals the course of my life, demonstrating that God knew the purpose He had for me even while the thorns of life tried to derail me. He used those thorns to shape and mould me into the purpose He has for me today. He was with me all the while.

Today I have a choice. I can be bitter because of all that has happened, or I can choose to be better and seek God's joy.

In the writing of this book, I have found healing and risen from the ashes of my former life. I can now leave my past behind, no more looking back with regret.

My friends say that I am an adventure to be with us, because there's always some kind of drama going on and they get to share in it with me. Well, walking with God is always an adventure. We never know where He'll take us.

One thing I do know for sure is that I'm a walking miracle. To God be the glory!

There are several reasons why I opened up my private life to share with others. This book began when my daughters-in-law, Lane and Adele, suggested that I write my story for my grandchildren. They hoped their kids would read the book and glean some valuable guidance for their lives.

Then my pastor heard about my past and asked me to share my story in church. So I wrote down the details of what I could share in a ten-minute talk. He then took pity on me by asking questions, to make it a smoother talk.

When I finished speaking that day, several people came up to me with tears in their eyes. They told me that what I'd shared had revealed to them the area of their own lives that they needed to revisit and deal with. One woman even mentioned that if I ever wrote a book about my life, she would buy it. This helped me see the profound effect I could have by sharing my testimony.

After speaking to the congregation, God called me to go back to the twelve-step Bible study with Fay and help her out. At the end of a three-month study, she asked me to share my testimony at our round-up dinner, a special event she always hosted at the end of a study to celebrate its completion.

This time, I wrote and shared a more in-depth version of my story. It helped that I had kept notes from what I'd talked about in church. I expanded on those notes and turned them into a small booklet which I could read from.

After sharing, I felt very uneasy and embarrassed about my life, but I got pretty much the same reaction from the people who heard me speak as those who had heard me at church. A dear friend came up to me afterward in tears and revealed, in front of everyone, that she had lived many of the same abusive experiences.

Not long after, I heard the Lord speak to me: "I want you to write the whole story and tell people everything that really happened." Now I felt overwhelmed. I really didn't want to share my life with everyone, but God revealed to me how Satan builds strongholds in the secrets of our lives and reinforces them by silence. When we break the silence and share our stories, we break the strongholds of shame, embarrassment, and fear. We soon find that we are free, having taken what the devil intended for harm and working it out for good. Every time we tell our stories, more and more people are able to be delivered, given hope, and set free. Through us, God is glorified.

Therefore confess your sins to each other and pray for each other so that you may be healed. The prayer of a righteous person is powerful and effective. (James 5:16)

I saw myself as a person of no consequence. In other words, I had no value. Even people who were lower down in the gutter than I was had value in my eyes. But I learned long ago that when God tells me that He wants me to do something, I need to do it. If God wanted me to write my story, I knew He had an important purpose for it.

No matter what I faced in life—an alcoholic and abusive father, sexual abuse, love gone bad, near-death experiences, cheaters, divorces, drugs, alcohol, surgeries, and even murder—I survived it to tell my story, and it is ultimately a story of God's love and grace. I was a liar, a thief, a fornicator, and many other sinful things, but for God and His mercy this book would never have been written and I would never have found the healing, freedom, and peace I have today.

"Why did I have to go through all this?" I asked God one day, out of curiosity.

His answer was profound: "When I formed you, I placed the book inside you, but you had to live it in order to write it. I have a purpose for the book."

This book is truly about God's grace, and what God is saying is very simple: "I don't care about your past, but I can change your future, if you'll let Me."

For You

You are precious in the eyes of the Lord
It was for you that Jesus was born
The Father sent Him down from above
To walk as a man demonstrating love
Love so deep, hard to comprehend
Forgiveness He showed, which confused educated men
Healing the sick, raising the dead
Casting out demons, multitudes He fed
Rich and poor, fat and thin
Black and white, don't matter to Him
You are precious, never forget
For you He came with no regret

There is no sin so deep that God isn't deeper still! If you are sincere and want to be ready to meet Jesus, pray aloud this simple prayer from your heart:

Lord Jesus, I come before You just as I am. I am sorry for my sins. I repent of my sins. Please forgive me. In Your name, I forgive all others for what they have done against me. I renounce Satan, evil spirits, and all their works. I give You my entire self, now and forever. I invite You into my life and accept You as my Lord, God, and Saviour. Heal me, change me, and strengthen me in body, soul, and spirit.

Come, Lord Jesus, cover me with Your precious blood and fill me with Your Holy Spirit. I thank You, Lord Jesus, and shall follow You every day of my life. Amen!